חיים של ברכה

CHAYIM shel BRACHA

CHAYIM *shel*
BRACHA

A commentary on Mesechta Berachos

Rabbi Chaim Goldberger

Copyright © 2020 by Mosaica Press

ISBN: 978-1-946351-94-4

All rights reserved. No part of this book may be used or reproduced or transmitted in any form or by any means, electronic or mechanical, including photocopying, recording, or by any information storage and retrieval system, without written permission from the publisher.

Published by Mosaica Press, Inc.
www.mosaicapress.com
info@mosaicapress.com

בס"ד

HaRav Yochanan Zweig, shlita
Rosh HaYeshiva

Rabbi Yitzchak Zweig
President

יום שני לסדר 'איש אשר רוח בו וסמכת את ידך עליו' התשע"ט

לכבוד תלמידי יקירי ידידי ורעי הרב חיים גולדברגר שליט"א רב דק"ק כנסת ישראל, מינעאפאליס,

הגיע לידי ספרך החשוב חיים של ברכה על מסכת ברכות ועברתי עליו כמשאת הפני וראיתי חיבור מיוחד במינו איך שהבאת ללומד את ההבנה והעומק ביסוד הגמרא להבין את הסוגיא בשלימותה בבהירות והסבר נפלאה.

כבר מזמן היותך בישיבתנו ראינו שנועדת לגדולות הבנתך בלימוד הגמרא היתה יוצאת מן הכלל ומסירותך ללימוד ולתורה הם שזיכוך להגיע להשגים כאלה.

יהי רצון שחפץ השם בידך יצלך להמשיך להרביץ תורה וללמד לעם ישראל איך ללמוד את תורתו מתוך הרוחה שפע ונחת יחד עם נו"ב הרבנית תחי' בבריאות איתנא ונהורא מעליא בביאת גואל במהרה בימנו אמן.

בברכת התורה ובאהבה והערכה,

יוחנן משה צוייג

4000 Alton Road
Miami Beach, FL 33140

Tel: (305) 534-7050
Fax: (305) 534-8444

ALFRED AND SADYE SWIRE COLLEGE OF JUDAIC STUDIES

www.talmudicu.edu

כולל אברכים
דמינעאפאליס

הרב חיים שמחה גיבער
ראש הכולל

ב"ה

יום ב' מרחשון ער"ח מ"ק לפ"ק מינעאפאליס יצ"ו

אנא פעם היה לי הזכות את האומר ביקר חיים של כבוד אדר"ג
ידיד ה', ועט"ר האשכול הגדול והמופלא ה"ה הרה"ג ר' חיים יצחק קלצקי
שליט"א אשר ישא ברכות מאת ד' על פעולתו במינעאפאליס, ובוא
ואמרי קצת מאותן הדברים אשר ראה פה כדי לחזק את המורה
ולהוסיף ולהבין מן הדברים וכן באמת ראיתי לגדולות יש ומורה
פה ולהגדיל בעניני יום השאיני והשלישית. ועוד אף אני הדרא
את דרכו ויגמר ספרו את חיבורו בעזרת אלקים הטובה כדי לזכות
אלו הבאים לדבר ד', וכדי קטנ מחד ישודה הגדול הזה. ויהי רצון
לפני אא"ז אא אשא"מי הוא יזכו כיון בקיום הטוב ולהלוך בדדריו
ו הנה בהנהגוותו על הצפה יזכה לחזות ולצאת ואל הלחיים על
כל טוב אמת. ויראו ולבו שמחה לזווחה בכל עת וזמן. ויהי נעם
אבינו שבמים עליהם הפעל ב', דברים פיו'. ישפיע, ויכונ והיאת מרובה
בין גוף ובין נפש, ועבד ואל והרגלות בכל שלום הפעל!

אני עבדו ואהבו-
חיים שמחה גיבער
ראש הכולל

2930 Inglewood Avenue
St. Louis Park, MN 55416
PHONE (952) 926-3242

שמואל קמנצקי
Rabbi S. Kamenetsky

2018 Upland Way
Philadelphia, PA 19131

Home: 215-473-2798
Study: 215-473-1212

ר"ח חשון, תש"פ

Dear Rabbi Goldberger,

    Your work on Brochos is wonderful and many will בס"ד enjoy it. You are bringing out the best of the inyanim in the Mesechta and many people will benefit from this.

    My ברכה is that you continue to be מחדש on many subjects that the public will enjoy. Your writings will enrich those who study them with many sugyos.

My heartfelt brochos and wishes for much hatzlocha.

S. Kamenetsky

Table of Contents

Preface XIII

Chapter One
Me'eimasai

2	דף ב.
9	דף ב:
14	דף ג.
17	דף ד.
23	דף ה.
25	(1) דף ו.
31	(2) דף ו.
34	(1) דף ח.
40	(2) דף ח.
43	(3) דף ח.
48	(1) דף ט.
50	(2) דף ט:
52	(1) דף י.
58	(2) דף י:
61	דף יב:

Chapter Two
Hayah Koreh

70	(1) דף יג.
72	(2) דף יג.
76	(3) דף יג.
81	(1) דף יד.
86	(2) דף יד.
90	דף טו.

Table of Contents

(1) דף טז.	95
(2) דף טז.	98
דף טז:	100

Chapter Three
Mi She'meiso

דף יז:	106
דף יח.	111
דף יח:	114
דף כ.	119
דף כ:	123
דף כב:	129
(1) דף כג.	138
(2) דף כג.	142
(1) דף כד.	144
(2) דף כד.	150
(1) דף כה.	154
(2) דף כה.	158
(3) דף כה.	161
(1) דף כה:	168
(2) דף כה:	173
(3) דף כה:	178
(4) דף כה:	185
(5) דף כה:	196
(1) דף כו.	202
(2) דף כו.	209

Chapter Four
Tefillas Ha'shachar

(3) דף כו.	214
דף כו:	223
דף כט:	226

Chapter Five
Ein Omdin

דף לב:	234

Chapter Six
Keitzad Mevarchin

238	דף לה.
241	דף לה:
245	דף לו. (1)
251	דף לו. (2)
254	דף לו. (3)
265	דף לז:

Chapter Seven
Sheloshah She'achlu

272	דף מה.

Chapter Eight
Eilu Devarim

280	דף נא:

Chapter Nine
Ha'roeh

288	דף נז.

Preface

מה נמלצו לחכי אמרתך מדבש לפי

How sweet to my palate are Your words; more than honey to my mouth. (Tehillim 119:103)

When I wrote the preface to my first book, *The Six Steps of Bitachon—a Practical Guide to Divine Providence*, I spent many paragraphs thanking those people who inspired me to live a life of Torah study and *avodas Hashem*—those ideals that brought me to writing my first book.

In this preface, I'd like to focus on those inspirational individuals to whom I have to offer thanks for my initiative to write on *Mesechta Berachos*.

Learning in Yerushalayim in 1983, I lived with an uncle—may he live and be well—R' Menashe Goldberger and his family, who at the time lived in an apartment in the Zichron Moshe neighborhood off Rechov Yaffo in the heart of the city. His next-door neighbor was an *adam gadol* by the name of HaRav Yitzchok Soloveitchik. Rav Yitzchok, while a quintessential Yerushalmi, Rosh Yeshiva of a classic Brisker yeshiva—Yeshivas Shaarei Simcha, named for his grandfather HaRav Simcha Soloveitchik, brother of Rav Chaim, *zt"l*—that he had founded in Zichron Moshe, had actually been raised in America, spoke English like an American, and gave me the hope that I might be able to meet and have a personal relationship with a *gadol*.

Preface

I took steps to make his acquaintance, and my dream came true when I was invited one Shabbos to join the Rav and his family for *shalosh seudos*. I had been learning *Mesechta Berachos*, and I knew I wanted to come in to meet him with some kind of Torah question I could ask. I thought of a question I felt was sufficiently acceptable, and I presented it to the Rav.

It had to do with a Gemara that seems to repeat itself. On *daf* 7a, the Gemara says: "Rav Yochanan said in the name of Rav Yose: How do we know that we should not attempt to appease someone (*ein meratzin*) in the moment of his anger? Because the *pasuk* says, '[When] my face will change, then I will be reconciled with you.'" Then again on *daf* 7b, the Gemara repeats the exact same teaching! I thus asked Rav Soloveitchik why the Gemara needed to repeat on *amud beis* what it just taught us on *amud alef*.

The Rav expressed satisfaction with the question, and he gave me an answer, which I recorded after Shabbos in a notebook. To my delight, I came across this notebook as I was preparing this *sefer* for publication. The *maimra* on *amud alef*, he had explained, was teaching the lesson of *ein meratzin* as it applies to Hashem—*bein adam l'makom*. The *maimra* on *amud beis* applies the lesson to one's fellow—*bein adam l'chaveiro*.

I remember being enchanted by the Rav's answer. I found it utterly fascinating how much depth could be contained in something as disarmingly simple as a repeated passage of Aggadah. That excitement lay quietly in my heart for a long time, but eventually it emerged, and I owe a debt of *hakaras hatov* to Rav Soloveitchik for lighting a spark in a young *bachur*'s *neshamah*.

Now while that incident may have involved *Mesechta Berachos*, my real motivation to work on *Berachos* in particular came from a different individual. Rabbi Chaim Cohen became our neighbor when we moved into the Woodside community in Silver Spring, MD, in 1975. What impressed me about him then (and still today) was that he was an accomplished *talmid chacham* as well as a successful professional and businessman. I remember how he had accepted upon himself to completely master one *mesechta*—his "Olam Haba Mesechta," as he would call it—and the one he chose was *Berachos*. He wrote a *sefer* on *Berachos*

Preface

and shared a number of his insights with me. I always dreamed of being able to respond in kind. This *sefer* is my thanks for Rabbi Cohen's inspiration; one of his insights can be found in my piece on *Perek Sheloshah She'achlu*.

A number of the *shiurim* I have given on the *mesechta*—*shiurim* that make up the body of much of this *sefer*—were classes I was privileged to teach to a remarkable group of *baalei batim* in Atlanta, GA, between the years 1991 and 1993. These were men who, for various reasons, were able to spend their mornings in the old Kollel Beis Medrash daily until 11:00 AM. It was HaRav Menachem Deutsch, as head of the Atlanta Scholars Kollel, who gave me the go-ahead to run a morning yeshiva for these men. That experience led to similar projects in communities I have served in Lowell, MA, and Minneapolis, MN; many of the results of the efforts put into those projects over the years can be found on these pages. Other *shiurim* were developed as a result of talking in learning with my son, Yaakov, and learning *b'chavrusa* with my son, Moshe. May Hashem bless them both with constant flowing streams of *hirhurei Torah*, *tefillah*, and *teshuvah*.

I did mention Rav Simcha Weinberg in my first introduction, but a special mention goes to him here. It was his challenge to me this past Rosh Hashanah that encouraged me to accept upon myself to publish this *sefer* this year. It was also he who pushed me to write my first *sefer*, and it is always he who has seen my potential long before I have and insisted I bring it out into reality. In all his ways, Rav Simcha, *shlita*, continues to keep the vision of my great Rebbe, his father Moreinu v'Rabbeinu HaRav Yaakov Weinberg, *zt"l*, vividly alive and personally accessible.

There is no one who can make a busy rav or executive feel like an *avreich* in kollel more than a wife. Without my dear wife's unwavering commitment to my accomplishments in Torah, without her sacrifice of the hours gone into working on my *sefer* that would have been hours spent at home, I would not have been able to realize this effort in our *avodas Hashem*. *Sheli v'shelachem, shelah hi*.

I owe an enormous debt of gratitude to my Kollel *chavrusa*, Rav Yehuda Wolin, *shlita*. Rav Yehuda came to my attention well-recommended by

Preface

my son, Yaakov, who knew him from yeshiva in Passaic. I was excited when he approached and asked to make a learning *seder* with me, and I quickly recognized it as a Heaven-sent opportunity to ask him to use our *chavrusa* time to review each and every one of the *shiurim* that would make up this *sefer*. A *talmid chacham* of unique ability, Rav Yehuda graciously agreed, and the *chelkei Torah* found on these pages bear his scholarly imprint and approval. Speaking of the Kollel, it is universally acknowledged that the Minneapolis Community Kollel has catapulted the city of Minneapolis to the top of the ranks of small-size *mekomos haTorah* in America, and that is due to the enormous dedication of the Rosh Kollel HaRav Chaim Gibber, *shlita*, from whom I have had the *zechus* to drink of his Torah, his *middos*, and his *mehalech ha'chaim* for close to forty years and who has so kindly agreed to append a *haskamah* to this volume. I have great appreciation as well for the *meyased haKollel*, HaRav Moshe Tuvia Lieff, *shlita*, a respected Torah authority and colleague who left a lasting mark on Minneapolis, and for the current *menahalei haKollel*, including my beloved nephew, HaRav Avigdor Goldberger, *shlita*. May the Kollel continue to grow and flourish and provide inspiration to the community, to other communities, and to all Klal Yisrael.

The *chiddushim* themselves are of a singular style, and it is a style I owe entirely to Mori v'Rabi HaRav Yochanan Zweig, *shlita*. The format consists of asking a variety of questions—all designed to make it clear that there is some fundamental understanding missing from our comprehension of the *sugya*. A principle, referred to in the *shiurim* as the *"yesod,"* is then introduced, and the rest of the *shiur* demonstrates how the application of this novel insight circumvents or answers all the original questions.

The Rosh Yeshiva has now raised more than an entire generation on his unique *derech* of learning. Whether the *yesodos* I put forth in answer to my questions live up to his standards is something I can only hope for, but that any ability I have to ask the questions comes directly from the *shiurim* and *ris'cha d'Oraisa* I heard from the Rosh Hayeshiva is something I can state with certainty, and it was a great personal *kavod* for me to present the manuscript for his *haskamah*. Hashem should bless the

Rosh Yeshiva and his family with *arichas yamim v'shanim* in good health, and Hashem should bless the yeshiva that it should spread its wings out from Miami Beach to the whole world as it continues to supply water from the wellsprings of the Rosh Yeshiva's Torah to a nation thirsty to drink from its depths.

As always, Rav Yaacov Haber and Rav Doron Kornbluth and their worthy team have shown themselves to be ideal partners in my Torah-publishing endeavors. May Hashem bless them, their families, and the Mosaica Press publishing house, and allow them to continue their trailblazing efforts to be *mekadesh shem Shamayim b'rabim*.

May Hashem Yisbarach continue to nurture and support me, ever supplying me with new goals and the means to carry them out. May He bless my wife and children, my parents, my mother-in-law, our extended families, my *talmidim*, and all our beloved friends and acquaintances.

I have chosen to name this treatise on *Mesechta Berachos*, *Chayim shel Bracha*, as a tribute to my parents, Gus and Betty Goldberger, they should live in good health *ad me'ah v'esrim*. My parents started me off on a life of Torah, founding a day school in our hometown when I was old enough to attend one. They continued to steer me in the same direction all through my youth, and this achievement is a tribute to their vision. My mother's name is Chaya Bracha, making me a genuine Chaim (Yitzchak) shel Bracha. I have also set the stage for me to allude to my father's name next, *im yirtzeh Hashem*, in a *sefer* to come on *Mesechta Shabbos*, which I hope to call *Chayim shel Shalom*, a nod both to my father's name, Shlomo, and to the blessing of *shalom* brought upon us by the Shabbos. May the speedy arrival of Ben-David enable all my future publications to be both written *and* published in Yerushalayim *Ir Ha'kodesh, tibaneh v'tivased bim'heira b'yameinu*, Amen.

Erev Rosh Hashanah 5780

Chapter One
Me'eimasai

דף ב.

מתני׳ מאימתי קורין את שמע בערבין משעה שהכהנים נכנסים לאכול בתרומתן עד סוף האשמורה הראשונה דברי ר׳ אליעזר וחכמים אומרים עד חצות רבן גמליאל אומר עד שיעלה עמוד השחר מעשה ובאו בניו מבית המשתה אמרו לו לא קרינו את שמע אמר להם אם לא עלה עמוד השחר חייבין אתם לקרות ולא זו בלבד אמרו אלא כל מה שאמרו חכמים עד חצות מצותן עד שיעלה עמוד השחר הקטר חלבים ואברים מצותן עד שיעלה עמוד השחר וכל הנאכלים ליום אחד מצותן עד שיעלה עמוד השחר א"כ למה אמרו חכמים עד חצות כדי להרחיק אדם מן העבירה.

What is the beginning of the daily time span allotted to recite the nighttime k'rias Shema? It is that time that Kohanim enter [their homes] to eat their terumah portions. [And the time span continues] until the end of the first watch period, according to Rabbi Eliezer. The Sages say it is until midnight. Rabban Gamliel says it is until dawn. One time, [Rabban Gamliel's] sons returned home late from a wedding [and had missed the Sages' deadline of midnight]. They addressed their father, "We have not yet recited Shema." Rabban Gamliel responded, "If dawn has not yet broken, you remain obligated to recite it. Moreover, wherever the Sages called for a midnight deadline, the allotted mitzvah time span actually extends until dawn, e.g., the burning of the fats and limbs [called to be completed by midnight] is a mitzvah that extends until dawn, and all sacrifices that are to be eaten by midnight—these too can be eaten until dawn. Then why did the Sages say they are to be completed by midnight? In order to distance a person from committing a transgression."

דף ב.

1. The Mishnah tells us that the beginning of the time span for reciting nighttime *k'rias Shema* is the time when Kohanim enter to eat *terumah*. The Gemara clarifies that this time is *tzeis ha'kochavim* (dark)—the moment three stars are visible in the night sky. Why not just say so? asks the Gemara. It is in order to teach us that Kohanim eat *terumah* at night (after the day of their *mikveh* immersion ends), and that they need not wait until they bring their *korban* the next day. The question is, why is this bit of information relevant here? *K'rias Shema* is an obligation for all Jews, not just Kohanim. **Why do we need to be discussing rules for Kohanim in a Mishnah teaching us about *k'rias Shema*?**

2. The Gemara proceeds to ask two questions:
   - What was the author of our Mishnah last discussing that led him to now discuss *k'rias Shema*?
   - Why is he beginning with nighttime *k'rias Shema* rather than daytime *k'rias Shema*?

   The Gemara's first answer is that he had been discussing the verse, "*u'v'shochbecha u'v'kumecha*—when you go to sleep and when you arise." This answer resolves both questions, since *u'v'shochbecha u'v'kumecha* is both addressing *Shema* and placing the two daily recitations in order. The Gemara then offers an alternative answer: He had been discussing the verse, "*va'yehi erev va'yehi boker*—and it was evening and it was morning." The problem is that this verse—being about *maaseh Bereishis*, not *k'rias Shema*—only serves as an answer to the second question! **Why would the Gemara add an answer that only resolves *one* of two questions when it already has an answer that resolves them *both*?**

3. The Gemara tells us that the source for the dispute over whether or not Kohanim must wait to eat *terumah* until after they have

Berachos 2a

brought their *korbanos* is the verse, "*u'va ha'shemesh v'taher,*" which can be read either as, "when the [day ends] they are pure," or as, "when the [next day begins] they can make themselves pure." **The argument for the latter is actually very flimsy, as the word *v'taher* is *never* used to mean that one can make oneself pure. Why does the Gemara even bother to consider this proposal**, which Rabbah bar Rav Shila quickly dispenses with by saying, "If that's what it meant, it should have said *v'yitaher*"?

4. This discussion marks the beginning of the Talmud. One might have expected the Talmud would begin with a topic of broad and momentous importance. Instead, it seems to be dealing with a rather narrow topic—one routine daily recitation—consisting of picayune details, many of which are not even adhered to in standard Jewish communities (see *Rashi*, *Tosafos*, and *Rosh*). **Why was *zman k'rias Shema shel arvis* selected as the choice for how to begin Shas?**

Yesod

In order for the Gemara to make sense, it must be that the second answer (*va'yehi erev va'yehi boker*) offered to the two questions actually answers them both. *K'rias Shema* is a twice-daily recitation of our mission as a nation. The question is, what is it that compels our implementation of that mission? Is it a *maaseh Shamayim*—act of God, as effected through nature, i.e., the day shifting to night and night shifting to day, that naturally compels us to take stock of our mission as it presents itself anew and to declare it at both shift changes by reciting *Shema*? Or is it a *maaseh adam*—act of man, i.e., our changes from wakefulness to sleep and vice versa are what compel us to take stock and declare the mission of our oncoming life segment? The first answer holds *k'rias Shema* is triggered by a *maaseh adam* (*u'v'shochbecha u'v'kumecha*). The second holds *k'rias Shema* is triggered by a *maaseh Shamayim* (*va'yehi erev va'yehi boker*).

AS WE SAID, the source for the dispute over whether or not Kohanim must wait to eat *terumah* until after they have brought their *korbanos* is the verse *u'va ha'shemesh v'taher*. The dispute surrounding this verse revolves around the same question as the one at the beginning of the Gemara. Does the Kohen become pure as the result of a *maaseh Shamayim* (i.e., the setting of the sun naturally and automatically makes him pure), or a *maaseh adam* (i.e., his action of bringing the *korban* is what makes him pure)?

WHY IS THE purification of a Kohen linked to *k'rias Shema*? It is because of what *k'rias Shema* stands for. *Rashi* explains in Chumash (*Devarim* 6:4):

> Hear O Israel: Hashem, who is now only our God [Hashem Elokeinu], Hashem [will be]
> One [God, accepted as such throughout the whole world] [Hashem Echad].

K'rias Shema is the declaration that one day, *our* acceptance of Hashem as God will spread to the entire world.

WHAT WILL HAPPEN when that blessed day comes? That is what our Mishnah and Gemara are coming to teach.

RIGHT NOW, OUR Kohanim serve in a role relevant only to the relationship between God and the Jewish People. But come the future, there will be a need for Kohanim to serve in a role relevant to the newly restored relationship between God and the whole world.

Those Kohanim of the future will not be limited to the descendants of Aharon. All the Jewish People will be Kohanim to the world, as the verse says, "And you shall be for me a kingdom of Kohanim and a holy nation" (*Shemos* 19:6).

KOHANIM ARE RELEVANT to *Shema*, because it is the *Shema* that predicts the day when Kohanim writ small will grow to become Kohanim writ large.

Berachos 2a

NOW LET US consider the following question: Are our Kohanim representatives of us to God, or representatives of God to us? I would suggest that if they represent us, their actions should be rightfully considered no more than *maaseh adam*. But if they are representatives of God, the actions they take should be considered *maaseh Shamayim*, just as the actions of any ambassador or diplomat are considered the actions of his home country.

This is the dispute being played out in the pages of our Gemara. Both in its discussion of the source of *k'rias Shema* and in its discussion of Kohanim eating *terumah*, the Gemara wants to know if we are dealing with *maaseh Shamayim* or *maaseh adam*. The matter is crucial. If we conclude we are dealing with *maaseh adam*, then mundane acts by ordinary people are just mundane acts. But if we are dealing with *maaseh Shamayim*, everything a "Heavenly diplomat" does has to be seen as if it is being done by Hashem Himself, *k'v'yachol*!

BY CITING RABBAH bar Rav Shila's reasoning, the Gemara comes to the conclusion that Kohanim eating *terumah* ought to be considered *maaseh Shamayim*. This is powerful, as it provides a clear explanation for the entire mitzvah of *terumah*, including why it must be eaten in the strictest of purity, why a non-Kohen who eats it is *chayav misah*, why it is fundamentally different from Levitical *maaser* (which remains a *maaseh adam*), and why *m'd'Oraisa* even a single kernel of grain constitutes *terumah*.

At the same time, the Gemara earlier, by favoring *u'v'shochbecha u'v'kumecha* over *va'yehi erev va'yehi boker*, had concluded that reciting *k'rias Shema* is to be seen as *maaseh adam*.

BUT THAT GEMARA, in maintaining the alternative view about *k'rias Shema* as a *hava amina*, is actually teaching us something extraordinary. It is teaching us that *k'rias Shema* being associated with *maaseh adam* may be true for now, when we are at the stage of "Hashem Elokeinu" but not yet "Hashem Echad." In the future, however, when the world recognizes Hashem's unity and all Israel is a "kingdom of Kohanim and a holy nation," we who recite *k'rias Shema* twice a day will transition into individuals whose actions will start to be seen as *maaseh Shamayim*, as we will all become Hashem's ambassadors to the rest of the world. This means our every action—going to sleep, waking up, eating, drinking, conversing, etc.—will cease being mundane and will become actions that every non-Jew on earth will seek to connect to in his quest to become connected to God! This is the true significance of *k'rias Shema*, and this is why our Gemara carries on in somewhat unusual fashion, as it is building the case for what *Shema* will someday be all about, even if it is not about that now.

AS EVIDENCE TO this idea, we need merely reexamine the rest of the Mishnah. Rabban Gamliel made it clear that *k'rias Shema* includes a *harchakah*—a fence set up to distance ourselves from transgressing. Where else do we find the need for such *harchakos*? In our Mishnah, they are needed for *avodas ha'korbanos* (*hekter chalavim* and *korbanos ha'ne'echalim*). This makes sense, as what both *Shema* and *korbanos* have in common is that both have a connection to being *maaseh Shamayim*—actions that appear human on the surface but in fact serve as the means by which Heaven gets its matters taken care of in this physical world. These two mitzvos require *harchakos* because mortal beings performing *maaseh Shamayim* cannot afford to make mistakes. Humans are prone to mistakes. Hence, the *harchakos* are there to insulate our efforts. There is one other mitzvah that requires *harchakos*, and now we can understand why. It is the mitzvah of observing *hilchos niddah*, and now we can explain that it, too, requires *harchakos* because it too consists of human actions that—in effecting the potential creation of a new soul—are in fact *maaseh Shamayim* like *Shema* and *korbanos*.

IT IS NOW clear why Shas begins with the *sugya* of *k'rias Shema*, as the Talmud—through the learning of its contents and the performance of its teachings—is the vehicle by which we use the mitzvah of *Shema* to propel us from the world of *maaseh adam* to the future world—predicted right in the *Shema* itself—where all our deeds become *maaseh Shamayim*. Indeed, *k'rias Shema* actually contains the formula for

Berachos 2a

reaching that lofty goal: loving God, instilling Torah in our children, doing mitzvos, and remembering *yetzias Mitzrayim*.

FAR FROM A tangential topic filled with inscrutable detail, *k'rias Shema* is the distilled essence of everything for which Judaism stands, the particulars of which are to be dealt with exhaustively as the pages of the Talmud unfold.

דף ב:

אמר מר בשעה שהכהנים נכנסין לאכול בתרומתן ורמינהו וגו'.

Said the Master: At the time that Kohanim enter [their homes] to eat their terumah. And we ask [from a Beraisa], etc.

Our Mishnah says that the earliest time one can say *k'rias Shema* at night is when the Kohanim enter to eat their *terumah*. (Let's call this time "Kohanim.")

Beraisa #1 says the earliest time for *k'rias Shema* is when *ani'im* come in to eat their meal of bread and salt. (We'll call this "*ani'im*.")

Beraisa #2 quotes Rabbi Meir saying the earliest time is when people come in to eat their meal on Erev Shabbos ("*ani'im*") and quotes *Chachamim* saying the time is "Kohanim."

[*Beraisa #3* brings *z'man kiddush* as Rabbi Eliezer's view, "Kohanim" as Rabbi Yehoshua's view, Kohanim's immersion time as Rabbi Meir's view, "*ani'im*" as Rabbi Chanina's view, and the time when regular people eat their weeknight meal as Rav Achai's view.]

THE GEMARA BRINGS a *kashya* on the Mishnah from *Beraisa #1*. Mishnah says "Kohanim"; *Beraisa* says "*ani'im*." The Gemara's problem with this is, how can we have a *Beraisa* disputing our Mishnah?

The Gemara tries to answer that there is no dispute, as "Kohanim" and "*ani'im*" are one and the same time.

The Gemara challenges this answer by quoting *Beraisa #2*, where "*ani'im*" and "Kohanim" are cited as being competing positions, thus proving they cannot be one and the same time.

The Gemara resolves this challenge by pointing out that the challenge from *Beraisa #2* is built on the assumption (as explained in *Rashi* 2b, s.v.

9

Berachos 2b

m'she'he'ani and s.v. *b'arvei Shabbasos*) that the time when people come in to eat their meal on Erev Shabbos is synonymous with the time when *ani'im* come in to eat their meal of bread and salt on weeknights. If we simply abandon this assumption, we will have no problem from *Beraisa* #2. "*Ani'im*" and "Kohanim" we will say are one and the same time, and the time when people come in to eat their meal on Erev Shabbos is a different time.

MY QUESTION IS: How are we OK with that? If we don't like *Beraisos* disputing our Mishnah, how are we OK with *Beraisa* #1, which now includes a position, attributed to Rabbi Meir, that the proper time for starting *k'rias Shema* at night is not "Kohanim" or "*ani'im*," but rather the time when people come in to eat their meal on Erev Shabbos (which we'll call "Erev Shabbos")? This position is in dispute with our Mishnah! It must be that we are OK with it because we will say it is only the view of Rabbi Meir, and he is a lone opinion, a *da'as yachid*, about which we are not concerned if it disputes our Mishnah, which is the view of the *Chachamim*. So then why not just say, in response to the original *kashya* on the Mishnah from *Beraisa* #1, that we are not concerned about the "*ani'im*" view in *Beraisa* #1, as it is merely the view of a *da'as yachid*, either Rabbi Meir (as seen in *Beraisa* #2) or Rabbi Chanina (as seen in *Beraisa* #3)? Let us simply say it is not a concern for us, as our Mishnah ("Kohanim") represents the view of *Chachamim*. Why do we instead become so troubled by *Beraisa* #1 that we try to make it so "*ani'im*" and "Kohanim" are one and the same?

IT SEEMS THAT the entire issue here is something different. In truth, there never was a need for the Gemara to ask a "*v'raminhu*" *kashya* just because we found a *Beraisa* somewhere with a position different from our Mishnah. The proof to this is that we see the Gemara was not bothered by the fact that the very same *Beraisa* #1 also contains a view that the end of the time allotted for *k'rias Shema* (*sof z'man k'rias Shema*) is in agreement with none of the opinions offered in our Mishnah, but is rather *ad sha'ah she'omed l'pater mitoch se'udaso*. The halachah of *sof z'man k'rias Shema* remains like the *Chachamim* in our

Mishnah despite this competing view in the *Beraisa*, and nobody is asking *v'raminhu*!

The issue here is that the minute we find the *z'manim* of *k'rias Shema* expressed as being governed by when "*ani'im*" begin and end their *seudah*, *k'rias Shema* has been converted from a mitzvah whose parameters are defined by a *maaseh Shamayim* to a mitzvah whose parameters are defined by a *maaseh adam*. The Gemara that went to all the trouble to bring Rabbah bar Rav Shila's use of *Beraisa* #2 to prove that *u'va ha'shemesh v'taher* meant the *maaseh Shamayim* of *tzeis* as opposed to the *maaseh adam* of Kohanim bringing *korbanos* (as a way of showing that we need to use *va'yehi erev va'yehi boker* not *u'v'shochbecha u'v'kumecha* as the source for *k'rias Shema* and have *k'rias Shema* be understood as *maaseh Shamayim*) is going to have it all destroyed if a *z'man* is found that is not linked to *tzeis ha'kochavim*! **That** was the *kashya* from *Beraisa* #1.

The Gemara deflects this by asserting that "*ani'im*" is not a distinct *z'man* dependent on *maaseh adam*. "*Ani'im*" is just another way to refer to "Kohanim," but the governance is still that of "Kohanim," and it is exclusively *maaseh Shamayim*.

But then we have a challenge from *Beraisa* #2. *Beraisa* #2 shows definitively that "*ani'im*" is its own *z'man*, and, untethered from *tzeis ha'kochavim*, this *z'man* is going to have to be governed by and described as *maaseh adam*!

TO DEFLECT THIS challenge, the Gemara reminds us that "Erev Shabbos" and "*ani'im*" might not be synonymous (and, thus, the assumption as explained by *Rashi* would no longer be the correct way to understand "*ani'im*"). This will allow us to maintain that "*ani'im*" is the same as "Kohanim" and is *tzeis* (*shitas Chachamim*); the other view in *Beraisa* #2 (*shitas* Rabbi Meir) is at *sh'kiah* (which is when people actually do come in to eat their meal on Erev Shabbos); and all *z'manim* remain governed by a *maaseh Shamayim*.

But then the Gemara is faced with *Beraisa* #3. If "*ani'im*" is the view of Rabbi Chanina, and "Kohanim" is the view of Rabbi Yehoshua, then "*ani'im*" and "Kohanim" cannot be one and the same, and we again are

Berachos 2b

faced with the fear that *"ani'im"* is a stand-alone *z'man* that is governed by human actions—*maaseh adam*. This means that all the opinions on this matter are governed by *maaseh adam*. Rabbi Eliezer's view is governed by when people make *kiddush*. Rabbi Yehoshua's view is governed by when Kohanim go in to eat. Rabbi Meir's view (here in *Beraisa* #3) is governed by when Kohanim immerse (although Rabbi Yehudah is not sure about Rabbi Meir). Rabbi Chanina's view—no longer linked to the *maaseh Shamayim* of *tzeis ha'kochavim*—is governed by when poor people sit down to eat. Rav Achai's view is governed by when regular people gather to eat.

WE WOULD HAVE been OK with one or two minority views in *Beraisa* #3 being in the camp of *maaseh adam*, as long as the preponderance of opinions are aligned with *maaseh Shamayim*. But if every opinion about *z'man k'rias Shema* rests on a *maaseh adam*, wails the Gemara, how can we maintain our thesis that *k'rias Shema* is based on *maaseh Shamayim*?

Wait, says the Gemara, maybe we can try one more thing. Maybe *z'manei k'rias Shema* are indeed governed by *maaseh Shamayim*, it's just that *"ani'im"* is an **earlier** *z'man* than "Kohanim." That way, we can say that *ani'im* is *sh'kiah*, "Kohanim" is *tzeis*, and *k'rias Shema* is a *maaseh Shamayim* after all!

No, the Gemara sadly replies. Rabbi Eliezer's view of Friday night *kiddush* is already linked to *sh'kiah*. If Rabbi Chanina's *"ani'im"* time were *sh'kiah*, Rabbi Chanina and Rabbi Eliezer would be duplicate opinions. *"Ani'im"* must be later than "Kohanim," and **all the opinions must be linked to *maaseh adam*:** *"Ani'im"* is the first one after "Kohanim" or *tzeis*, as we have no reason to say it is later than anything other than "Kohanim"; regular people on Friday night (Rabbi Meir's *shitah* from *Beraisa* #2) is next (see *Rashi* 3a, s.v. *kashya d'Rabbi Meir ad'Rabbi Meir*), as they can eat earlier on Friday night than they can on weeknights since all the food is already prepared and ready (*Rashi*, s.v. *b'arvei Shabbasos*); latest of all is the time when regular people eat their meal on weeknights, when they first have to prepare the meal and then they can sit and eat. And according to the *is d'amri* in *Rashi* (2b, s.v. *nichnasim* *l'hasev*), these last two times merge, as the author of the last *shitah* (Rav Achai) was talking about Friday night, not weeknights.

THE GEMARA'S FINAL conclusion is to support the determination we made on *amud alef*—that *k'rias Shema*, according to our Mishnah, is a *maaseh adam*.

Berachos 3b

דף ג:

ת"ר ארבע משמרות הוי הלילה דברי רבי ר׳ נתן
אומר שלש וגו׳.

The Rabbis taught: The night is divided into four watch periods, these are the words of Rebbi. Rabbi Nasan says three, etc.

1. What is the root of the *machlokes* between Rabbi Eliezer (with Rabbi Nasan) and Rabbi Yehudah HaNasi (Rebbi) over whether there are three *mishmaros* at night or four?
2. Rebbi's source for his position that the night has four *mishmaros* is that while David awoke at midnight, he is still described in the *pasuk* as having two *mishmaros* ahead of him (*kidmu einai ashmoros*). This can only be true if there are four *mishmaros* at night. But then the Gemara challenges the idea that David awoke at midnight based on the assumption that "*neshef*" means the beginning of the night. The Gemara resolves the conflict in three ways (David was already up by midnight; David dozed until midnight; David learned until midnight and was then roused to sing praises), all of which dispense with the notion that David first woke up at midnight. If so, Rebbi's source no longer exists, since *kidmu einai ashmoros* can now start from *neshef*, not from midnight, and there can be only three *mishmaros* and David will still have two ahead of him. What happens to Rebbi's position in light of our Gemara?

Yesod

Rebbi will deflect the challenge of the Gemara by not agreeing to the assumption that *neshef* means the beginning of the night. Rebbi will say that *neshef* is a word that covers the entire night or any part thereof. So when David says he awoke at midnight, the *pasuk*, "*kidamti ba'neshef va'ashavei'a*" poses no contradiction. And thus Rebbi can continue to argue that the night consists of four *mishmaros*.

THIS WILL HELP us understand something larger: Which opinion did Rebbi adopt in our Mishnah? With the opinions named being Rabbi Eliezer, the Rabbis, and Rabban Gamliel—and Rabban Gamliel agreeing in essence with the Rabbis, just disagreeing over the issue of a fence—it seems safe to say that Rebbi's position would be that of the Rabbis and not that of Rabbi Eliezer.

What is that issue? What is the meaning of "*u'v'shochbecha*"? Is it when people go to sleep (beginning of the night) or when people **are** asleep (the entire night)? Rabbi Eliezer holds the former; Rebbi holds the latter.

THAT ISSUE IS the same as the issue about the word *neshef*. Does it mean the beginning of the night (Rabbi Eliezer) or does it mean the entire night (Rebbi)?

THIS REFLECTS A very broad and defining difference between the two Sages. According to Rabbi Eliezer, Torah words and thoughts cover the least territory that they can be said to cover. We are in no position to take any liberties beyond what we know to be the Torah's intent. In *Pirkei Avos*, he was described as a "limed pit that never lost a drop" (*Avos* 2:8), restricting his Torah conclusions only to that which he heard directly from his *rebbe*. Both the words *u'v'shochbecha* and *neshef* can refer to no more than the beginning of the night. According to Rebbi, in contrast, our mission is to take the Torah and expand it, extrapolating it out over inherently understood principles. In his case, that led to Rebbi taking the ultimate liberty of writing down the Oral Torah, a step he took because he applied his own innate understanding to help determine what was desired by Hashem to be done on behalf of the Torah. That same expansiveness allows him to translate both *u'v'shochbecha* and *neshef* as referring to the whole night.

Berachos 3b

THIS *MACHLOKES* WILL become crucial as we encounter the Gemara's next topic—determining God's will even as we acknowledge our inherent uncertainty about it. This discussion is introduced by the Gemara presenting the distinction between God's *"ba'chatzos"* and man's *"ka'chatzos."* It continues with David's checking with advisors and the Sanhedrin about matters of State, and with Mephiboshes about matters of halachah (where you will notice that one checking is done first and the other is done afterward). From there it continues to David's uncertainty of his own piety in light of the possibility of his having sinned. Throughout the entire upcoming Gemara, we will have to apply the opposite worldviews of Rebbi and Rabbi Eliezer in order to gain the fullest understanding of these critical life matters.

דף ד:

אמר מר קורא ק״ש ומתפלל מסייע ליה לר׳ יוחנן
דאמר ר׳ יוחנן איזהו בן העולם הבא זה הסומך גאולה
לתפלה של ערבית רבי יהושע בן לוי אומר תפלות
באמצע תקנום וגו׳.

Said the Master: One recites k'rias Shema and then davens [Shemoneh Esreh]. This supports the view of Rabbi Yochanan, for Rabbi Yochanan said: Who is [certain to be] a resident of the World to Come? He who connects [the berachah of] geulah to tefillah at Maariv. Rabbi Yehoshua ben Levi [disagreed and] said: The tefillos were set between [the morning and nighttime recitations of Shema], etc.

Rabbi Yochanan and Rabbi Yehoshua ben Levi have a dispute over whether *k'rias Shema* of night should be said before or after *Amidah*. Rabbi Yochanan says before, and that one who does so and is thereby *somech geulah l'tefillah* even at night is a *ben Olam Haba*. Rabbi Yehoshua ben Levi says there is no reason to be *somech geulah l'tefillah* at night, because there was no *geulah* at night—the *geulah* was by day. Much more important is to bracket the two daily recitations of *k'rias Shema* around the daily *tefillos*—*tefillos b'emtza tiknum*.

WE PASKEN LIKE Rabbi Yochanan, because a *Beraisa* that we cited in support of *Chachamim* holding like Rabban Gamliel and just adding a fence to make it midnight suggested that the proper order of evening events is *k'rias Shema* first before *Amidah*.

Berachos 4b

This is troublesome for several reasons:

1. Who even needed that *Beraisa*? Did we not know without the *Beraisa* that the *Chachamim* are mandated to make fences? Don't we know it from the first Mishnah in *Avos*? *Bichlal*, didn't we already know from our Mishnah itself that, at least according to Rabban Gamliel, the *Chachamim* said *chatzos* in order to distance people from sin (made a fence)? Who needed our entire Gemara? And then because of an unnecessary *Beraisa* we *pasken* like Rabbi Yochanan?

2. *Paskening* like Rabbi Yehoshua ben Levi would have made so much more sense. All the halachic compromises we made in the opening *sugya* would have been avoided! We would not have needed to add an early extra *Shema*, putting forth the somewhat forced explanation of *la'amod l'tefillah mitoch divrei Torah*, if *Shema* didn't have to be before *Amidah*. We could have davened *Maariv* (*Amidah*) early in shul with no halachic problem, without *k'rias Shema*, and waited until we were home alone after dark to say *k'rias Shema*. We would have had no reason to separate *k'rias Shema* from its *berachos*, and no one would have had to accept the halachic stretch that the *berachos* ostensibly assigned to *k'rias Shema* (and bearing its name) are actually *milsa b'anpei nafsha* and can be said when davening early *Maariv*, which we only do in order to accommodate *geulah l'tefillah*, which would have been unnecessary had we *paskened* like Rabbi Yehoshua ben Levi. Nobody would have had the urge to wait on *k'rias Shema* until saying *k'rias Shema al ha'mitah*, forcing *Rashi* into the unlikely suggestion that *k'rias Shema al ha'mitah* is enough for the mitzvah of nighttime *k'rias Shema*, since everyone would have been happy to say it immediately at *tzeis*, being the first time all evening they would be saying it (having not said it at all during *Maariv*). Why are we rejecting this elegant *shitah*, one that had so cleanly fit in with the Mishnah and our entire *sugya* up until *daf* 4b?

דף ד:

3. **Rabbi Yehoshua ben Levi is right.** *Geulah ma'alyasa* did not take place until morning. Rabbi Yochanan even agrees to this! So why should we commemorate *geulah me'urta*, even if it is somewhat connected to the ultimate *geulah*? What did the preliminary nighttime *geulah* really accomplish?
4. The Gemara on *daf* 9a–b seems to suggest the opposite of our *sugya*. It argues, in the name of Rabbi Abba, that *geulah* took place at night. All that took place by day was "*yetziah*." If anything, this should indicate that the primary *semichas geulah l'tefillah* should be at night, with *geulah l'tefillah* by day only an afterthought. Why does our Gemara treat it the opposite?
5. Why do we refer to the Exodus as "*yetzias Mitzrayim*" as opposed to "*geulas Mitzrayim*"?

Yesod

I would like to suggest that our attachment to the halachic position of Rabbi Yochanan is related to the same issue our entire Gemara has really been all about from the beginning.

The first thing to note is that the *Beraisa* here tells us not that the *Chachamim* made fences to the rules **of the Torah**, but rather that they made fences *l'divreihem*—to their **own** teachings, *d'Rabbanans*.

What is the significance of *d'Rabbanans*? What status do they have?

Let us consider an imaginary parallel to the Gemara's comparison of the *geulah* of night to the *geulah ma'alyasa* of morning.

Imagine the *geulah* of night as representing *divrei Chachamim* (*mitzvos d'Rabbanan*) and the *geulah* of day as representing *divrei Torah* (*mitzvos d'Oraisa*). It certainly would be accurate to call *d'Oraisas* "*ma'alyasa*" just as the *geulah* of daytime is referred to as "*ma'alyasa*." So next we can ask: What rank, if any, does the lesser *geulah* have in light of the greater *geulah*? That is the *machlokes* of Rabbi Yehoshua ben Levi and Rabbi Yochanan. Rabbi Yehoshua ben Levi holds the lesser *geulah* has no ranking in the face of the greater *geulah*. Rabbi Yochanan holds the lesser *geulah* stands in its own right, despite the existence of a greater *geulah*, and that is why we must be *somech geulah l'tefillah* as much at

Berachos 4b

night as we do by day. In the parallel we have imagined, Rabbi Yehoshua ben Levi would hold that *divrei Chachamim*, like the non-ranking *geulah* of night, rate no status when compared with *d'Oraisas*. Rabbi Yochanan, in contrast, would hold they do—and therefore, according to him, *d'Rabbanans* can require fences just like *d'Oraisas*, *d'Rabbanans* can grant *Olam Haba* just like *d'Oraisas*, and *d'Rabbanans* can carry the death penalty just like *d'Oraisas*. Precisely the *machlokes* as displayed in our Gemara!

What is another way to frame this *machlokes*? It is simply this: Rabbi Yehoshua ben Levi holds *divrei Chachamim* are *maaseh adam*, while Rabbi Yochanan holds *divrei Chachamim* are *maaseh Shamayim*.

And it all flows perfectly in the Gemara. What have we been discussing prior to this in the Gemara? The status of Kohanim. What was the Kohanim's role within the Jewish People? They were the teachers of Torah. Who fills in for their role after their stature ebbs? Clearly, it is the *Chachamim*. Our Gemara, having determined that Kohanim are to be considered representatives of God (*maaseh Shamayim*), goes on to *pasken* like Rabbi Yochanan that the *Chachamim* and their teachings are similarly to be considered *maaseh Shamayim*.

With this, we can explain the awkward halachic stretches we were made to accept in the opening *sugya*. Had we determined that *divrei Chachamim* are *maaseh adam*—sound teachings from good and wise but mortal leaders considered representatives of the people—the *Chachamim* would have been recognized as coaches, top-notch trainers helping to prepare the Jewish People to effectively fulfill their roles in the service of Hashem. Fences they might make would have carried no more significance than any self-improvement commitments entered into voluntarily; their own fences would not require additional fences; and compliance would neither confer Divine reward nor carry serious punishment for neglect. And most importantly, their enactments would need to make rational sense, because no personal trainer can expect a client to adhere to instructions that appear to the client to be irrational.

But once we have determined that *divrei Chachamim* are *maaseh Shamayim*, everything changes. Far from mere coaches, *Chachamim* are Divine agents, and their rulings are imbued with transcendent truth.

They must be adhered to with strictness parallel to *divrei Torah* (except where Torah itself permits leniency); they carry Divine reward and serious penalty; they require their own fences for protection; and, most importantly, they need not make rational sense or be elegant to command our obedience. We can be told that an early *k'rias Shema* can be strictly for the purpose of *la'amod b'tefillah mitoch divrei Torah*; that *birkas k'rias Shema* can be successfully uncoupled from *Shema*; that *Maariv* can be early even while *Minchah* is late—and all for the purpose of connecting *geulah* to *tefillah* of *Maariv*. If such is as the *Chachamim* have decreed, teaches Rabbi Yochanan, like whom we *pasken*, their decrees are *maaseh Shamayim*, and we must obey these *mitzvos d'Rabbanan* with as much seriousness as if we had heard them *mi'pi haGevurah*.

Now we can talk about *yetzias Mitzrayim* versus *geulas Mitzrayim*.

Of the four *lashonos* of *geulah* found in *Parashas Va'era*, none actually necessitate that Israel physically leave Egypt. Only the fifth *lashon* (*v'hevesi*) calls for an actual "*yetzias*" Mitzrayim.

Furthermore, at the *Bris Bein Ha'Besarim*, Avraham was promised *yetzias Mitzrayim*, not *geulas Mitzrayim*. However, Moshe's original request of Pharaoh—"Let us go and worship for three days in the *midbar*"—would have yielded *geulas Mitzrayim* but not *yetzias Mitzrayim*.

Perhaps we can suggest as follows: *Geulas Mitzrayim* is our restoration to God, while *yetzias Mitzrayim* is our restoration to the Godly strain we carry within ourselves. This explains the promise to Avraham, where only the latter would guarantee that we would have the internal motivation to reclaim the Land. It explains *rechush gadol*, because this is all about guaranteeing Avraham that we would feel good about ourselves, something that *rechush gadol* is able to supply. But only *geulah*, not *yetziah*, can be linked to *tefillah*, because we cannot pray to the Godliness within ourselves. And only a *geulah* that is *maaseh Shamayim* can yield a link to *tefillah* (as *maaseh adam* is connected to *yetzias Mitzrayim*, not *geulas Mitzrayim*, and does not have the ability to connect us to anything beyond the best part of ourselves). But when it is linked to *tefillah*, the fact that our *divrei Chachamim* is considered *maaseh Shamayim* gives the nighttime *geulah* as much punch in forging this link as daytime *geulah*. Like *shitas* Rabbi Yehoshua ben Levi, on the other hand, *divrei*

Chachamim is considered *maaseh adam*, and thus it has no power to be linked to *tefillah*. Only *geulah ma'alyasa*, i.e., *divrei Torah*, are considered *maaseh Shamayim* and can forge a connection to *tefillah*, and thus only the daytime *berachah* of *geulah* can be connected to *tefillah*. Nightime offers a better representation of the relationship of *divrei Torah* to *divrei Chachamim*. *K'rias Shema* (*divrei Torah*) creates the parameters around the *avodah* day, and *tefillos* (*divrei Chachamim*) simply find their subservient place within those parameters.

With this we can understand how sometimes in *kiddush* we emphasize *maaseh bereishis* (*maaseh Shamayim*) and sometimes *yetzias Mitzrayim* (*maaseh adam*). We also understand how it was *yetzias Mitzrayim*, not *geulas Mitzrayim*, that led to *kabbalas haTorah*, because *kabbalas haTorah* is *mashlim adam*, not *shamayim*.

Moshe succeeded at *yetzias Mitzrayim* because he functioned in the context of *maaseh adam*. He failed at bringing us into Eretz Yisrael because at Mei Merivah he reverted to acting in the context of *maaseh Shamayim*. This, as we have said, addresses our *geulah* from Mitzrayim, but it leaves our full *yetziah*, the original concern of Avraham Avinu at the *Bris Bein Ha'Besarim*, still short of completion.

דף ה.

א"ר יצחק כל הקורא ק"ש על מטתו כאלו אוחז חרב של שתי פיות בידו וגו׳.

Rabbi Yitzchak says: Saying k'rias Shema al ha'mitah is like one who is holding a double-edged sword, etc.

1. Rabbi Yitzchak says: Whoever says *k'rias Shema al ha'mitah* is like one who is holding a double-edged sword (with which to kill *mazikin*—Rashi). Then, the same Rabbi Yitzchak says: Whoever says *k'rias Shema al ha'mitah*, *mazikin* will be removed from him as if by birds. If the second statement is true, who needs the first? Since he won't be removing the *mazikin*, why does he need the double-edged sword?

2. After *darshening l'chumei reshef* to mean *mazikin*, the Gemara returns and *darshens* it to mean *yissurin*. On this, Reish Lakish says that one who is *oseik baTorah* will have *yissurin* flee from him. Before, *ein oaf ela Torah* was understood to mean *ha'korei k'rias Shema al mitaso*—one who recites the bedtime Shema. Why does it now change to *kol ha'oseik baTorah*—one who gets involved in Torah study?

3. Reish Lakish only says that *yissurin*—like *mazikin*—will depart from him. Why doesn't he also restate Rabbi Yitzchak's other point—that he will be given a double-edged sword?

4. Rabbi Yochanan says Reish Lakish's point is too obvious, and the real message is that if someone is capable of being *oseik baTorah* and does not do so, he will be the recipient of horrible *yissurin*. What is the *machlokes*?

Berachos 5a

Yesod

This *sugya* is connected to the *machlokes* between Rabbi Yishmael and Rabbi Shimon Bar Yochai on *daf* 35b regarding whether a person should work for a living or be *oseik baTorah* and have his *melachah* done for him by others. Rabbi Yitzchak gives two conflicting statements about one who says *k'rias Shema al ha'mitah* because he is referring to two different types of people. The type that follow Rabbi Yishmael and do their own *melachah* receive a double-edged sword with which to do their own killing of the *mazikin*; the type that follow Rabbi Shimon Bar Yochai and have their *melachah* done by others have the *mazikin* removed by others too without their direct efforts.

From Rabbi Yitzchak, one would not discern a difference between whether one chooses the approach of Rabbi Yishmael or that of Rabbi Shimon Bar Yochai; they just seem to be two parallel alternatives to be chosen according to each individual's *techunas ha'nefesh*. So Reish Lakish comes along and says the approach of Rabbi Shimon Bar Yochai (*kol ha'oseik baTorah*) is superior. In what way? In that one who does so will be protected not only from *mazikin* but also from *yissurin*, whereas the "*baalabos*" type will not be given any kind of sword to fight against *yissurin*.

To that, Rabbi Yochanan exclaims—That's *p'shita*! Of course an *oseik baTorah* will get protection from *yissurin*. It's *b'feirush* in the *pasuk*. The *chiddush* here needs to be stated more powerfully. The two options are not just parallel alternatives. In fact, if one is capable of exclusively learning, like Rabbi Shimon Bar Yochai, and instead chooses the path of Rabbi Yishmael, he will face *yissurin mecho'arin*.

דף ו: (1)

אמר רבי חלבו אמר רב הונא כל הקובע מקום
לתפלתו אלהי אברהם בעזרו וכשמת אומרים לו אי
עניו אי חסיד מתלמידיו של אברהם אבינו ואברהם
אבינו מנא לן דקבע מקום דכתיב וישכם אברהם בבקר
אל המקום אשר עמד שם ואין עמידה אלא תפלה
שנאמר ויעמוד פינחס ויפלל.

Rabbi Chelbo cited Rav Huna: Whoever establishes a fixed place for his prayer, the God of Avraham will come to his aid. And when he passes on, they will say of him, "So humble, so pious! He was among the disciples of Avraham Avinu!"

And how do we know that Avraham Avinu established a fixed place for his prayer? We know, for it is written, "Avraham woke up early the next morning [and went] to the place where there he had stood [the day before]" (Bereishis 19:27). And "stood" is a reference to prayer, as it says, "Pinchas stood and prayed" (Tehillim 106:30).

The way this Gemara is generally understood, the evidence that Avraham established a fixed place to pray is the fact that he went back the next morning to the same spot he prayed in the day before. This would be an acceptable proof if it said he went back the next morning *to pray*. But the verse does not say he went back the next morning to pray. It says he went back for a different reason:

He looked out over the area of S'dom, Amorah, and the entire plain, and beheld that the smoke of the earth rose up like the smoke of an oven. (Bereishis 19:28)

Berachos 6b

Avraham went back to survey the destruction, not to pray. If so, what source is there that one should establish a fixed place for prayer? Additionally, what is so special about establishing a fixed place to pray that should earn one such lofty accolades as "humble" and "pious"?

The *Rosh* insists that it is not enough to establish a fixed shul, but that one must establish a fixed spot in that shul. He bases it on a *Yerushalmi* that suggests David HaMelech had a certain spot from which he would consistently pray. *Talmidei Rabbeinu Yonah* are bothered by this insistence. Since the whole shul is a place of prayer, why should it matter where in the shul you choose to daven? Instead, *Rabbeinu Yonah* learns that the need to daven in one spot comes from a different *Yerushalmi* that says that one who davens alone at home, it is as if he is building firm iron walls around himself, which *Rabbeinu Yonah* understands to be talking about one who fixes a set spot in his home for prayer. The problem is that it now emerges that no one is learning the obligation to set a fixed spot in shul from the example of Avraham Avinu. And yet the halachah continues to say that one who does so will be considered a disciple of Avraham, basing it on our Gemara. This point is therefore difficult for *Rabbeinu Yonah* because even if Avraham Avinu did fix a specific spot, it was not in his home. And furthermore, it is difficult for the *Rosh* because if all Avraham did was pick a general place to daven, and it was from David HaMelech that we learn we are to pick a specific spot, shouldn't the title "disciple of Avraham Avinu" apply even to one who just picks a general place to daven?

I would like to suggest there is a third way to learn, and that is the *shitah* of the *Rambam*. The *Rambam*'s language is:

> How does one prepare one's place for davening? He should stand in a low place and turn his face toward the wall. He should open windows or openings facing Yerushalayim in order to pray facing them. And he should...establish a spot for his davening constantly [tamid]. (Hilchos Tefillah 5:6)

If the *Rambam* holds that one is obligated to establish a fixed spot the way the other Rishonim understand it, why does he not say that

דף ו:

first? What he should be saying is that he must select a fixed spot in shul that is low and near a wall (to whatever extent such fixed spots are available). Furthermore, what can he possibly mean by "*tamid*"? The establishment of a davening spot is something that happens once, not constantly. If he meant one must daven in the same spot constantly, he could have said so. But one cannot be "*kove'a*" (establish) a spot for davening more than once! Finally, if the *Rambam* is learning like the other Rishonim, he is doing a poor job of clarifying whether he sides with *Rosh* or *Rabbeinu Yonah*. How can the *Rambam* leave so unclear whether he is talking about shul or about home?

IT SEEMS TO me the *Rambam* understands the Gemara differently than the other Rishonim. According to the *Rambam*, what Avraham Avinu did was daven in one spot, i.e., standing still. Without Avraham's example, it would be permissible to daven while walking around from spot to spot as long as you remain standing and not sitting, as prayer is called "*Amidah*," which requires standing (but in theory does not require standing still). The Gemara's proof is that when the *pasuk* refers to what Avraham did the day before, when he prayed, it says, "to the place where he had prayed," i.e., the spot. Avraham Avinu had prayed standing still in one spot, says the Gemara, and his God will assist anyone else who does the same.

With this, we can answer all our questions. Avraham never established a "*makom kavu'a*" in the commonly understood meaning of that phrase, not at home and not at shul. This is why the *Rambam* gives no indication as to which of those two he holds of. He does not hold of that obligation at all! And we now understand why the *Rambam* chose to use the word *tamid*. He does so because to choose to daven in a fixed **position** is something one must do every time he davens *Shemoneh Esreh* (no matter what shul and no matter which seat).

But everybody does this, you might ask. We all daven every *Shemoneh Esreh* rooted in one place with our feet together. What is so great about this practice that it earns one the special accolades of "humble" and "pious"?

For the answer to this, we must remember that just because one performs the physical expression of a mitzvah, it does not always mean one has fulfilled the entirety of that mitzvah. For example, one who is circumcised may be in physical compliance with the mitzvah. But if he is not *shomer ha'bris* and engages in wanton sexual misconduct, can he truly be said to be observant of the covenant represented by the mitzvah of *milah*? Similarly, the mitzvah of *tefillah* is to address God via the words of *Shemoneh Esreh* and thereby offer Him an act of service. If you are reciting the *Amidah* standing still with your feet together, but your mind is wandering off in all directions and is hardly still at all, can you truly be said to be in fulfillment of this mitzvah? The way the *Rambam* understands the *sugya*, the accolades of "humble" and "pious" belong to the one who makes sure every *tefillah* he ever says is said with his mind as rooted in place as his feet—solidly focused on the One to whom he is speaking. "Humble" because the definition of humility is making sure to give appropriate space to others; and "pious" because piety involves the giving to Hashem that is part of being in a real relationship with Him, something that eludes one who cannot even focus on His presence during the intimate moments of *tefillah*.

According to which approach does the halachah go?

Shulchan Aruch (*Orach Chaim* 90:19) pointedly does not quote the above Gemara when *paskening* the halachah (even though *Mishnah Berurah* §59 does). It would be difficult for him to do that, as the Gemara does not really give a mandate for *k'vias makom* as much as it sets it up as a supreme act of devotion (he will be called *chassid*, i.e., one who goes *lifnim m'shuras ha'din*). He seems to take his *p'sak* from the words of the *Rosh*, who says this halachah in the name of Rabbi Tanchum b'Rabbi Chiya in *Perek Tefillas Hashachar* in the *Yerushalmi*.

No one seems to challenge the *Rambam's pshat* in this Gemara, so the *Mechaber* can *pasken* the halachah from the *Rosh* and still be learning like the *Rambam* in the Gemara.

The only problem with this approach is that if our Gemara is the source for standing in one place, why does the *Rambam* in another halachah (Halachah 5:4) *pasken* like the Gemara on *Berachos* 10b, where

Rabbi Yose bar Chanina says a *mispallel* must daven with his feet together due to *ragleihem regel yesharah*—that angels stand on one single straight leg?

The answer is that davening with one's feet together was not Avraham's innovation either. Let's understand what Avraham did. He was *"kove'a makom."* What does it mean to be *"kove'a makom"*?

Being *"kove'a makom"* has a parallel. It is being *"kove'a seudah."* A number of halachos in *hilchos berachos* depend upon whether or not one has been *"kove'a seudah."* The definition of being *"kove'a seudah"* is the following: One is said to be establishing a fixed place for his meal when he indicates—by his words, actions, and/or choice of foods—that he is committing himself not to leave the table until the eating session (the meal) is over.

The same is true of being *kove'a makom*. One is said to be establishing a fixed place for his *tefillah* when he commits himself not to leave his davening position until the *tefillah* session (his *Shemoneh Esreh*) is over. This is the innovation of Avraham Avinu, and he did it as a way of underscoring the direct interaction with Hashem that is the definition of *tefillah*. Without this innovation, all the *din* of *ragleihem regel yesharah* would require is that when you are actively at prayer, your feet must be together. But, theoretically, you could stand with your feet together for *Avos*, move around, stand again with your feet together for *Gevuros*, and do the same for every *berachah* of *Shemoneh Esreh*.

Avraham Avinu showed that this would make one's davening an act of one-way devotion at best, but not a conversation with God. Be *kove'a makom* all the time (*tamid*), as the *Rambam* says, and you become a disciple of Avraham's ability to communicate with God, and, assuming you master it internally, an *anav* and a *chassid*. Indeed, the Gemara's actual phrase is *"omrim lo"* (they say **to** him) not *"omrim alav"* (they say **about** him). This is because we cannot praise a person in his lifetime for accomplishments that are taking place internally. But after he dies, the *malachim* will say to him, "We are aware of how you davened, and we know you are an *anav* and a *chassid*."

Halachah l'maaseh, one should set up a regular seat in shul, like the *Shulchan Aruch paskens* in accordance with the *Rosh*, and a regular

Berachos 6b

davening area at home, like the *Magen Avraham* in accordance with *Rabbeinu Yonah*. And he should stand with his feet together when he says the nineteen *berachos* of *Shemoneh Esreh*, like Rabbi Yose bar Chanina. But much more importantly, he should first establish—every time before he sets out to daven—that he is initiating a "davening session" that he commits not to interrupt until all nineteen *berachos* are said. And during that entire session, he should be focused on no thoughts other than the words he is saying and the One to whom he is saying them. He is still *yotzei tefillah* if he falls short, but his reward is great should he succeed.

דף ו: (2)

אמר רבי חלבו אמר רב הונא היוצא מבית הכנסת אל
יפסיע פסיעה גסה אמר אביי לא אמרן אלא למיפק
אבל למיעל מצוה למרהט שנאמר נרדפה לדעת את
ה׳ אמר רבי זירא מריש כי הוה חזינא להו לרבנן דקא
רהטי לפרקא בשבתא אמינא קא מחללין רבנן שבתא
כיון דשמענא להא דרבי תנחום א״ר יהושע בן לוי
לעולם ירוץ אדם לדבר הלכה ואפילו בשבת שנאמר
אחרי ה׳ ילכו כאריה ישאג וגו׳ אנא נמי רהיטנא.

Rabbi Chelbo quoted Rav Huna: One who exits a shul should not take broad steps. Abaye commented: This is true only of leaving shul, but to go to a shul, it is a mitzvah to run, as it says, "Let us chase after knowledge of God" (Hoshea 6:3).

Said Rabbi Zeira: Whenever I saw rabbis running to hear Torah lectures on Shabbos, I used to think they were violating Shabbos. But ever since I heard Rabbi Tanchum say in the name of Rabbi Yehoshua ben Levi, "One should always run to a halachic talk [alt., to do a mitzvah], even on Shabbos, as it says, 'Go after Hashem like a roaring lion (Hoshea 11:10),'" I too run.

1. Rav Huna seemed clear enough on his own that his rule was only about exiting a shul. Why when Abaye was teaching that it is a mitzvah to run *to* shul did he first have to reiterate that Rav Huna's rule forbidding running only applies to leaving shul?
2. Rabbi Zeira's message is not about shuls; it is about Shabbos. What is it doing here?

Berachos 6b

3. Why was Rabbi Zeira's focus only on rabbis? Did no one else attend Shabbos lectures? Did no one else but rabbis violate Shabbos by running?

--- ***Yesod*** ---

There are two possible reasons why one should not take broad steps (*p'si'a gasah*) upon leaving shul. One is for the same reason that one should not engorge oneself while eating (*achilah gasah*)—it is beneath one's human dignity to conduct oneself in a wild manner. According to this reason, why is it stated specifically with regard to leaving shul? Because when leaving shul, one might find cause to justify running, for instance, when his prayers ran long and he is now late for his work. Thus, it needs to be emphasized that the need to maintain human dignity applies even when one is leaving shul and might have a justifiable cause. But undoubtedly, according to this reasoning, one would be equally prohibited from running *to* shul (or anywhere else) when acting wild has no justification.

Abaye subscribes to a different reason. He has no problem with running per se. Acting wild is a problem only when one is being self-indulgent, as when one is eating wildly. Running to shul is praiseworthy, for one is in wild pursuit of knowledge of God—a good thing, according to the verse in *Hoshea*. And even running *from* shul would be honorable in theory if it resulted from, as *Rashi* suggests, a wish to linger in shul as long after prayers as possible, even to the point where you now have to run to get to work.

Except for one thing. People who will see you run away from shul will not know that your running is due to your love for Hashem and your desire to wring more time out of your shul visit. You will give the impression—albeit unintended—that you are glad to be leaving now that davening is over and that you simply can't get away fast enough. Thus the "I love Hashem so much" message that running might have been making will have to defer to the inferior understanding of those who would bear mistaken witness. That is how Abaye interprets Rav Huna, and that is why he must begin by repeating what *he* understands to have been Rav Huna's implication—as a way of countering the view of those who might have understood Rav Huna the other way.

Now we understand why Rabbi Zeira's message is here. It is not here to tell me *chiddushim* in *hilchos Shabbos*. It is here to support Abaye's interpretation of Rav Huna. If Abaye is not right, and running is *prima facie* an act of undignified conduct, Rabbi Zeira—even if he ever did manage to come across a justification for the rabbis' act (they're about to miss the start of the *shiur!*)—certainly never would have engaged in this frowned-upon practice himself! By Rabbi Zeira revealing his total reversal in light of Rabbi Tanchum's teaching, we see that Abaye is on solid ground in interpreting Rav Huna's law as he does.

We also understand why Rabbi Zeira's observation emphasized rabbis. When he thought running was a form of conduct too undignified for Shabbos, perhaps he could be *melamed z'chus* on ordinary people, whose sense of self-dignity may not be high enough for their running to qualify as *chillul Shabbos*. But rabbis? They have dignity they know they must maintain. From them it is certainly *chillul Shabbos*!

We now also understand the importance of Rabbi Zeira concluding by telling us that he too now runs. Just like when there is a need to do a *melachah* on Shabbos to save a life, and the act may look like *chillul Shabbos* to the uninformed but it is really not, it becomes especially incumbent on the rabbis, Rabbi Zeira included, to lead the way by taking action themselves as a way of clearly demonstrating to all that not only is the act not a Torah violation, but that it is an act of Divine service!

דף ח. (1)

Abba Binyamin says: An individual's personal prayer is heard [by God] only in shul, as it says, "Lishmo'a el ha'rinah v'el ha'tefillah—In the place of rinah [joyful sounds], there shall be tefillah." (Berachos 6a)

[Rabbi Yochanan said in the name of Rabbi Shimon Bar Yochai:] What does it mean when it says, "Va'ani sefilasi l'cha Hashem eis ratzon"? When is it a desirable time to pray? At the time when the tzibbur is praying. [Therefore, when praying at home, one should align one's personal prayer time with that of the tzibbur.] (Ibid., 8a)

Tefillas ha'tzibbur is heard always; and even if the tzibbur contains sinners, God never rejects the prayer of the masses. Therefore, a person should always connect himself with the tzibbur. And he should not daven alone as long as he is able to daven with the tzibbur. But really a person should always go in the morning and the evening to shul, for an individual's personal prayer is heard at all times only in shul. And anyone who has a shul in his city and does not daven there is called a bad neighbor. (Rambam, Hilchos Tefillah 8:1)

1. The *Rambam*, in *Hilchos Tefillah* 8:1, *paskens* like Abba Binyamin (quoted above from *Berachos* 6a) and not like Rabbi Yochanan (quoted above from *Berachos* 8a; nowhere does the *Rambam* rule that one should align his personal prayer time to that of the *tzibbur* when praying at home alone). But if he rejects the Gemara on 8a, why does the *Rambam* go on and say that one should not pray alone as long as he is able to pray with a *tzibbur*?

The source for the value of praying with a *tzibbur* (directly or by at least aligning with their davening time) is the Gemara on 8a. If he rejects the Gemara telling us it is important to daven *at the same time* as the *tzibbur*, from where does he know that it is important to daven *together* with a *tzibbur*?

2. After the quote from Rabbi Yochanan, the Gemara continues and says Rabbi Yose bar Chanina actually learned this out from a different *pasuk*—"*b'eis ratzon inisicha.*" This is a very unclear statement. Rabbi Yochanan had learned a number of different things from his *pasuk*. What was it that Rabbi Yose learned from the different *pasuk*? Did he learn that there exists a special *eis ratzon* for *tefillah*? That the *eis ratzon* is when the *tzibbur* is davening? That one davening at home should align his timing to the time of the *tzibbur*'s davening? All three? Whichever answer you choose, it is going to be difficult to reconcile what comes next, because the Gemara right after says that Rav Acha bar Rabbi Chanina learns it out from a third *pasuk*, "*hein Keil kabir v'lo yim'as*—See, God is mighty and will not reject in disgust." Whatever you may think Rabbi Yose was learning out from his *pasuk*, how could Rav Acha have learned any of those things from *his pasuk*, which does not even *mention* the time of a *tzibbur*'s prayers (*sha'as tefillas ha'tzibbur*)?

3. With the *Rif*'s *girsa*, the Gemara works out a little better. According to the *Rif*, there is a three-way *machlokes* as to which *pasuk* is the source for the halachah that personal prayer is heard only in shul. Rabbi Yochanan says it is from *va'ani sefilasi*; Rabbi Yose bar Chanina says it is from *b'eis ratzon inisicha*; Rav Nachman (the correct name according to *Rif*'s *girsa*) says it is from *hein Keil kabir*. What is this *machlokes* all about?

Yesod

The *Rambam* does not reject the Gemara on 8a. He just learns it differently than anyone else.

Berachos 8a

According to the *Rambam*, this is a *sugya* that teaches halachah, but the *sugya* begins not with the halachic statement as first quoted from Rabbi Yochanan but rather with the story that leads in to Rabbi Yochanan's quotation.

The story is found toward the bottom of 7b:

> Rav Yitzchak asked Rav Nachman why he failed to come to shul to daven. Rav Nachman answered that he was too weak. "Why didn't you arrange a minyan in your house?" asked Rav Yitzchak. "It would have been too much trouble for me," answered Rav Nachman. Rav Yitzchak persisted. "Why did you not ask the shaliach tzibbur to inform you when davening time was [so you could align your tefillah to that of the tzibbur]?" "Why all that trouble," responded Rav Nachman. Answered Rav Yitzchak? "Because of Rabbi Yochanan's teaching: 'What do we learn from the pasuk of va'ani sefilasi...eis ratzon? That there is an eis ratzon for tefillah and it is at the time when the tzibbur is davening.'"

Let us begin by answering our last question. The *machlokes*, as presented by the *Rif*, is over the meaning of *"ein tefillaso shel adam nishma'as ela b'veis ha'knesses*—Individual prayer is heard only in shul." Rabbi Yochanan holds "only in shul" means "only with the *tzibbur*." (This is exactly how the *Tur paskens*: One should daven only in shul with the *tzibbur*, for Rabbi Yochanan said, "Personal prayer is heard only in shul," meaning "with the *tzibbur*."[1])

Rabbi Yose bar Chanina agrees but alters the source, as Rabbi Yochanan's *pasuk* says nothing to indicate it is about *tefillas ha'tzibbur*, since it is about David HaMelech's private prayer. (Rabbi Yochanan would counter that the *pasuk* does not **have** to say anything about *tzibbur*. All we need is for the *pasuk* to tell us there is such a thing in prayer as an *eis ratzon*. As we already know that the ideal *tefillah* is a *tzibbur* davening in shul, we will automatically understand that such time is the *eis ratzon*.) So Rabbi Yose sources the halachah in *b'eis ratzon inisicha*, which although it is in *lashon yachid*, is actually talking about the singular entity of Klal Yisrael as a whole, so it really is about *tefillas ha'tzibbur*.

Rav Nachman disagrees with the entire premise. He agrees that the halachah is lauding *tefillas ha'tzibbur*, but not the **time** of *tefillas ha'tzibbur*, rather the **experience** of *tefilas tzibbur*. The halachah is saying one should daven in shul with a minyan not because being with the minyan connects you to a **more receptive time** for Hashem to hear the davening, but because being with a minyan connects you to a **more powerful davening activity** (one that has so much spiritual power that Hashem will never reject it).

The story in the Gemara on 7b captures this *machlokes* perfectly in the dialogue between Rav Yitzchak and Rav Nachman. Rav Nachman says, "Why all that trouble? I certainly would have made a minyan in my home because of the importance of a minyan if not for the fact that it was too difficult for me, but why would there be a need for me to align my private davening with the *tzibbur*'s minyan time? I hold the source for the halachah that personal prayer is heard only in shul is the *pasuk* of *hein Keil kabir v'lo yim'as*, which makes no mention of any *eis ratzon*!" Rav Yitzchak, holding like Rabbi Yochanan and Rabbi Yose bar Chanina, says no; the source is one that contains *eis ratzon*, and you should have davened at the time of *sha'as tefillas ha'tzibbur*. The story, as it appears in our Gemara, is exactly the same *machlokes* as as that which was spoken out directly according the *Rif*'s version of the Gemara! It is also the reason why the *Rif* has Rav Nachman as the *bar plugta* instead of Rav Acha bar Chanina.

Now on to the *Rambam*. Unlike the *Tur*, the *Rambam paskened* like Rav Nachman *against* Rabbi Yochanan. He did this because a *Beraisa* (see *tanya nami hachi* on 8a) supports the view of Rav Nachman (or Rav Acha bar Chanina, in our *girsa*) that the source *pasuk* is *hein Keil kabir v'lo yim'as*, and the halachah is about the power of the *tzibbur*, not the power of *sha'as tefillas ha'tzibbur*. Therefore, he first *paskens* to make sure to be part of (not necessarily daven with, just be part of) a *tzibbur*, even of sinners, in order to be counted in with their never-rejected *tefillas ha'tzibbur*. Next, he *paskens* to try if possible to daven with a minyan for your own *tefillah* even if you must be outside of shul, but

Berachos 8a

only because we learn that Rav Nachman would have done so had he felt up to it. But then he *paskens* like Abba Binyamin on 6a, that really, for your own davening, *tefillah* in a shul is essential.

We have thus answered all our questions:

1. The *Rambam* can *pasken* that we do not have to align our davening with the time of the *tefillas ha'tzibbur* and can still *pasken* we should try to arrange a minyan at home if we cannot be in shul because he does not reject the Gemara on 8a; he simply holds it begins with the story on 7b and he follows the example of Rav Nachman.
2. Rabbi Yose can learn about *eis ratzon* issues from his *pasuk* and still Rav Acha can learn that there are no *eis ratzon* issues, because in learning from *his pasuk*, Rav Acha is rejecting the basic premise of Rabbi Yochanan and Rabbi Chanina that *tefillah* has an *eis ratzon*, just the way it is in the *girsa* of the *Rif*.
3. The *machlokes* between Rabbi Yochanan and Rabbi Chanina on one side and Rav Acha (or Rav Nachman) on the other, just like the disagreement between Rav Yitzchak and Rav Nachman in the story, is whether the advantage of *tefillas ha'tzibbur* is that it is a better time of davening (Hashem is more receptive—*maaseh Shamayim*) or that it is a better method of davening (our unity makes us more powerful—*maaseh adam*).

With this, we can also answer a major *kashya* on the *Yerushalmi* (*Berachos* 54a). Rabbi Yochanan there praises a *yachid* who davens at home. All the *mefarshim* ask: But doesn't the *Mechaber* in the *Shulchan Aruch pasken* that a *yachid* should daven in shul? Why doesn't he follow this statement of Rabbi Yochanan here in the *Yerushalmi*? The answer we can now give is that while the *Tur* might *pasken* like Rabbi Yochanan, *Shulchan Aruch* actually *paskens* like the *Rambam* who rejects Rabbi Yochanan! *Tur* and Rabbi Yochanan hold what is important is **when** a *yachid* davens. The *Rambam* and *Shulchan Aruch*, who *pasken* like Rav Nachman, hold what is important is **where** a *yachid* davens. And while it is true that *Shulchan Aruch* does rule that one should try to align his private *tefillah* to the time of the *tefillas ha'tzibbur*, that is only *l'ravcha* *d'milsa* to be *choshesh* for both *shitos* where you can do both. It does not mean that he *paskens* like Rabbi Yochanan. And just like *Shulchan Aruch* rejects Rabbi Yochanan in the *Bavli*, he rejects Rabbi Yochanan in the *Yerushalmi*.

And since, according to Rav Nachman, getting a minyan when you are already not davening in shul is just something to do if you are reasonably able but is not absolutely essential, and davening in shul for an individual is essential as per Tanya Abba Binyamin, it seems almost plausible to argue that where you have the two options, davening *b'yechidus* in shul may actually be a better choice than davening *b'tzibbur* outside a shul.

L'halachah, of course, consult with your Rav.

Berachos 8a

דף ח. (2)

תניא נמי הכי רבי נתן אומר מנין שאין הקב"ה מואס בתפלתן של רבים שנאמר הן אל כביר ולא ימאס וכתיב פדה בשלום נפשי כי ברבים היו עמדי.

A Beraisa also states: Rabbi Nassan says: From where do we know that God is never repulsed by the prayer of the many? From the fact that it says: "Behold, God is powerful and He does not repel." And it says: "He redeemed my soul through my peaceable activities, for the multitudes were with me."

1. The *Rambam* uses the above Gemara to begin Chapter 8 of *Hilchos Tefillah*: "The prayer of the community is constantly accepted. Even if sinners were included among them, God is not repulsed by the prayer of the many." But since when am I supposed to be concerned about the prayer of the community? Isn't my objective to get my personal prayer heard?

2. The *Rambam* has to dispel the notion that if there are sinners in the minyan, God would reject the prayer of the entire minyan. That makes it sound like I should daven alone better than having to rely on the fact that God never rejects the community's davening. Or is he saying that I should be concerned that perhaps I am the sinner? The *Rambam*'s next line certainly suggests the latter when it says, "Therefore, a person must connect himself up with the community." But is that what I should want? Should my goal be no bigger than to simply not have my prayer rejected? And if I am a sinner, my *tefillah* is being rejected anyway; all that is being accepted is the *tefillas ha'tzibbur* of which I happen to be a part. What about having me strive to not be a sinner and have

דף ח.

my *tefillah* accepted on its own merit? Moreover, why should Hashem reject the *tefillah* of a sinner? At least he is calling out to God. Isn't that something of value?
3. The *Rambam* says that communal prayer is constantly accepted. So why do we say only that God "is not repulsed" by such prayer?
4. The basis for the *Rambam's* "*l'fikach*" (therefore) is that communal prayer is always accepted. This must mean that my own *personal* prayer is at risk of not being accepted. But the *Rambam* goes on to say that the only place private prayer is accepted at all times is in shul, implying that in shul, private prayer *is* accepted at all times. So why do I need a minyan to guarantee the acceptance of my *tefillos*? Let me just daven *b'yechidus* in a shul!
5. And if you want to respond and say that what the *Rambam* means is that you need a *tzibbur* to have a guarantee of your *tefillah's* acceptance, and even that guarantee is only effective when the davening is done in shul, then why does the *Rambam* say *tefillaso* (his prayer) when a more accurate term would have been *tefillasam* (their prayer)?
6. Why does the *Rambam* omit the halachah that one should align his davening time with that of the *tzibbur*?
7. What is the difference between the two successive lines in the *Rambam*: "A person must connect himself up with the community," and "He should not daven alone anytime he is able to daven with the community"?

Yesod

The *Rambam* is saying the following:

There are two distinct issues: *tefillas ha'tzibbur* and *tefillaso*. *Tefillaso* is the prayer the individual says on his own behalf. *Tefillas ha'tzibbur* is the prayer the *shaliach tzibbur* says on behalf of the whole *tzibbur*. An individual functions on both levels. He is an individual, and he is also a member of the community. He stands to benefit from both *tefillos*.

The *Rambam* does not mean there are sinners in the minyan. Instead, he means to say that there are sinners in the *community*. They are not

41

necessarily davening. But one might think their very membership in the community might doom the *tzibbur*'s *tefillah*. To dispel that notion, we have the *pasuk* to teach us that God is never repulsed by a community's prayer, and therefore one should never hesitate to **connect** with a community (the *Rambam* is not talking about davening together with them), even a community that includes sinners. This will gain for one his *tefillas ha'tzibbur*.

The other issue is one's own personal *tefillah*. Does one do that alone or with a minyan? Don't daven alone when a minyan is available, says the *Rambam*. But no one is guaranteeing that one's personal *tefillah* will be accepted—even with a minyan—at all times. That guarantee is only for the *tefillas ha'tzibbur*. The only guarantee available for a personal prayer is that if it is done in a shul, it will be accepted. So go for a minyan, absolutely, but not at the cost of not being in shul. An individual davening alone in shul has a greater guarantee of his personal prayer being accepted than that same person davening with a minyan outside of a shul. His communal prayer is taken care of as long as he is a connected member of the community. (Note that in halachah 4, the *Rambam* does not define *tefillah b'tzibbur* as everyone starting their *Shemoneh Esreh* at the same time.)

And why does the *Rambam* insert that shul is the only place individual prayer is accepted *at all times* (*b'chol eis*)? Because his source for this halachah is the story about Rav Nachman (7b at the bottom) who would have gathered a minyan at home had it not been too much *tirchah* for him. If shul is the only place personal prayer is *ever* heard, why should he have bothered at all to gather a home minyan? From the fact that he would have bothered, *Rambam* knows that shul is the only place individual prayer is heard *at all times*. Personal prayer is indeed heard at home, just not at all times. It is still worth the effort, therefore, whenever shul davening is not an option, to gather a minyan at home, as long as the *tirchah* involved does not render the effort unreasonable.

דף ח. (3)

אמרו ליה לר׳ יוחנן איכא סבי בבבל וגו׳.
They said to Rabbi Yochanan, "There are old men in Babylonia," etc.

The steps in this Gemara of the *sabei b'Bavel* are as follows:
- Rabbi Yochanan was surprised there were old men in Bavel until he learned that they go to shul.
- Once he learned that they attend shul, Rabbi Yochanan said it matches what Rabbi Yehoshua ben Levi told his sons to do in order to live a long life.
- Rabbi Acha bar Chanina sources the idea in the *pasuk*, "*Ashrei…lishkod al dalsosai…ki motza'i matza chaim.*" This is a confirmation that one who attends shul will live a long life.
- Rav Chisda says one should enter two doors when entering shul. Two doors? The measure of two doors, clarifies the Gemara.
- *Rashi* says this means one should enter at least two door-lengths in. *Rabbeinu Yonah* does not agree and lets you stay near the entrance if that is your *makom kavu'a*. Instead, he says, you should wait the length of time it takes to walk two door-lengths after entering the shul before commencing your davening.
- Rav Chisda quotes a *pasuk* in *Tehillim* to show that Hashem loves the "gates of excellence in halachah" more than He loves the shuls and study halls. Ulla's statement supports this when he says, "From the time the Beis Hamikdash was destroyed, God has nothing in His world other than the four *amos* of halachah." Upon hearing that, Abaye switched from davening at shul to davening at home, where he studied Torah.

Berachos 8a

- The Gemara relates how Rabbi Ami and Rabbi Assi, despite having their choice of thirteen shuls in Teverya, would daven only "between the pillars where they would learn."
- Rabbi Chiya bar Ami quotes Ulla to say that greater is the one who benefits from his own handiwork even than one who fears God, as the word "*ashrecha*" applies to both, but the phrase "*tov lach*" is reserved for the one who engages in *yegias kapayim* (his own handiwork).

1. "Door-lengths" is a very odd way to measure either distance or time. Doors come in such a variety of sizes! Why would Rav Chisda measure anything by this reference?
2. What was the *hava amina* before the Gemara clarified that "two doors" meant "the measure of two doors"? Did anybody ever seriously consider the possibility that one would have to walk through two different doors to enter a shul if that was otherwise unnecessary? Was the idea that one would have to walk through the same door twice? Why?
3. In the *Yerushalmi*, Rav Chisda implies we are talking literally about two doors (not the **measure** of two doors), since he emphasizes how the *pasuk* says "*dalsosai*" and not "*dalasi*," and "*pesachai*" and not "*pischi*." What could this mean?
4. How does going to shul give one long life?
5. Elsewhere in the text, Rava notes to Rafram bar Papa how Rav Chisda was the great champion of shuls. According to the Rishonim's explanation of our Gemara, he's not a champion of shuls—he's a champion of davening! What is Rava saying?
6. Why is "halachah" referred to as "the four *amos* of halachah"? Halachah is not physical that it should be deemed as taking up space!
7. Why do we need to know how many shuls there were in Teverya in which Rabbi Ami and Rabbi Assi did not daven?
8. What is the need for the specific construction details in the phrase: "*Beinei amudei heicha d'havu garsi*—Between the pillars

where they would learn"? Who needs to know that *batei midrashos* were constructed using pillars?

9. How can it be that one who benefits from his own handiwork is even greater than one who fears God?

Yesod

The *Rambam* (*Hilchos Tefillah* 8:2) learns that the reason to enter through two doors (be *nichnas shnei pesachim*) is not to concentrate better in shul but to fulfill a *pasuk*. With this *Rambam*, we can learn the whole Gemara differently:

The purpose of a shul is to function as a miniature Beis Hamikdash, a *mikdash me'at*. The Beis Hamikdash was required to have more than one door, as we see in the *haftarah* of *Parashas haChodesh*.[2] In order for a shul in *chutz la'aretz* to be effective, it must remind you of the Beis Hamikdash. Having to walk through two doors makes you think of the two-door minimum requirement for the Beis Hamikdash, and it is that awareness that turns the shul into your *mikdash me'at*.

Jews can live without the Beis Hamikdash because the Beis Hamikdash itself is just a reminder. The three *matanos* that are *nikneis b'yissurim* are Torah, Eretz Yisrael, and *Olam Haba*. Beis Hamikdash is not mentioned as one of them. That is because Beis Hamikdash is not the purpose of this world. The Beis Hamikdash is a reflection of God's presence in this world, external to our own selves. But our mission as the Jewish People is not to connect to the external manifestation of the *Shechinah*; it is to reveal the existence of the *Shechinah*'s internal manifestation, i.e., God's presence in this world as it resides within us. Connecting to the external, which is done via the Beis Hamikdash, just helps us do our job a little better.

Even Avraham Avinu failed to recognize this at first. After arriving in Eretz Canaan, he started traveling in a southerly direction, toward what would later become the city of Yerushalayim.[3] In a Chumash *shiur* I once gave on the topic, I suggested Avraham went south intending to reveal the *makom haMikdash*. Instead Hashem brought a famine and forced him out of the Land. "That is not your primary mission," Hashem was saying to Avraham, "internal development is!" And so upon returning from Egypt, Avraham proceeded to engage in the revelation of the *Shechinah*'s internal presence as found within Eretz Yisrael. (The other two Avos, Yitzchak and Yaakov, carried on the mission of internal *Shechinah* revelation as well, each in his own unique way.)

(As an interesting aside, when we look deeper into Avraham Avinu, we find that Avraham's life story lies beneath the surface of a Mishnah we recite daily at the beginning of *Shacharis, eilu devarim she'adam ochel peiroseihem*:

- *Kibud Av v'Em*—Avraham had a keen sensitivity to the mitzvah of *kibud av*.[4]
- *Gemilus Chassadim*—Avraham was Judaism's Pillar of Kindness.
- *Hashkamas Beis Ha'medrash*—The *pasuk* describes Avraham as getting up early in the morning.
- *Hachnasas Orchim*—The three desert travelers who became Avraham's guests.
- *Bikur Cholim*—A mitzvah Avraham learned from Hashem's visit to his sickbed.
- *Hachnasas Kallah*—Avraham brought Rivkah to Yitzchak.
- *Levayas Ha'meis*—Avraham buried Sarah.
- *Iyun Tefillah*—Avraham analyzed and recasted his prayer for S'dom.
- *Hava'as Shalom*—Avraham took action to quell the quarrel between his shepherds and the shepherds of Lot.

The Mishnah tells us that these mitzvos confer some measure of reward yet in this world. Why might that be? I would suggest that what these activities have in common is that they all bring out the *Shechinah*'s presence within us, and the earthly "reward" they generate can be used to assist us in carrying the internal revelation yet deeper. This certainly seems to have been true of Avraham, who found the latter part of his life filled both with blessing of all kinds and with renewed spiritual undertakings.[5])

Associating yourself with two doors at shul connects you to the Beis Hamikdash, which strengthens your ability to do your job of revealing the inner *Shechinah*. If a shul happens to have two doors, let your intention be to use them to make that connection to the Beis Hamikdash. If not—and Bavli shuls apparently did not—one could have a legitimate *hava amina* to walk through the one door twice. But seeing how that creates unnecessary repetition, one can be *yotzei* the *inyan* of two doors by having *kavanah* for the Beis Hamikdash connection while fulfilling the **measure** of two doors, either in space or in time.

That is how one connects to Hashem's external presence in Bavel. But Rav Chisda explains that there is an even better approach. As great a champion of shuls as he may have been, nevertheless Rav Chisda teaches that Hashem actually prefers *sha'arim ha'metzuyanim b'halachah*—"gateways" or "doors" that "open" via insightful halachah study. This is what **Hashem** uses as a reminder of the Beis Hamikdash; halachah is how He infuses His external *Shechinah* into our lives. This, then, is the meaning of the "four *amos* of halachah." Halachah is the only aspect of Torah that can force us to physically adjust to accommodate the *ratzon* Hashem, the same way another person's physical presence can compel us to adjust our own.

Based on this, Abaye began davening at home. He discovered that he could connect to the external *Shechinah* through his *avodah* in Torah learning (all the while that his Torah itself was expanding his connection to the inner *Shechinah*). Rabbi Ami and Rabbi Assi had thirteen shuls in Teverya (thirteen is the same *gematria* as *echad* and *ahavah*). With these shuls and their *gematria* significance, they could have used them to attain a real connection to *yichud Hashem*! Nevertheless, even such a profound connection was still only a connection to Hashem's external Presence, so they preferred to get a connection where they learned. But they still needed the idea of "two doors." That they got by having *kavanah* that the two pillars surrounding them while they davened would effect the same reminder power for them as two actual doors.

Yegi'as kapayim is a reference to someone working on what is *ikar*—his primary mission. Being a *yorei Shamayim* is an outstanding achievement, but it is just the assistance; it **helps** us to fulfill our primary purpose. *Tov lach* is the *Olam Haba* you can have right here in this world as you reveal *Olam Haba* as being this world's true inner component.

דף ט: (1)

מתני' מאימתי קורין את שמע בשחרית משיכיר בין תכלת ללבן ר' אליעזר אומר בין תכלת לכרתי וגומרה עד הנץ החמה ר' יהושע אומר עד שלש שעות שכן דרך מלכים לעמוד בשלש שעות הקורא מכאן ואילך לא הפסיד כאדם הקורא בתורה.

From when do we recite k'rias Shema in the morning? From when one can distinguish between blue and white. Rabbi Eliezer says between blue and green. [And one may finish] up until sunrise. Rabbi Yehoshua says you have until three hours, for it is the way of kings to arise three hours into the day. After that, reading k'rias Shema [is not wrong as it] remains no worse than reading Torah.

The Mishnah says that the daytime *z'man k'rias Shema* begins when there is enough light to distinguish between blue and white (*techeiles v'lavan*). The Gemara asks, what does "between blue and white" mean? It can't mean to distinguish between a fleece of blue wool and a fleece of white wool, as that can be distinguished even in the darkness! Rather it means enough light to distinguish between "the blue in it and the white in it."

Rashi explains the Gemara is still referring to fleece. The Mishnah is talking about one fleece whose dye did not penetrate uniformly. There must be sufficient light to distinguish between the blue patches in the fleece and the white patches in it—a distinction that cannot be easily made at night.

Tosafos says the Mishnah is not talking about one fleece. It is talking about the blue and white fringes on the tzitzis. *Tosafos* says this because the Gemara in *Menachos* says that *z'man k'rias Shema* is dependent on the mitzvah of tzitzis (triggered, thus, by its *techeiles* and *lavan*).

How can we defend *Rashi* when *Tosafos* is bringing a *mefurash* Gemara against his *pshat*?

Rashi is simply explaining the Gemara, which clearly links the discussion in the Mishnah to fleeces of wool. The Gemara in *Menachos* is fine. Tzitzis remains a reminder for the beginning of *z'man k'rias Shema* by containing, and therefore reminding us of, the two colors we have to distinguish in a fleece of wool in order for there to be enough light to begin the *Shema*. (And who is going to be standing there every morning with a fleece of wool, anyway?) Tzitzis is a reminder of the colors that define the standard, but it is the standard (and the light conditions associated with that standard) that ushers in the mitzvah of *k'rias Shema*, not the colors themselves.

This illustrates a key difference between *Rashi* and *Tosafos*. *Tosafos* explains the halachah, while *Rashi* explains the Gemara. (This may be why the three are referred to as גפ"ת, *gephet*—Gemara, *Perush Rashi*, and *Tosafos*.)

דף ט: (2)

מתני׳ מאימתי קורין את שמע בשחרית משיכיר בין תכלת ללבן ר׳ אליעזר אומר בין תכלת לכרתי וגומרה עד הנץ החמה ר׳ יהושע אומר עד שלש שעות שכן דרך מלכים לעמוד בשלש שעות הקורא מכאן ואילך לא הפסיד כאדם הקורא בתורה.

From when do we begin reciting k'rias Shema in the morning? From when one can distinguish between blue and white. Rabbi Eliezer says between blue and green, [and you may finish] up until sunrise. Rabbi Yehoshua says you have until three hours, for it is the way of kings to arise three hours into the day. After that, reading k'rias Shema [is not wrong, as it] remains no worse than reading Torah.

1. In the first Mishnah, we had Rabbi Eliezer, based on his reading of *u'v'shochbecha* as meaning "when people are going off to sleep," saying we could read *k'rias Shema* a few hours into the night. We had Rabban Gamliel, based on his reading that *u'v'shochbecha* means "as long as people are sleeping," saying one could read *k'rias Shema* all night long. Here, we have opinions (*Tanna Kama*/Rabbi Eliezer and Rabbi Yehoshua) saying we could read *k'rias Shema* a few hours into the day. Where are the opinions representing Rabban Gamliel's point of view arguing that one could read *k'rias Shema* all day?

2. If *Tanna Kama* and Rabbi Eliezer are really saying that sunrise is *sof z'man k'rias Shema*, how is it possible to explain the Gemara on 3a that lists sunrise as a daily *siman* to wake people up to

say *k'rias Shema*? According to their opinions, wouldn't sunrise wake-up be too late to then say *k'rias Shema*?

Yesod

Tanna Kama and Rabbi Eliezer are not saying sunrise is *sof z'man k'rias Shema*. They are saying sunrise is the time you will need to end your recital of *k'rias Shema* if you want to be *somech geulah l'tefillah* in the ideal way (like the *vasikin*). Rabbi Yehoshua, on the other hand, is describing actual *sof z'man k'rias Shema*, and the two sides are not disagreeing.

But we *pasken* neither like *Tanna Kama*/Rabbi Eliezer nor like Rabbi Yehoshua; instead, we *pasken* like Shmuel on *daf* 8b, who *paskens* like Rabban Gamliel that the meaning of the *pasuk*, according to most authorities, is "as long as people are sleeping." The unspoken but obvious parallel to this would have to be "as long as people are awake" or all day long. And that is our *psak*. The only reason it is not stated as such is because if we would wait until later in the day to say *k'rias Shema*, we would miss *tefillah b'zmanah*. So the Mishnah simply says it is no worse than reading Torah. But in theory, we have all day to say the daytime *k'rias Shema* just like we have all night to say the nighttime *k'rias Shema*.

This is not to say one should leave his daytime *k'rias Shema* for the afternoon. It is to say, however, that if one should ever find himself in the afternoon having missed *k'rias Shema* in the proper morning time, he should not be cavalier about saying it in the afternoon. "*Lo hifsid k'adam ha'korei baTorah*" should be seen as his **minimum** benefit. But according to how we *pasken*, he may well still be given full credit for being *yotzei* the daytime *k'rias Shema*.

Berachos 10a

(1) דף י.

ואמר ר׳ יוסי בר׳ חנינא משום ר׳ אליעזר בן יעקב מאי דכתיב לא תאכלו על הדם לא תאכלו קודם שתתפללו על דמכם.

Rabbi Yose ben Rabbi Chanina said in the name of Rabbi Eliezer ben Yaakov: What does it mean in the Torah when it says, "Do not eat on the blood"? It means: Do not eat [in the morning] before you have davened for your blood [i.e., your life].

The halachah tells us we are not permitted to eat in the morning before we daven. The source is a verse in *Sefer Vayikra* (19:26): "*Lo tochlu al ha'dam*—Do not eat over blood." According to Aryeh Kaplan, the verse is also a reference to an obscure idolatrous practice that called for a bowl of blood to be placed on the table while eating.[6]

Our Gemara renders it as follows: "'Do not eat over blood'—do not eat until you have prayed for your blood (i.e., do not [choose] eat[ing] over [the welfare of your] blood)."

This seems a strange way for the Torah to teach us not to eat before davening. Why not say simply, "Do not eat before morning prayers," "Do not seek to satisfy your own needs before first greeting God in prayer," or even "Do not eat before first praying for your life"? Why is the focus specifically on praying for your "blood"?

In *Parashas Bereishis*, God confronted Kayin after he killed his brother, Hevel: "What have you done? The voice of your brother's blood is crying out to me from the ground. And now you shall be cursed, from the ground that opened its mouth to accept your brother's blood from your hand."[7]

The commentaries argue over whether the ground's act was a good one or not. According to *Rashi*, the ground acted incorrectly by absorbing Hevel's blood, but the *Mizrachi* super-commentary cites a Gemara in which the ground's action is described as *"l'tovah"* (for the good). What is the essential issue underlying this dispute?

In *Parashas Acharei Mos*, we are given a mitzvah called *kisui ha'dam*: *"V'shafach es damo v'chisahu b'afar"* (*Vayikra* 17:13). Anytime we slaughter a kosher bird or non-domesticated animal (i.e., not sheep and cows), we are required to absorb the blood of its slaughter into earth and to cover the blood with earth (*Chullin*, chap. 4). Why only birds and wild animals? And why does the language in the verse that teaches us this mitzvah refer to the slaughter as *"sh'fichas damim"* (bloodshed), a term universally understood to mean murder and the term the Gemara uses to describe one of the three *yehareg v'al ya'avor* (lit., "be killed and don't transgress") sins of Judaism? In fact, why is it that the terminology "shedding of blood" refers exclusively to loss of life and not to the mere drawing of blood, when, if anything, in the laws of Shabbos we find the opposite according to some Rishonim—that the *melachah* violated by the mere drawing of blood is referred to as *"netilas neshamah"* (taking of life)?

THE STARTING POINT for this analysis requires understanding the nature of blood. We are all familiar with the composite origin of the human being: His body originates from dust and unto dust will return, the soul comes from On High and will return there after death separates it from the body. But what about his blood? Where should that return to? On the one hand, it is material, suggesting it should go down to the earth, but admittedly it does not have the automatic association with earth as the clay matter of the body does. The Torah does identify blood, at least in an animal, with the *nefesh* (soul). Should blood then be considered to stem from a Higher Origin?

Rambam describes the world as being composed of four essential elements: fire, earth, air, and water.[8] Applying these four elements to the construction of the human being, it seems to me that while the body's foundational element is clearly earth, and the spirit's could be either air

Berachos 10a

or fire, we could make a comfortable argument that blood's originating element is water.

OK, so where does it return when it leaves the body?

Good question.

On the second day of Creation, water was divided:

"God made a space amidst the water that divided between the Lower Waters and the Upper Waters" (*Bereishis* 1:7). The issue that will address all our questions is the need to determine which blood originates in which of the two waters.

LET US BEGIN with the mitzvah of *kisui ha'dam*. The Torah requires us to cover the blood of birds and wild animals. If we can accept for a moment that all birds, by virtue of their capacity for flight, have at least a sense of independence and freedom if not actual wildness, we could say that the Torah requires covering the blood of wild creatures and requires no such covering for domestic ones. I would explain this to be saying that the blood of animals that have surrendered their freedom for the security of domesticity comes from the Lower Waters. Lower Waters are waters over which we as human beings have dominance, thus the slaughter of *beheimos* requires no special treatment for the discarding of its blood and is not among those kinds of slaughter referred to in the Torah as "bloodshed."

Taking the life of an animal containing blood produced of Upper Waters, on the other hand, is quite a different act. We have no inherent rights over Upper Waters—only those God has given us. Spilling such blood is bloodshed because it involves the removal of Upper Waters from a casing in which God placed it. It is bloodshed when we take it from a wild animal, and what makes it bloodshed is the fact that we are displacing a variety of blood over which we have no rights. Now, it may be permissible for us to do it—we find in the rest of nature that it is not a sin for a stronger animal to prey on a weaker one—but as human beings with a Divine spirit, it is incumbent upon us to recognize when we have used our superior strength to create an imbalance in nature.

Now let us take it to the next step. In general, how do we rectify it when we cause an imbalance in nature through our actions? We bring a sacrifice, a *korban*, in the course of which we cause blood (*zerikas ha'dam*) to be absorbed into earth (*mizbei'ach adamah*). Here too, although no actual sin was done, we enact a kind of "*zerikas ha'dam*" in order to atone for the imbalance we have created by displacing blood that had belonged to the Upper Waters. Indeed, for this purpose we were granted use of this blood.

"For this, I have given you the blood, to gain atonement" (*Vayikra* 17:11). Not the atonement of domestic animals' blood sprinkled onto the *Mizbei'ach*; rather the atonement of wild animals' blood covered in earth via *kisui ha'dam*.

We have explained the origin of the blood of different kinds of animals. What about the blood of man? As free and independent beings, we ought to be able to classify our blood as sourcing in the Upper Waters. But we do not always act in a manner consistent with free beings. In fact, every time we sin, we show ourselves to be chained to the demands and desires of our bodies. The truth is that our blood is composed of a mixture of Lower Waters and Upper Waters. Every time we choose to perform the will of God over our own will, we enable the Upper Waters' component of our blood to master and control the Lower Waters within us. When we choose sin, we choose to surrender ourselves and become dominated by Lower Waters; this is why we need the body of a domestic animal, which too has surrendered its Upper Waters' blood, in order to gain atonement (using fire as a kind of "elevator element" to cause the lower material to ascend upward).

Now we can examine the action of the ground in swallowing up the blood of Hevel. Hevel was a *tzaddik* and his blood was of the Upper Waters. It should have been left atop the ground, either to remain and demand revenge (like the blood of the prophet Zechariah[9]) or to evaporate and return to its source. The ground was wrong in absorbing it. But, as *Rashi* puts it, it repeated its earlier error. During Creation, God said to make trees whose wood tasted like its fruit. The earth disobeyed and produced trees with inedible wood.[10] Why did the earth do this? Because it thought it was trying to do good. "If the wood tastes like the fruit," reasoned the earth, "people will consume the wood and the trees will not survive." Here too, the do-gooder earth thought the same thing:

Berachos 10a

"If Kayin does not receive atonement for his crime, heinous as it might have been, mankind will not survive." The earth's error in both cases is clear. In a world run by God, its survival or survival of its species is not our concern. God will worry about that. Our one and only mandate is to obey God's commands and do His will.

With this, I believe we can explain the puzzling language of the halachic prohibition against eating before davening. When God separated the Lower Waters from the Upper Waters, the Lower Waters protested bitterly and have continued ever since to attempt to reconnect to their counterpart above.[11] I suggest that God's resistance to their re-unification is out of concern that the Lower Waters will dominate and overwhelm the Upper Waters upon their reunification, obliterating the permanent character of the Upper Waters.

If I am correct thus far, then the solution to this cosmic dilemma lies in man. In man, Upper Waters' blood is mixed with Lower Waters' blood. If he maintains the proper relationship between them, i.e., by keeping from sin and thereby preventing the Lower Waters from dominating, he enables the two Waters to reunite within his being.

Is all of this real in any meaningful way? Absolutely. In traditional Jewish thought, water is a representative symbol for pleasure. Just as water will fill any available container up to its contours, a person will naturally take as much pleasure as his time, body, or the rules will allow. The difference between Lower Waters and Upper Waters is that Lower Waters represent physical and material pleasures—good food, pleasant temperatures, comfortable surroundings—while Upper Waters represent higher pleasures, including those of the spirit—spirited conversation, human solidarity, connection to God.

If the battleground between these two forces translates into the daily struggle within man to choose the stimulation of an early morning Torah class over the comfort of another hour in a feather bed; the satisfaction of discipline over the instant gratification of indulgence; the pleasure of spiritual growth over the stability of security—it becomes clear that eating a self-indulgent meal before davening gives the Lower Waters' component of your blood a distinct and unfair head start on the day. And thus we have the precision wording of the halachah: "Do not eat before praying over your blood," i.e., pray first, thereby giving your blood a fair chance to have its Upper Waters ingredient successfully dominate its Lower Waters part.

דף י: (2)

מתני' בית שמאי אומרים בערב כל אדם יטה ויקרא ובבקר יעמוד שנאמר ובשכבך ובקומך ובית הלל אומרים כל אדם קורא כדרכו שנאמר ובלכתך בדרך אם כן למה נאמר ובשכבך ובקומך בשעה שבני אדם שוכבים ובשעה שבני אדם עומדים א"ר טרפון אני הייתי בא בדרך והטתי לקרות כדברי ב"ש וסכנתי בעצמי מפני הלסטים אמרו לו כדי היית לחוב בעצמך שעברת על דברי ב"ה.

Beis Shammai say: In the evening, each person should recline and recite k'rias Shema, and in the morning he should stand, as it says, "And when you lie down and when you get up." Beis Hillel say: Each person should recite it as he is, as it says, "As you go on your way." If so, why does it say, "When you lie down and when you get up"? It means at the time when people lie down, and at the time when people get up. Said Rabbi Tarfon: I was once traveling, and I lay down to recite k'rias Shema in accordance with Beis Shammai, and I became endangered on account of bandits! They said to him, "You deserved your guilt, for you transgressed the words of Beis Hillel."

In the Mishnah, we find a *machlokes* between Beis Hillel and Beis Shammai over how to interpret the words *u'v'shochbecha u'v'kumecha*. Beis Shammai hold the Torah requires actual *sh'chivah* and actual *kimah*; thus one would have to lie down to recite the evening *Shema* and stand up to recite the daytime *Shema*. Beis Hillel disagree and claim that the Torah is merely dictating *z'manim*—the time when people go to bed and the time people arise. We *pasken* like Beis Hillel, but a number of questions remain:

1. If we *pasken* like Beis Hillel, why does the Gemara on *daf* 11a spend so much time trying to explain the *shitah* of Beis Shammai?
2. The Gemara brings a story where students of Beis Shammai reprimand a scholar for sitting in his sukkah with his table inside the house. The scholar's action was permitted according to Beis Hillel, but Beis Shammai's concern was *shema nimshach achar shulchano*—maybe he will be drawn after the table back into his house. If this is a legitimate concern, why do Beis Hillel not share it?
3. What is the basis for the dispute over whether specific postures are required for *k'rias Shema* or not?

Yesod

The way we have been learning throughout this *mesechta*, we can say that the *machlokes* at the beginning of the *sugya*—whether *k'rias Shema* is a *maaseh Shamayim* or a *maaseh adam*—is actually the *machlokes* between Beis Shammai and Beis Hillel. The two *iba'is eimas* on *daf* 2a are the two possible positions the Tanna of the opening Mishnah could be taking, and the Gemara is trying to find out which one it is he sides with. Does he side with Beis Hillel—*maaseh adam*—in which case the obligation of *k'rias Shema* is learned out from *u'v'shochbecha u'v'kumecha* (acts of man), or does he side with Beis Shammai—*maaseh Shamayim*—and the obligation is learned out from *va'yehi erev va'yehi boker* (acts of God)?

We have explained in the Gemara's conclusion that the Tanna of our Mishnah sides with Beis Hillel. For now, *k'rias Shema* is a *maaseh adam*. But, as you recall, the Gemara also concluded that Kohanim already today are *maaseh Shamayim*. And someday soon, when the promise of *k'rias Shema* reaches its actualization, we will all become Kohanim. When that day arrives, all our actions will become *maaseh Shamayim*. It should be obvious, then, that our *k'rias Shema* too will shift from being *maaseh adam* to being *maaseh Shamayim*, and we will effectively *pasken*

Berachos 10b

like Beis Shammai. This is why the Gemara spends as much time as it does discussing a *shitah* that is currently irrelevant, even so much that one who follows it deserves to die, as they told Rabbi Tarfon. Nevertheless, because it will be *halachah l'asid lavo*, it is discussed at length in our Gemara.

Indeed, this is the reason Beis Shammai learn that *k'rias Shema* requires *sh'chivah mamash* and *kimah mamash*. Once our act of *k'rias Shema* is seen as *maaseh Shamayim*, all our otherwise mundane activities come to be seen as *maaseh Shamayim*, even acts as banal as going to sleep and getting up. Our very postures become expressions of the Divine, and this becomes reflected in the halachah. As we have seen, it is all not for now, but it will be the reality of the future.

Now we can explain the dispute about the sukkah. Beis Shammai hold the sukkah is *maaseh Shamayim*. It is a space created by God (via our agency) to draw His presence down closer to us, thus extra care must be taken to prevent the possibility of our being drawn out of it into our homes. Beis Hillel hold the sukkah is a *maaseh adam*. It is a space we create to draw ourselves up into His Presence. Beis Hillel thus reason that if we ourselves are the ones who created this venue as a means to draw close to God, in what danger are we of being drawn out of it? We are the ones who made it out of our desire to be closer to God, and there is no concern that we will be tempted to leave!

דף יב:

ואמר רבה בר חיננא סבא משמיה דרב כל השנה כולה אדם מתפלל האל הקדוש מלך אוהב צדקה ומשפט חוץ מעשרה ימים וגו'.

Said Rabbah bar Chinena Saba in the name of Rav: All year long, a person davens "Ha'Keil Hakadosh" and "Melech Ohev Tzedakah u'Mishpat," except for the Ten Days, etc.

1. Why is Rav's statement introduced with, "All year long, a person davens '*Ha'Keil Hakadosh*" and "*Melech Ohev Tzedakah U'Mishpat*"? If you want to tell me what to do during *Aseres Yemei Teshuvah*, tell me. But why does that need to be prefaced with what we do all year?
2. It is not clear from Rabbi Elazar whether he is agreeing with Rav and just adding that *b'dieved* one who said *Ha'Keil* instead of *Hamelech* need not repeat it with the correction, or whether he is disagreeing with Rav and saying we should all say *Ha'Keil Hakadosh l'chatchila* and even Rav should agree to this *b'dieved*? Why isn't Rabbi Elazar clearer?
3. Rabbi Elazar's justification applies to *Ha'Keil Hakadosh*, not to *Melech Ohev Tzedakah U'Mishpat*. One would assume, then, that even he—the more *meikel* of the two—would still require one who failed to say *Hamelech Hamishpat* to repeat it properly. So why do we find that, in halachah, only one who says *Ha'Keil Hakadosh* must repeat, not one who says *Melech Ohev Tzedakah U'Mishpat*? Whose *shitah* is that?
4. It would seem from the Gemara that Rav Yosef and Rabbah are trying to take sides in the *machlokes* between Rav and Rabbi

Elazar. But if they are, why do they not just say, "*halachah k'Rav*" or "*halachah k'Rabbi Elazar*"? And why do they cite their respective *shitos* in such absolutist forms (Rav Yosef—"*Ha'Keil Hakadosh* and *Melech Ohev Tzedakah U'Mishpat*; Rav—"*Hamelech Hakadosh* and *Hamelech Hamishpat*") with no suggestion that anyone might hold one is acceptable *b'dieved* for the other, especially when it was hardly clear at all in the original *machlokes* that Rav and Rabbi Elazar held their views in such absolutist terms?

5. And if they are not trying to take sides in the original *machlokes*, from where are they getting their *shitos*, and why are they ignoring Rav and Rabbi Elazar?
6. We always say *Rabbah v'Rav Yosef, halachah k'Rabbah*. So why does our Gemara need to state "*v'hilchesa k'Rabbah*"?
7. Assuming Rabbah is going with *shitas* Rav, the question regarding *b'dieved* must be dealt with. So why does the *Rambam pasken* like Rabbah only to completely ignore the issue of whether one who inadvertently recited the wrong *berachah* must repeat it correctly?
8. Why anyway is it so important to replace *Ha'Keil* with *Hamelech* during the *Aseres Yemei Teshuvah*? And if the reason is the word "*melech*," why do we also have to change *Melech Ohev Tzedakah U'Mishpat* when that already has "*melech*" in it?
9. *Keil* and *melech* are constantly being used interchangeably (see the prayer *Yishtabach*). What is the significance of these words that they should generate such debate?
10. *Rambam* says that even though *teshuvah* and *tze'akah* are always good, they are especially good during the *Aseres Yemei Teshuvah* (*hilchos Teshuvah* 2:6). But then he says this is only for an individual; a *tzibbur* has this kind of access all the time. Why should an individual not have this access all the time, and if he does not, why does he have it during the Ten Days, and how does the *Rambam* know this?

Yesod

The difference between *Keil* and *melech* is that *Keil* describes God's unilateral power, while *melech* focuses on the fact that we have accepted Him upon ourselves as our Sovereign.

The appropriate word for the time period of the *Yamim Nora'im* is certainly *melech*, on the basis that God has requested, "*Tamlichuni aleichem*—Make me your king" (*Rosh Hashanah* 34b).

But there is a problem. The Torah says, "*Som tasim alecha melech*—Place a king over you" (*Devarim* 17:15). According to the Vilna Gaon, all singular words in the Book of *Devarim* are meant to refer to the singular entity of Klal Yisrael. This means that it is only a *tzibbur*—which is known to be the authoritative representative of the entire Klal Yisrael—that is able to appoint a king. An individual cannot appoint a king. Thus it makes no sense for an individual to adopt the phrase *Hamelech Hakadosh* as a response to "*Tamlichuni aleichem*" when no individual has that authority!

AND SO, WHEN Rav comes along and says we should say *Hamelech Hakadosh* during the *Aseres Yemei Teshuvah*, *Rashi* is quick to point out that it is expressly **not** for the purpose of being *mamlich Hashem*: "It is because during these days He expresses His *malchus* in the way He judges the world" (*Rashi*, *Berachos* 12b).

We are not coronating G-d; that is something we cannot do as individuals. We are merely acknowledging the fact that He exercises the judgment role of *malchus* during this time.

This is why Rav prefaces his words with what we say all year long. In his view, on the technical level what we say during the year we *should* also be saying during the *Aseres Yemei Teshuvah*, were it not for the fact that, *m'svara*, we want to make mention of this special aspect of His *malchus*. It is also why Rabbi Elazar adds that *b'dieved*, *Ha'Keil Hakadosh* is good enough, both because it was anyway the technically correct words to say and because it does carry a reference to Hashem judging during the *Aseres Yemei Teshuvah*, even if it is not a specific reference to the idea that this judgment is an aspect of His *malchus*. Rav would not

Berachos 12b

disagree, and this would be the halachah if the Gemara had stopped then and there.

BUT THE GEMARA does not stop there. It asks *"Mai havei alah"* and introduces Rav Yosef and Rabbah. What is that for?

I would like to suggest that there is another *shitah* inhabiting our Gemara.

The *machlokes* we have tracked throughout this *perek* of *Berachos* debates whether different concepts in Judaism are to be seen as *maaseh Shamayim* or *maaseh adam*. In our chapter on *daf* 8a (1), we noted that Rabbi Yochanan was of the opinion that a *tzibbur* is a *maaseh Shamayim*.

This is highly relevant to our Gemara. A *yachid* (individual) has no way to engage in *"tamlichuni aleichem."* Only a *tzibbur* can do that. But what if a *yachid* is suddenly given the status of a *tzibbur*? Then, it stands to reason, even a *yachid* could get involved in *"tamlichuni aleichem."* But how could a *yachid* be given the status of a *tzibbur*? It can be done if you hold a *tzibbur* is *maaseh Shamayim*. Just as God could designate a collection of ten men as His vehicle to reach down closer to us, He could similarly designate a single *yachid* as that vehicle. According to the *Rambam*, that is exactly what happens during the *Aseres Yemei Teshuvah*. For those ten days, in His quest to reach down as close to us as possible, Hashem deputizes each individual and invests each one with the status of *tzibbur*. This is why we each have *tzibbur*-like access for those ten days. And with the status of a *tzibbur*, we can engage individually in *"tamlichuni aleichem."* And so we say *"Hamelech Hakadosh."*

BUT THIS IS all possible under one proviso—that we hold a *tzibbur* is *maaseh Shamayim*.

If it is *maaseh adam*, there can be no essential difference between how we form ourselves into a collective all year round, and how we form ourselves into a collective during the days of *Yamim Nora'im*.

This is our Gemara. Rav holds *tzibbur* is *maaseh adam*. We do not get invested with any special Heavenly status during the *Aseres Yemei Teshuvah*. We do say *"Hamelech Hakadosh,"* but it is not for the purpose of fulfilling *"tamlichuni aleichem."* It is just in order to make mention of God's seasonal activities. And thus Rabbi Elazar adds to it and says *b'dieved*, *Ha'Keil Hakadosh* would still work.

BUT, AS WE mentioned, there is another, unspoken *shitah* inhabitating our *sugya*. It is the *shitah* of Rabbi Yochanan. Rabbi Yochanan holds a *tzibbur* is *maaseh Shamayim*. With *shitas* Rabbi Yochanan, it is conceivable that we could perform "*tamlichuni aleichem*," as we have shown.

RAV YOSEF AND Rabbah hold like *shitas* Rabbi Yochanan. So first of all, they both disagree with Rav (and his cohort, Rabbi Elazar) that there could be any *b'dieved* back-up plan. Either we are *yechidim* invested with a *din tzibbur* or we are not. If we are, then we must say *Hamelech Hakadosh* and fulfill "*tamlichuni aleichem*." If we are not, then it is completely inappropriate to say *Hamelech Hakadosh*. Rav Yosef holds we are not invested with *din tzibbur*, hence the only appropriate phrase available to us is the only one we can say as *yechidim—Ha'Keil Hakadosh*. Rabbah, who just happens to be the source in *Rosh Hashanah* 34b for the *maimra* of "*tamlichuni aleichem*," holds we are invested with *din tzibbur*, hence we can fulfill "*tamlichuni*" even as individuals, hence we both can and must say *Hamelech Hakadosh* and *Hamelech Hamishpat* during the *Aseres Yemei Teshuvah*, and even *b'dieved* we must go back and correct our mistake.

WHY HAMELECH HAMISHPAT? What was wrong with *Melech Ohev Tzedakah U'Mishpat*? Now it becomes clear. "*Melech*" is a reference to Hashem as king, but it is not an act of *hamlachah*. "*Hamelech*" is an act of *hamlachah* (which is why we begin the *Shacharis* of *Yamim Nora'im* with "*Hamelech*"). During these Ten Days, says Rabbah, we are required to be *mamlich* Hashem as the King of holiness and also to be *mamlich* Him as the King of justice.

Rambam is in an interesting predicament. In *Hilchos Rosh Hashanah*, he *paskens* like Rav against Rabbi Yochanan. To be consistent, it would seem he should *pasken* like Rav (and Rabbi Elazar) here as well, and *Hamelech Hakadosh* should be said without any connotation of actual *hamlachah* and one should be *yotzei b'dieved* with *Ha'Keil Hakadosh*. But when he brings the halachah, he brings it like Rabbah that one is to say *Hamelech Hakadosh* and *Hamelech Hamishpat*, without the *Rambam* saying a word about not having to go back and correct it if you inadvertently said it wrong (thus clearly implying you *would* have to correct it, as the obligation remains hanging over you until it has been fulfilled). Why does he bring the halachah this way? This is the answer to our earlier question. It is because the Gemara says *"v'hilchesa k'Rabbah,"* that is to say, the halachah for the *Aseres Yemei Teshuvah* follows Rabbah (in accordance with *shitas* Rabbi Yochanan), **even if the rest of the year you *pasken* like *shitas* Rav.**

IT IS FROM this that *Rambam* knows that Hashem grants us special *tzibbur* status even as individuals during the *Aseres Yemei Teshuvah*. Even if He recognizes *tzibbur* year-round as a *maaseh adam*, He adopts it as *maaseh Shamayim* during these Ten Days. And for that duration, while it is *maaseh Shamayim*, He extends its reach all the way down to us as *yechidim* and invests us each individually with the unlimited access and the *hamlachah* power of a *tzibbur*.

Endnotes

1. *Tur, Orach Chaim* 90.
2. *Yechezkel* 46:9.
3. *Rashi* on *Bereishis* 12:9.
4. Ibid., 11:32.
5. See *Bereishis* 24:1, 25:1, and 25:8.
6. See Aryeh Kaplan, *The Living Torah*, note on *Vayikra* 19:26.
7. *Bereishis* 4:10–11.
8. Rambam, *Mishneh Torah, Yesodei HaTorah* 3:10.
9. See *Gittin* 57b.
10. See *Rashi, Bereishis* 4:11 and 1:11.
11. *Bereishis Rabbah* 5:4.

Chapter Two
Hayah Koreh

Berachos 13a

(1) דף יג.

מתני׳ היה קורא בתורה והגיע זמן המקרא אם כוון לבו יצא.

Mishnah—If he had been reading Torah, and the time for reciting *k'rias Shema* arrived, if he focuses his attention he has fulfilled his obligation.

Gemara—[The Mishnah does not mean that the person is required to focus his attention on the fact that he is intentionally performing a mitzvah, since mitzvos do not require intent. Rather, it means] he must focus his attention on the fact that he is reading [as opposed to proofreading].

1. How is it possible that one could be *yotzei k'rias Shema* while engaged in an ordinary review of *pesukim*? Which *pesukim* was he reading? If he was reading in *Parashas Va'eschanan*, he might be reading the *pasuk* of *Shema* and the first paragraph (*V'Ahavtah*), but if he would intentionally jump after that to *Parashas Eikev* for *V'Hayah im shamo'a* and to *Parashas Shelach* for *Va'yomer*, he's not doing an ordinary review of *pesukim*—he's deliberately reciting *k'rias Shema*!

2. And if you want to say he is only reading the first paragraph, how is he *yotzei k'rias Shema*, which at least *m'd'Rabbanan* requires three paragraphs?

3. The Gemara says he was proofreading, and in order to be *yotzei*, he has to focus his attention to reading. Why did we need a Mishnah to tell me this? Is there anyone who believes one could possibly be *yotzei k'rias Shema* by uttering letters (see *Rashi*) in a proofreading exercise?

Yesod

The Mishnah is describing someone who had been proofreading, got up to the *pasuk* of *Shema*, realized it was *z'man k'rias Shema*, and wanted to be *yotzei*. He is already reading, as we clearly had no *hava amina* that uttering letters is an act of reciting *k'rias Shema*. And mitzvos do not require intent. So what is the Mishnah requiring?

One possibility is that the Mishnah is requiring not that he be reading, but that he be **exclusively** reading. In other words, the *hava amina* is that he could read the *pesukim* but continue to proofread at the same time. The Mishnah is telling us that while you may not have to have intent to perform a mitzvah, and you may not have to understand more than the first *pasuk* (as we will see on *amud beis*), *k'rias Shema* is still a statement, a pledge, and a declaration. No declaration is valid if it is made while multitasking.

Rashi is not saying there was a *hava amina* one could be *yotzei k'rias Shema* by uttering letters. The *hava amina* was that you could be *yotzei k'rias Shema* by reading the *pesukim* aloud while continuing to do the proofreading you were doing while you had been uttering the letters. The Mishnah is coming to teach us that you cannot.

Now we understand why the Mishnah needs to concern itself only with the first paragraph of *Shema*. Certainly your intention was always to recite *k'rias Shema* in its entirety, and after the first paragraph you have every intention to jump to *Eikev* and *Shelach*. But because you had been in the process of proofreading when you got up to *Shema*, it was your hope to continue your proofreading through the end of that paragraph simultaneously with making it into the beginning of your *k'rias Shema*. The Mishnah is teaching us that this practice would make your *k'rias Shema* invalid.

דף יג. (2)

ת"ר והיו שלא יקרא למפרע וגו'.

The Rabbis taught: "And they shall be"—that one may not read the words in inverted order, etc.

ת"ר שמע ישראל ה' אלהינו ה' אחד עד כאן צריכה כוונת הלב דברי רבי מאיר וגו'.

The Rabbis taught: "Hear, O Israel, Hashem is our God, Hashem is One"—until here concentration is required, says Rabbi Meir.

The *sugya* in *Berachos* 13a–b sets one *Beraisa* off against another. In one *Beraisa*, Rabbi Akiva tells Rabbi Eliezer that one's *kavanah* is required not just until *al levavecha* but for the entire first *perek*. In another, Rabbi Acha in the name of Rabbi Yehudah tells the *Tanna Kama* that his *kavanah* is not required for the entire *k'rias Shema* but just for the first *perek*.

The first *Beraisa* could be talking about the *chiyuv* to be *mekabel ol malchus Shamayim*, as one Mishnah does suggest that the first *perek* of *k'rias Shema* is *kabbalas ol malchus Shamayim* and the second *perek* is *kabbalas ol mitzvos*. The second *Beraisa* cannot be about *kabbalas ol malchus Shamayim*, as there is no source that entertains the possibility that *kabbalas ol malchus Shamayim* lasts longer than the first *perek*. So the *kavanah* as discussed in the second *Beraisa* must be about something else.

ACHARONIM ASK: IF both *Beraisos* anyway conclude that we need *kavanah* in the first *perek*, what's the difference if we say *halachah k'Rabbi Akiva* or *halachah k'Rabbi Acha*? *Tzlach* wants to say that one *Beraisa* is saying *tz'richah kavanah* and the other is saying that *keivan she'kivein*

דף י:ג.

perek alef shuv eino tzarich. According to this, the first one is saying that *kavanah* is needed even *b'dieved*, implying that the second *perek* requires *kavanah* too, at least *l'chatchila*; the second *Beraisa* is saying that no *kavanah* is needed for the second *perek*, not even *l'chatchila*.

This *Tzlach* is difficult to accept, though, as the different terms are easily explained by the nature of the arguments. In one, the starting point is that only a few lines need *kavanah*, so the response is that more needs *kavanah*; in the other, the starting point is that much more needs *kavanah*, so the response is that no *kavanah* beyond one *perek* is needed. There is simply no evidence to support the suggestion that these phrases are references to *l'chatchila* and *b'dieved*. The way we are proposing to learn in this *shiur*, the Acharonim's question doesn't even begin. The difference is vast. Like Rabbi Akiva, the purpose of the *kavanah* is for *kabbalas ol malchus Shamayim*, and the requirement to stand is for *kavod haShechinah* and would apply, therefore, even if one had previously been sitting. Like Rabbi Acha, the purpose of *kavanah* is for better concentration, not *kavod*, and the requirement to stand is for better concentration as well. That kind of *kavanah*, as we will see, applies only when one had previously been walking.

WHEN SHMUEL IN the *Yerushalmi* says, "*Tzarich l'kabel ol malchus Shamayim me'umad*" (just as Abaye says regarding *kabbalas p'nei haShechinah* in *Kiddush Levanah*, "*hilkach tzarich l'memra me'umad*"), he means you **must** stand for the first three *pesukim*. (It would apply to the entire first *perek* according to Rabbi Akiva).

But when this concept gets said over in the *Bavli*, it is said over generically ("One should stand for *al levavecha*—we mean until *al levavecha*"). Why? What happened to the message that the purpose of the standing is for *kabbalas ol malchus Shamayim*?

The answer has to be that the generic presentation found in the *Bavli* is because of *shitas* Rabbi Yochanan, who rules that one must stand for the whole first *perek*. If Rabbi Yochanan meant to say like Rabbi Akiva that *kabbalas ol malchus Shamayim* extends for the entire first *perek*, we would understand what he means that one must stand for the first *perek*; it would be for *kavod haShechinah*.

Berachos 13a

But we know Rabbi Yochanan does not hold *halachah k'Rabbi Akiva*! He holds *halachah k'Rabbi Acha*, that concentration is needed not for the whole *k'rias Shema* but **just** for the first *perek* (like the second *Beraisa* above). The purpose behind this kind of standing is in order to enable the person to have better concentration, not for *kavod haShechinah*. So the *Bavli*—sensitive to the view of Rabbi Yochanan—cannot make a blanket statement that standing is for *kavod haShechinah* of *kabbalas ol malchus Shamayim*. Rabbi Yochanan doesn't agree!

But the fact remains that all *shitos* other than Rabbi Yochanan hold *amidah* **is** because of *kabbalas ol malchus Shamayim* (like the first *Beraisa*), and *l'halachah* we don't *pasken* like Rabbi Yochanan. We know this because Rabbi Yochanan holds one is required to stand for the entire first *perek*, while the *Rambam paskens* one must stand only for the first *pasuk*.

Well and good, you might say, but evidently we don't *pasken* like Rav Nassan bar Mar Ukva—the source for the *inyan* of standing. Rav Nassan says one must stand through *al levavecha*, while we hold one must stand only until the end of the first *pasuk*.

So like whom do we in fact *pasken*? The answer is clear. We *pasken* like Rabbi Meir. The real question we need to ask is what exactly is the view of Rabbi Meir? Does Rabbi Meir ascribe to the approach of Rabbi Akiva, like whom there is a *din* of *kabbalas ol malchus Shamayim*, or does he go with the approach of Rabbi Acha (as Rabbi Yochanan does), like whom there is just a plain mitzvah of *k'rias Shema* without an added layer called *kabbalas ol malchus Shamayim*?

To say that Rabbi Meir goes with Rabbi Acha is very difficult. First of all, how could he justify such a broad *machlokes* with the *Tanna Kama*, who holds *k'rias Shema* needs *kavanah* for the entire *k'riah* (or at least for the two *perakim* that contain a reference to *al levavecha/chem*) while he (Rabbi Meir) holds it needs *kavanah* for just one *pasuk*!? Second, like Rabbi Acha's approach, how could we understand Rabbi Meir dropping the *kavanah* requirement after the first *pasuk*? At least like Rabbi Akiva, a case could be made to end *kavanah* after the first *pasuk* from within the framework of *kabbalas ol malchus Shamayim*, because historically the statement *"Shema Yisrael..."* was first uttered by the sons of Yaakov as a testimony made before their father that they were *mekabel* God's Unity, and the end of the first *pasuk* was where the B'nei Yaakov's statement of acceptance came to an end. But what makes the end of the first *pasuk* a stopping point according to Rabbi Acha's view?

Far better is to say Rabbi Meir goes with Rabbi Akiva and thus *kabbalas ol malchus Shamayim*. This is well supported by the subsequent Gemara (about lengthening the *dalet*), which itself is about *kabbalas ol malchus Shamayim*, both here and in the *Yerushalmi*.

So *paskening* like Rabbi Meir is *paskening* like Rabbi Akiva but simply limiting its application to the first *pasuk*. If so, the *tzarich la'amod* of Rav Nassan bar Mar Ukva is also to be understood as an element of *kabbalas ol malchus Shamayim*. Rav Nassan, of course, holds like Rabbi Eliezer, so he says one must remain standing through the words *al levavecha*. Rabbi Akiva holds it must be the whole *perek*. Rabbi Meir holds the first *pasuk*. But they all agree the purpose of standing is for *kabbalas ol malchus Shamayim*. So if we are in fact required to stand up because of *kavod Shamayim*, why are we not obligated to stand up for the first *pasuk* if we had been sitting? The answer is we indeed should have been obligated. The reason we are not is only because of Beis Shammai. **If we were to stand up for *k'rias Shema* from a sitting position, it would not look like we were being *mekabel ol malchus Shamayim*. Rather, it would look (at least during the morning *Shema*) as if we were trying to follow the ruling of Beis Shammai**, who requires one to physically arise as a way of acting out "*u'v'kumecha*," an act for which Rabbi Tarfon was told he was virtually *chayav misah* for having followed Beis Shammai! Thus, *l'halachah*, the only available way to fulfill the *inyan* of *amidah* is in a scenario where one had up until then been walking.

And we emerge with a *chiddush l'halachah*, Tosafos says, that standing for *k'rias Shema* is merely a *mitzvah min ha'muvchar*, and that is true in most applications. But as we have shown, in the one scenario where one had been in the middle of walking around when he reached or otherwise decided to say *k'rias Shema*, he would be obligated to stop walking and remain standing still (through at least the first *pasuk* if not through *al levavecha*) *m'ikar ha'din*!

Berachos 13a

דף יג. (3)

בפרקים שואל מפני הכבוד ומשיב ובאמצע שואל מפני היראה וגו׳.

Between paragraphs [of the Shema], one may greet another out of honor and may respond to a greeting; and in the middle of a paragraph, one may respond out of fear, etc.

1. In the *sugya* of *b'emtza sho'el mipnei ha'yirah*, both *Rambam* and *Shulchan Aruch pasken* like Rabbi Yehudah that within a *perek* one can be *sho'el mipnei ha'yirah u'meishiv mipnei ha'kavod*. Yet, *Shulchan Aruch* adds that during the *pasuk* of *Shema Yisrael*, one should not interrupt at all, not even *mipnei ha'yirah*. Why does the *Rambam* omit this *halachah*?

2. It seems plausible that the difference between *shitas* Rabbi Meir and *shitas* Rabbi Yehudah is linked to the difference between how the two understand why we need special *kavanah* in specific parts of *k'rias Shema*. As we showed in our preceding chapter, Rabbi Meir holds the *din* of extra *kavanah*—which he assigns to the first *pasuk* alone—is for *kabbalas ol malchus Shamayim*. Rabbi Yehudah disagrees and holds that any special *kavanah*—whether for the first *pasuk*, until *al levavecha*, the whole first *perek*, or the entire *k'rias Shema*—is in order to generate extra concentration. If Rabbi Meir holds it is for *kabbalas ol malchus Shamayim*, we know *kabbalas ol malchus Shamayim* equals *kabbalas p'nei haShechinah*, as we find there is a *din me'umad* in *Kiddush Levanah* for the same reason we have a *din* that *k'rias Shema* must be done *b'amidah*, meaning we are engaged in *kavod haShechinah* at the moment of *kabbalas ol malchus Shamayim*. So,

says Rabbi Meir, when we are called upon to be *mafsik*, *yirah* obligations of all types may trump *kavod*, but no other *kavod* obligation can trump *kavod haShechinah*. Rabbi Yehudah, on the other hand, holds the whole reason for special *kavanah* is for extra concentration, not for *kabbalas ol malchus Shamayim*, thus being *meishiv mipnei ha'kavod* is no less legitimate an interruption than interruptions made for *yirah*, the only caveat being that more latitude exists for *yirah* interruptions than for those due merely to *kavod*. And we *pasken* like Rabbi Yehudah in the *din* of being *mafsik*. But how, in fact, can we *pasken* like Rabbi Yehudah in the *din* of being *mafsik* if the rules for being *mafsik* are tied to what you hold the reason is for the extra *kavanah* in parts of *Shema*, and in that we *pasken* like Rabbi Meir and not like Rabbi Yehudah? The *din* of being *mafsik* should have to follow the *shitah* of Rabbi Meir!

Yesod

Rabbi Meir holds we have *kabbalas ol malchus Shamayim* in *k'rias Shema*, but it is only for the first *pasuk*. How will he justify not being allowed to interrupt throughout the entire *k'rias Shema* and its *berachos* if 98 percent of it is not involved in *kabbalas ol malchus Shamayim*? Apparently, Rabbi Meir will have to say that all paragraphs even just *affiliated* with *kabbalas ol malchus Shamayim* are to receive the same *din mafsik* as those parts directly engaged in *kabbalas ol malchus Shamayim*.

This is a difficult stretch to accept. Combined with the fact that we generally say *Rabbi Meir v'Rabbi Yehudah halachah k'Rabbi Yehudah*, that leads us to determine that in the matter of being *mafsik*, we will *pasken* like Rabbi Yehudah.

But what will we do in halachah with the first *pasuk*? There we hold like Rabbi Meir as Rava ruled. But isn't it incompatible to marry a set of interruption standards based on "extra concentration" to a *kavanah* requirement based on *kabbalas ol malchus Shamayim*?

The answer is that in the matter of *mafsik* we *pasken* completely like Rabbi Yehudah. For the one *pasuk* that we hold is engaged in *kabbalas ol malchus Shamayim,* **we are going to have to estimate what Rabbi Yehudah would have held for a** *kabbalas ol malchus Shamayim* **situation.** *Beis Yosef* cites a *Ramach* that we should make no interruptions at all during the *pasuk* of *Shema Yisrael,* and so this becomes our supposition, according to *Shulchan Aruch,* as to how much Rabbi Yehudah would allow a greeting to interrupt a *kabbalas ol malchus Shamayim* situation if there *were* such thing as a greeting interrupting a *kabbalas ol malchus Shamayim* situation.[1]

But then why does the *Rambam* not say this? He too *paskens* like Rabbi Meir for *kabbalas ol malchus Shamayim* on the *pasuk* of *Shema Yisrael* and like Rabbi Yehudah for *din mafsik.* Yet he draws no distinction between *emtza ha'perek* and *emtza ha'pasuk,* with no exception even for the *pasuk* of *Shema*! If he is not going to go with *Beis Yosef's* approach (brought in *Kesef Mishneh*), how will he be able to handle the problem of incompatibility between the two *p'sakim*?

The answer to this is that the *Rambam* noticed something interesting in the matter of extending the *din* of *emtza ha'perek* to *afilu emtza ha'pasuk.* He noticed that the *Yerushalmi* discusses it and the *Bavli* ignores it. Where did the *Yerushalmi* discuss it? In its prelude to the *din* of *assur likrotz*—the prohibition against signaling during your recitation of *k'rias Shema.* First, *Yerushalmi* extends the ruling of *mafsik b'emtza ha'perek* to *emtza ha'pasuk.* Then it goes on to say that Rav Yirmiyah always limited his permitted greetings interruptions during *k'rias Shema* to signaling (by hand or eye gesture); he never spoke. Rav Yonah did speak, but only because he had a *derashah* from *v'dibarta bam* permitting it.

Not only does the *Bavli* neither have this discussion nor learn this *derashah,* notices the *Rambam,* it actually uses *v'dibarta bam* to learn out that it is forbidden to make hand or eye signals during *k'rias Shema* because *k'rias Shema* must be said as a *davar keva* and not *arai.* **In other words, while the** *Bavli* **assumed you could speak during the permitted interruptions of greeting and required a** *derashah* **to know you could not make signals, the** *Yerushalmi* **assumed you could not signal during** *k'rias Shema* **and needed a** *derashah* **to know you could speak!** These positions are polar opposites of each other. What is going on here, wondered the *Rambam*?

דף יג.

The *Rambam's* conclusion is that we have a *machlokes* between the *Bavli* and the *Yerushalmi* over whether the greetings being permitted during *k'rias Shema* are fundamentally inimical to the proper recital of *k'rias Shema* and are permitted only *b'dochak*, or whether they are actually a fulfillment of the message of *k'rias Shema*—just as Avraham Avinu's greeting of the guests in *Parashas Vayera* was a fulfillment of his meeting with Hashem, not a contradiction to it—and are welcomed happily whenever they apply. What is supposed to be our correct attitude toward the interruptions? The *Bavli* holds that interrupting to offer or return greetings is a *fulfillment* of the mitzvah of *k'rias Shema*; the *Yerushalmi* holds it is a *contradiction* to the mitzvah.

Rambam paskens like the *Bavli* against the *Yerushalmi*. Thus when we try to speculate what Rabbi Yehudah would have said in a case of *kabbalas ol malchus Shamayim*, *Rambam's* answer is that he would have welcomed the interruptions the same there as he would have welcomed them anywhere else. We who add *kavanah* to the first *pasuk* of *Shema* in accordance with Rabbi Meir actually have a case of *kabbalas ol malchus Shamayim*, but still the halachah is exactly right—Rabbi Yehudah would have applied his *din mafsik* the same to Rabbi Meir's first *pasuk* as he would to any other *din mafsik* where the *kavanah* being interrupted was for extra concentration: *sho'el mipnei ha'yirah u'meishiv mipnei ha'kavod*. *Shulchan Aruch*, which acknowledges no *Bavli-Yerushalmi* dispute at all, holds the *Bavli* agrees with the *Yerushalmi's* view that these interruptions—even where permitted due to their halachic necessity—remain essentially contraindications to the proper recital of *Shema*, and thus, presented with the added factor of *kabbalas ol malchus Shamayim*, Rabbi Yehudah, he estimates, would have gone beyond his normal *din heter* and allowed no interruptions there at all. Since we hold like Rabbi Meir in the matter of *kavanah l'pasuk rishon*, says *Shulchan Aruch*, we *pasken* like *Ramach* that no interruptions can be made in the first *pasuk*.

Two questions remain:

1) Where in the *Rambam* do we see that he notices a *machlokes Bavli-Yerushalmi*, particularly when no one else does?

Answer: When *Rambam* brings the *din* of *asur likrotz*, he says it is because of our mandate to prevent *k'rias Shema* from being said *arai*.

Berachos 13a

That is the very reason the Gemara in *Yoma* (19b) gives in rejecting the other uses of *v'dibarta bam*, including the one the *Yerushalmi* uses to teach the *heter* of speaking when greeting during *Shema*; and it is also the reason *umnin* (craftsmen) remain idle from their work during the first *perek*. By citing this approach from the *Bavli* (as opposed to just quoting the halachah *stam*), it is clear that *Rambam* is openly rejecting the competing approach used by the *Yerushalmi*. *Tosafos*, on the other hand, uncouples the *din* of *assur likrotz* from the *din* of *umnin* and brings *assur likrotz* as a stand-alone *din* also for the purpose of promoting extra concentration. It is not to prevent *arai*, so we have no reason to reject any *v'dibarta bam derashah*, and the *Bavli* need not be arguing on the *Yerushalmi*. This is the view the *Shulchan Aruch* accepts.

2) But if, according to Rabbi Meir, only the first *pasuk* is *kabbalas ol malchus Shamayim*, how is it that the need to keep *k'rias Shema* from becoming *arai* extends, like the *Rambam*, to the entire first *perek*?

Answer: The opposite of *arai* is *keva*. By the *din* of *kove'a makom l'tefillaso*, *Rambam* defined *keva* by *tefillah* as making a commitment to hold a "session" of *tefillah* (just like we hold an eating "session" and call it being "*kove'a seudah*") in which you agree not to leave until the session is over. Actual *kabbalas ol malchus Shamayim* may be just the first *pasuk*, but the session in which it takes place is not over until the end of the first *perek*.

דף יד: (1)

אמר רבי יהושע בן קרחה למה קדמה פרשת שמע
לוהיה אם שמוע כדי שיקבל עליו עול מלכות שמים
תחלה ואחר כך מקבל עליו עול מצוות וגו'.

Rabbi Yehoshua ben Korcha said: Why is Parashas Shema [recited] before V'Hayah im shamo'a? In order that one should accept upon himself the responsibility of the kingdom of Heaven first, and only then accept upon himself the responsibility of the commandments, etc.

Tosafos on top of 14b is actually in reference to the Mishnah on 13a. Both the Mishnah and the *Tosafos* are difficult.

1. What is the thread that binds the disparate elements of the Mishnah? Reading the Torah when *z'man k'rias Shema* arrives seems unrelated to the law of interrupting *k'rias Shema* to greet people out of fear or honor, and both seem unrelated to the question of why *Shema* comes before *V'Hayah* and *V'Hayah* before *Vayomer*. What is the connection?
2. Why is the Mishnah unconcerned with addressing the question of how one could be *yotzei* the mitzvah of *k'rias Shema* even **with** *kavanah* if he isn't doing the *berachos* and all three paragraphs?
3. The Gemara concludes that the person was not really reading Torah but proofreading it. In order to be *yotzei*, he must have *kavanah* to read. This is totally not implied in the Mishnah. Why would the Mishnah be so abstruse about its meaning?
4. Why is Rabbi Yehoshua ben Korcha's teaching important? It does not seem to impart anything of halachic significance.

Berachos 14b

5. One version of Rabbi Yehoshua ben Korcha has him answering his question by saying, "*k'dei she'yekabel*." Another has him saying "*ela k'dei she'yekabel*." What is the meaning of this difference?
6. How could *Tosafos* entertain the notion that Rabbi Yehoshua ben Korcha could answer his question by saying the two paragraphs were written in their order because that is the order in which they are found in the Torah? Doesn't *Tosafos* realize Rabbi Yehoshua ben Korcha must have been aware of the existence of *Vayomer* and the fact that it appears first in the Torah but last in *k'rias Shema*?
7. How can *Tosafos* declare that it is because of *ein mukdam u'me'uchar baTorah* that we are not concerned with matching the order of the paragraphs of *k'rias Shema* to the order of their appearance in the Torah? The principle of *ein mukdam* teaches us that the Torah does not necessarily present its narratives in chronological order. It has nothing to do with the Torah's choice of the order of **appearance** of those narratives. It should not give us any license to say the Torah is *unconcerned* with the ordering of its paragraphs. If anything, we should say that the Torah's lack of chronological order is the price it is willing to pay *davka* so it **can** be precise and intentional about the ordering of its passages!

Yesod

There are two fundamental and opposite approaches to the service of God. One follows the idea that the most important thing one can do is imitate God by emulating His actions (and obeying His commandments, both of which are ways of following His will). The other says the highest service of God is to grow and cleave ever closer to Him.

THE FIRST IS the way of Avraham Avinu and follows the dictum, "Greater is *hachnasas orchim* than even communing with the Divine Presence." The second is the way of Yitzchak Avinu, who blazed the path of always overcoming greater and greater temptations in order to grow ever closer to God, and is based on the message in *Avos*, "Who is mighty? The one who vanquishes his *yetzer hara*."

WHEN THE MISHNAH starts out describing a man who was already reading Torah yet still must have a specific intention in order to be in fulfillment of *k'rias Shema*, it is taking the position that the *deveikus* in Hashem one has while engaged in reading Hashem's Torah is not enough to prevent him from having to walk away from the *deveikus* and shift into mitzvah-performance mode. This reflects the Avraham approach.

The next case in the Mishnah continues along the same lines. Despite the connection to Hashem one is undoubtedly enjoying while reciting *k'rias Shema*, it is still more important for one to interrupt this activity and greet those who should be greeted—over which Rabbi Meir and Rabbi Yehudah might differ on the details but not about the basic necessity of placing a proper greeting above the need for unbroken concentration.

To this presumption, Rabbi Yehoshua ben Korcha reacts, "Why do you think the Sages placed *Shema* ahead of *V'Hayah im shamoa*? *Shema* is about *deveikus* (*kabbalas ol malchus Shamayim* = *kabbalas p'nei haShechinah* = basking in the closeness of encountering the Divine); *V'Hayah* is about performing mitzvos. Rather [than saying one should abandon *deveikus* in order to do mitzvos] (this is the "*ela*" we pointed out in our list of questions), aren't the Sages teaching us that *deveikus* is a higher form of *avodas Hashem* than the performance of mitzvos, and that we should conduct ourselves like Yitzchak not like Avraham?"

Tosafos is merely noting that Rabbi Yehoshua ben Korcha's proof is only compelling if things *should* have been in the reverse. If *V'Hayah* should have preceded *Shema*, then the fact that the Sages advanced *Shema* is legitimate evidence that they intended Rabbi Yehoshua ben Korcha's point. But maybe, asks *Tosafos*, Rabbi Yehoshua ben Korcha should have considered the possibility that *Shema* should anyway have preceded *V'Hayah* because regardless of valid teaching reasons, the importance of maintaining the Torah's appearance order is paramount. That way, his proof is broken because now we do not know if *Shema* is first in order to teach us Rabbi Yehoshua ben Korcha's point or just

Berachos 14b

because it is first in the Torah. To this, *Tosafos* answers that Rabbi Yehoshua ben Korcha sees in *Vayomer* a paragraph that should have overridden its purpose in being last in *k'rias Shema* if appearance in the Torah were indeed paramount, and it should have been first. We see that just as *Vayomer* is not advanced for the sake of order when there is a purpose to having it displaced, so too *Shema* would not be advanced solely for the sake of order when there is a purpose to having it displaced.

Tosafos then likens this to *ein mukdam u'me'uchar baTorah*, but not because that describes our case. It does not! But it does show an example of where the Torah does not disregard a purposeful moving of a narrative out of chronological position solely for the sake of maintaining proper chronological order. Just as the Torah does not dismiss a purposeful arrangement simply for the sake of good order, we can say our Sages too would not dismiss a purposeful arrangement simply for the sake of good order. The purposeful arrangement would have been to put *V'Hayah*, which speaks to the masses, ahead of *Shema*, which speaks to the individual. This proves, concludes *Tosafos*, that Rabbi Yehoshua ben Korcha has a legitimate point. By promoting *Shema* ahead of *V'Hayah*, the Sages seem to be demanding the Yitzchak approach, not the approach of Avraham.

(TO THIS, RABBI Shimon Bar Yochai responds and says, "No! *Shema* was **rightfully** ahead of *V'Hayah*, and I don't mean because of its Torah order. And it is not because *deveikus* is more important than imitating God. Imitating God is service of the highest order. And the highest form of imitating God is teaching Torah, as that imitates God who is the *Melamed Torah L'Amo Yisrael*. But since one cannot teach what one has not learned, learning, which is found in the paragraph of *Shema* [*v'dibarta bam*], must necessarily precede teaching, which is found in *V'Hayah* [*v'limadetem osam*]. Thus, Rabbi Shimon Bar Yochai fights back against Rabbi Yehoshua ben Korcha, defending and championing the approach of Avraham.)

דף יד:

THE GEMARA, LOOKING for halachic consensus, prefers not to recognize *machlokes* if it can find a way to avoid it. So it uses the aversion to saying *mitzvos tzerichos kavanah* (which could have been explained had the Gemara been willing) in order to propose a weak—but halachically non-controversial—reading of *kivein libo likros* and *b'koreh l'hagiha*. It does a similar thing later on in 14b when it corners Rabbi Shimon Bar Yochai ("*Shema* doesn't only have learning to the exclusion of teaching and doing!"). That may be true, but it doesn't change Rabbi Shimon Bar Yochai's position. It only changes whether or not he has a proof to it. Once again, the Gemara is able to slip out of controversy and into a bland reading of both Rabbi Yehoshua ben Korcha and Rabbi Shimon Bar Yochai. ("You know, they were both just *darshening*—giving added reasons for the already accepted fact that *Shema* comes before *V'Hayah*. Rabbi Yehoshua ben Korcha gives one reason and Rabbi Shimon Bar Yochai offers *chada v'od*—another reason. Nothing to see here.")

THE GEMARA AVOIDS taking a strong position because it does not want to have to decide between the Avraham approach and the Yitzchak approach. It actually wants both, with the former approach more suited to the masses, whereas the latter—the approach of *deveikus*—is truly an individual and highly personal experience. This is indeed what *Tosafos* mean when they conclude in Rabbi Yehoshua ben Korcha that but for the notion that *deveikus* (*kabbalas ol malchus Shamayim*) is primary, *V'Hayah* should have been first "because it is in *lashon rabim*."

(IT IS INTERESTING to note that the key phrase in the *Shema* paragraph—*b'chol levavecha u'v'chol nafshecha u'v'chol me'odecha*—is demonstrably related to the life experiences of Yitzchak.

- *Levavecha*—according to *Rashi*, this refers to *sh'nei yitzarecha*, corresponding to *eizehu gibor* [Yitzchak's *middah*] *ha'kovesh es yitzro*
- *Nafshecha*—*afilu Hu notel es nafshecha* [*Rashi*] is a hint to *Akeidas Yitzchak*
- *Me'odecha*—suggests the *pasuk*, "*ad ki gadal me'od*" [Bereishis 26:13], describing Yitzchak's great wealth)

Berachos 14b

(2) :דף יד

רב משי ידיה וקרא ק״ש ואנח תפילין וגו׳.

Rav washed his hands, and recited k'rias Shema, and donned tefillin, etc.

1. What is the connection between the introduction of Rabbi Shimon Bar Yochai's addendum to our Mishnah's Rabbi Yehoshua ben Korcha and the story of *Rav mashi yadei*? If it is just about the story's connection to Rabbi Yehoshua ben Korcha, why not place it in the Gemara before the introduction of Rabbi Shimon Bar Yochai?

2. The Gemara had just established that Rabbi Shimon Bar Yochai was not arguing with Rabbi Yehoshua ben Korcha, just adding to him (*chada v'od ka'amar*). So then how, in explaining why Rav said Shema before putting on tefillin, can the Gemara say *Rav k'Rabbi Yehoshua ben Korcha sevira lei*? Rav holds like the opinion of Rabbi Yehoshua ben Korcha? It's not just the opinion of Rabbi Yehoshua ben Korcha—the Gemara just declared it to be everyone's opinion!

3. The Gemara's assertion is that Rav delayed performing the mitzvah of tefillin in order to wait until after he was *mekabel ol malchus Shamayim*. How does that make any sense? *K'rias Shema* itself is a mitzvah. How could he do that mitzvah before being *mekabel ol malchus Shamayim*?

4. Also, how does it make any sense that Rabbi Yehoshua ben Korcha holds you must be *mekabel ol malchus Shamayim* before engaging in mitzvos when one of the *peturim* in *k'rias Shema* is *oseik b'mitzvah patur min ha'mitzvah*—one engaged in a mitzvah is exempt from another mitzvah? How did one come to be

דף יד:

legitimately engaged in a mitzvah if he hadn't first prefaced it with *k'rias Shema* and its *kabbalas ol malchus Shamayim*?

5. After teaching us that Rabbi Shimon Bar Yochai taught us an additional reason why *Shema* should be before *V'Hayah*, why didn't the Gemara turn around and ask why Rabbi Yehoshua ben Korcha didn't also teach the reason of Rabbi Shimon Bar Yochai?

Yesod

We are misreading the Gemara. When we say that Rabbi Shimon Bar Yochai is *chada v'od ka'amar*, this is not to say that he and Rabbi Yehoshua ben Korcha agree. They continue to disagree, with Rabbi Shimon Bar Yochai saying *chada v'od*, and Rabbi Yehoshua ben Korcha saying *chada v'lo od*. What does this mean?

The Gemara postulates that Rabbi Yehoshua ben Korcha holds simply that the key factor is **order**. *Ol malchus Shamayim* must precede mitzvos whenever the two are paired. So *Shema* must precede *V'Hayah*, and *Shema* must precede the mitzvah of *hanachas tefillin*. And if the key is **order**, there is no room for any additional elaboration, so he holds *chada*—one reason—*v'lo od*—and no others.

That same Gemara postulates further that Rabbi Shimon Bar Yochai disagrees and says *chada v'od*. This is because Rabbi Shimon Bar Yochai holds the key factor is **importance**, not order. *Shema* must precede *V'Hayah* because it is more important, not because it is in better order, and thus there could always be additional reasons why *Shema* is more important, such as *Shema* containing *lilmod*, *l'lamed*, and *la'asos*, and *V'Hayah* containing only *l'lamed* and *la'asos*. Like Rabbi Shimon Bar Yochai, we would never think of extending this precedence to *asi'as mitzvos* for the following reason: Being about **importance** and not order, the logic would be that one cannot undertake to commit to mitzvos without first committing to the service of God, or the mitzvos will end up serving idolatry. That demands that *kabbalas ol malchus Shamayim* be done before *kabbalas ol mitzvos*. But with regard to *asi'as mitzvos*, we would have no such concern, as there is no *kabbalas ol malchus Shamayim* greater than a meticulous *asi'as mitzvah*. To put it another way, it is

Berachos 14b

only in the level of the theoretical that we are concerned that mitzvos without prior commitment to God will lead to idolatry. Once someone is actually engaged in the strict performance of mitzvos with all their details, there is no longer a fear of idolatry. So in its opening position, the Gemara concludes, in light of Rabbi Shimon Bar Yochai's approach, that Rav must hold like Rabbi Yehoshua ben Korcha if he insists on saying *Shema* before putting on tefillin.

But the Gemara responds, "No!" The *machlokes* between Rabbi Yehoshua ben Korcha and Rabbi Shimon Bar Yochai was not about order versus importance. Both hold the key factor is **importance**, but Rabbi Yehoshua ben Korcha holds that *ol malchus Shamayim* is more important than mitzvos, while Rabbi Shimon Bar Yochai holds that mitzvos are more important than *ol malchus Shamayim*. Therefore, first of all, Rabbi Yehoshua ben Korcha should have no reason to preface *asi'as mitzvos* with *kabbalas ol malchus Shamayim*, as that would be necessary only where the key is order, and, second, even if you should propose some reason that Rabbi Yehoshua ben Korcha might have us preface even *asi'ah* with *kabbalas ol malchus Shamayim*, Rav may actually hold like Rabbi Shimon Bar Yochai, not Rabbi Yehoshua ben Korcha, since he also was known to put on his tefillin *before* reciting *Shema*. So if he once was seen putting on his tefillin *after* reciting *Shema*, it must have been because that day his attendant brought them to him late.

We now understand why the Gemara waits until after introducing Rabbi Shimon Bar Yochai to bring *Rav mashi yadei*. The story is about Rabbi Shimon Bar Yochai as much as it is about Rabbi Yehoshua ben Korcha. And we understand why the Gemara says *Rav k'Rabbi Yehoshua ben Korcha sevira lei*. At that point, the Gemara contends that Rav disagrees with Rabbi Shimon Bar Yochai.

We also understand how the mitzvah of *k'rias Shema* is not self-contradictory in its being done before doing a *kabbalas ol malchus Shamayim*. Since the only issue is order, our only problem would be things that are out of order. Here the mitzvah and the *kabbalah* come simultaneously. They are not out of order, so there is no problem. Similarly, we can explain how one could be *oseik b'mitzvah* without a prior *kabbalas ol malchus Shamayim*. Again, since the only issue is order, there is only a problem when the two get presented to us at the same time. If the mitzvah began before it was time for *k'rias Shema*, it could be done without a problem; there is no essential need for a *kabbalas ol malchus Shamayim* to precede the performance of a mitzvah.

And we can understand why the Gemara did not ask why Rabbi Yehoshua ben Korcha did not teach Rabbi Shimon Bar Yochai's reason. Holding that the key factor is order, Rabbi Yehoshua ben Korcha would not agree that there could be any other reason!

Only one question remains: If Rabbi Shimon Bar Yochai truly holds mitzvos are more important than *ol malchus Shamayim*, why in fact is *Shema* before *V'Hayah*? The answer is an idea we mentioned above: **theoretical** versus **actual**. *Shema* must precede *V'Hayah* because in actual practice, despite the greater importance of the mitzvah of teaching over the *deveikus* of learning, learning must precede teaching or you will have nothing to teach. But where it is purely theoretical, such as in our tefillin, *V'Hayah* indeed does precede *Shema*.

Where is this?

In the tefillin of *Rabbeinu Tam*, where *Shema* and *V'Hayah* are reversed and *V'Hayah* in fact precedes *Shema*.

We would conclude, then, that one who follows the view of Rabbi Shimon Bar Yochai (and stresses the approach of Avraham over the approach of Yitzchak; see previous *shiur*) would want to be sure to conduct himself like those *minhagim* that wear the tefillin of *Rabbeinu Tam* in addition to the standard tefillin of *Rashi*.

Berachos 15a

דף טו.

מתני' הקורא את שמע ולא השמיע לאזנו יצא ר'
יוסי אומר לא יצא וגו'.

Mishnah—One who recites Shema but does not do so audibly has nevertheless fulfilled his obligation. Rabbi Yose says he has not fulfilled his obligation, etc.

1. Rabbi Yose and Rabbi Yehudah debate the question of whether or not one is required to speak the words of *k'rias Shema* audibly and whether or not one is required to speak the letters distinctly. It would seem that both of these requirements are enhancements of *Shema*. It seems strange to find two Tanna'im on opposite sides of these issues. Is it not logical that the champion of one of the enhancements would champion the other as well?

2. The first question can be dealt with if we accept that these are not general enhancements (read: *m'd'Rabbanan*) that can be understood as complementary embellishments of the performance of *k'rias Shema*, but are rather Torah injunctions ordained by fiat. This is indeed suggested by the Gemara attributing them to two differing interpretations of the word "*Shema*," with Rabbi Yose learning that it means, "Make audible to your ears that which you utter with your mouth," and Rabbi Yehudah learning that it means, "Make sure to hear—in whichever language you [best] understand." The problem with this is, then, how do we understand the halachah? Once we *pasken* like Rabbi Yehudah (which we do), our position should be that there is no source to make our reading of *Shema* (or any other spoken mitzvah activity) be audible. And yet, the halachah is clear that *l'chatchila* we

are supposed to say the words audibly, not just for *Shema* but for other mitzvos and *berachos* as well. How can this be?

3. This problem is already evident in the way we *pasken* like Rabbi Yehudah. Rav Chisda cites Rav Shila that the halachah is like the view of Rabbi Yehudah that has him in agreement with his Rebbe, Rabbi Elazar ben Azarya. This position is that *l'chatchila* one should say the words audibly, but *b'dieved* if one did not he is nevertheless *yotzei*. Here again, if these are *dinei d'Oraisa*, and we learn the word *Shema* is *not* teaching the need for audibility, what is causing Rabbi Yehudah to require audibility *l'chatchila*?

4. After the Gemara *paskens* like Rabbi Yehudah, Rav Yosef comes along and limits the *machlokes* between Rabbi Yose and Rabbi Yehudah only to *k'rias Shema* and not to any other *berachos* or mitzvos. In the end, after seeing that *bentching b'lev* is valid *b'dieved*, he concludes that for all other *berachos* and mitzvos one is *b'dieved yotzei* if he did not say the words audibly. First of all, what is the need for Rav Yosef after we have *paskened* like Rabbi Yehudah? Even if Rabbi Yose would want to keep battling and have all mitzvos be invalid without *shemi'as ozen*, Rabbi Yehudah has already said that even *k'rias Shema* itself is *yotzei b'dieved* without *shemi'as ozen*—all the more so all other mitzvos. And we *pasken* like Rabbi Yehudah! So why does Rav Yosef's comment matter? And there has to be an explanation, because the *Rif paskens* like Rabbi Yehudah and nevertheless brings down Rav Yosef *l'halachah*. Secondly, if we're going to say, as *Tosafos* does, that Rav Yosef rejects the whole *sugya* we just finished, and we *pasken* like Rav Yosef, why do we have an *amud* of Gemara discussing connections to *terumos*, Birkas Hamazon, and megillah that *l'halachah* have nothing to do with the *din* of *shemi'as ozen* by *k'rias Shema*? And finally, if we *pasken* like Rav Yosef that *sha'ar mitzvos* are unrelated, why does the halachah require *shemi'as ozen* by *sha'ar mitzvos* at all?

Berachos 15a

Yesod

Rabbi Yose and Rabbi Yehudah are actually involved in a very fundamental question: What is the nature of the mitzvah of *k'rias Shema*? According to Rabbi Yose, *k'rias Shema* is about bringing to the world the idea that things are not what they appear to the eye, and that much more important than drawing conclusions from what you see is to hear from someone who knows the truth how to understand the things that you appear to be seeing. *Hashme'a l'aznecha* is just the prerequisite for our being able to be *mashmi'a* truth to a world that otherwise relies only upon what it sees. According to Rabbi Yehudah, that would be a beautiful idea if the word *shema* meant "hear." But it doesn't; it means "understand." *Shema* hearkens back to the days when the *shivtei Kah* used it to convince their father Yaakov that they understood and internally accepted the idea of *yichud Hashem*.[2] It still means that today. And since internal clarity is the strongest guarantee of internal understanding, the word *shema* requires us to do those things that will enhance internal clarity, like using languages we understand (and, later in the Mishnah, using precision in our enunciation).

But that is true only according to one approach in the Gemara. Rav Chisda disagrees with this approach and challenges the notion that the *machlokes* Rabbi Yose and Rabbi Yehudah is about the nature of *k'rias Shema*. According to him, we cannot know the true nature of *k'rias Shema*; the only issue at hand is the issue of using the fullest possible form of speaking whenever we perform mitzvos with our speech, and that is accomplished by speaking audibly enough to hear our own words. The only *machlokes* Rabbi Yose and Rabbi Yehudah are having is whether *shemi'as ozen* is *m'akev* the mitzvah or is just required but not *m'akev b'dieved*.

Rav Chisda tries to establish that *terumos, Birkas Hamazon*, and *megillah* are all illustrations of the *machlokes* Rabbi Yose and Rabbi Yehudah—something that would be impossible if the entire *machlokes* were about the nature of *k'rias Shema*. But in the end, Rav Yosef says, "This is not the way to understand our Mishnah. It is not a universal *machlokes*, extending beyond *k'rias Shema* to *sha'ar mitzvos*. It is strictly about *Shema* and its fundamental nature."

[Interestingly, this is the same thing Rav Yosef does to Rav Chisda in another Gemara (*Sanhedrin* 41a). There, Rav Chisda cites many *Beraisos* as proofs that the Mishnah's purpose in promulgating mass *bedikos* of witnesses is to discover the truth. In the end, Rav Yosef says, "This is not the way to understand our Mishnah. Its purpose is not truth. Its purpose is *rachamim*, and it is promulgating mass *bedikos* as a way of getting the witnesses to conflict their testimony and thus be invalidated."]

Now let us understand the halachah. When we *pasken* like Rabbi Yehudah, it is not from *Rav Chisda amar Rav Shila*. That would be adopting Rav Chisda's understanding of the *machlokes*, making Rabbi Yehudah basically just "Rabbi Yose lite." The way we know this is not the way we *pasken* like Rabbi Yehudah is because we *pasken* like Rav Yosef, and understanding Rabbi Yehudah as "Rabbi Yose lite" is incompatible with *shitas* Rav Yosef.

So where do we *pasken* like Rabbi Yehudah, and why do we say in his *shitah* that *l'chatchila* we should do *shemi'as ozen* when he holds there is no source in the Torah for *shemi'as ozen*?

The answer is that we *pasken* like Rabbi Yehudah from *Amar Rav Tevi amar Rav Oshiya halachah k'divrei sheneihem l'hakel*.

What does it mean *halachah k'divrei sheneihem l'hakel*? Why not just say *ein halachah k'achad meihem*—in other words, we don't require *shemi'as ozen* and we don't require *dikduk osiyos*?

The answer is because we want our *k'rias Shema* to hold onto the fundamental meanings of both Sages. We want it to inspire us internally, as if the *pasuk* meant *Shema, b'chol lashon she'atah shomeia*, along with its resulting corollary, *dikduk osiyos*. And we want it to prepare us to change the world through the *ko'ach* of *mashmi'a*, along with its imperative *Hashme'a l'aznecha mah she'atah motzi mi'picha*. We don't need to be strict in halachah in order to make ourselves aware of these two perhaps competing principles we wish to jointly embrace. Having them both be *l'chatchila* will be enough to satisfy our purpose. And so *halachah k'sheneihem l'hakel*. And therefore, one should ideally be *mashmi'a* when reciting *Shema*, but only *l'chatchila*, because while we want to be aware

Berachos 15a

of Rabbi Yose's imperative, at the end of the day we *pasken* like Rabbi Yehudah, the *maikel*, and not Rabbi Yose.

All this is fine, but it doesn't explain *sha'ar mitzvos*. If we *pasken* like Rav Yosef, there should be no basis at all for requiring *shemi'as ozen* by all *berachos*, as the *Rambam* clearly does. Where does this come from?

The answer is: It comes from Rav Chisda.

Rav Chisda? Didn't we just finish saying we *pasken* like Rav Yosef against Rav Chisda?

Let's think. Just because we agree with Rav Yosef that the *machlokes* in our Mishnah is about *Shema*, it doesn't mean that we dismiss Rav Chisda. We just dismiss his interpretation of the Mishnah. But we can still agree with him that there is a requirement to use the fullest possible form of speaking when performing mitzvos with our speech. But understand that this is an entirely different *din* of *mashmi'a* than the one by *k'rias Shema*. The *din* of *mashmi'a* by *k'rias Shema* is designed to prepare us for the future use of the *ko'ach* of *mashmi'a* to change the mindset of reliance on science and visual observation and turn the world to *emunah b'Hashem*. That *din* doesn't really demand *shemi'as* **ozen** per se; its point is simply that we exercise the *ko'ach* of being *mashmi'a*, not that we have any real requirement of audibility. The one by *sha'ar mitzvos* is different. Its purpose is to have us do a proper act of speaking, which requires that we hear the words we are saying.

That is why the *Rambam* is precise in his choice of words as they appear in the two halachos. In *Hilchos K'rias Shema* (2:8), he says: "*Tzarich l'hashmi'a l'ozno* **k'shehu koreh**—One must sound out [the words] **when he is reading**." But in *Hilchos Berachos* (1:7), he puts it differently: "*Tzarich l'hashmi'a l'ozno* **mah shehu omer**—One must sound out **what he is saying**." And now the entire *sugya*, along with the halachah that emerges from it, is resolved.

דף טז. (1)

מתני׳ האומנין קורין בראש האילן ובראש הנדבך וגו׳.

Mishnah—Craftsmen read k'rias Shema at the top of a tree and on the top of a dovecote...

One who was engaged in his work [when he decided it was time for him to say k'rias Shema] must interrupt his work until he has read the entire first paragraph. Similarly, craftsmen must drop their work during the first paragraph. This is in order that their reading of Shema not be treated as a transitory activity. The rest is to be read as he was, and while engaged in his work. Even if he was standing on top of a tree or on top of a wall, he reads Shema where he is and recites its berachos before and after. (Rambam, Mishneh Torah, K'rias Shema 2:4)

How is this *Rambam* to be understood?

1. What is the difference between ordinary people and craftsmen? Why are ordinary people to "interrupt their work" while craftsmen are to "drop their work"?
2. Why does *Rambam* start in the singular, switch plural for craftsmen, then go back to singular at the end?
3. If the point of this halachah is to teach us that everyone must stop working to say *Shema*, why does the "Even if" lead to "he reads *Shema* where he is"? It should lead to "he nevertheless stops working"!
4. Why mention the *berachos* of *k'rias Shema* here?

Berachos 16a

Yesod

The Mishnah calls the people who are up a tree "*umnin.*" What is the *umnus* of being up a tree?

The *umnin* in the treetop were not harvesters. Those would have been called *po'alim*. The word *umnin* is related to "*Va'yehi* **omein** *es Hadassah*" (*Esther* 2:5), which, according to *Bereishis Rabbah*, literally means that Mordechai nursed her. Trees are grown in nurseries. The *umnus* that would put a craftsman in a tree is the *umnus* of tree husbandry.

There is a difference between a worker and a craftsman. The worker is driven by his desire to earn wages. The craftsman is driven by the call of the subject of his craft, its needs, and its perfection.

K'rias Shema must walk a very fine line. On the one hand, we are compelled to recite it as part of our regular activities—*u'v'lechtecha va'derech*. On the other hand, when we do incorporate it into our routine, we must make sure not to treat it as if it is our secondary focus. It must not be *arai*. The question being addressed in this *Rambam* is how to treat *k'rias Shema* as the primary focus of our activities without lifting it out of our regular routine.

One approach we cannot take is to step completely out of our daily activities and say *Shema*. This would only bolster the notion that we could not incorporate it into our routine without relegating it to also-ran status. We must welcome it into our routine but at the same time display enough deference so that it is clearly seen as primary.

For *po'alim*, this is done simply by interrupting their work. Since they are working only to make money, any interruption makes it clear that *Shema* is more important to them than moneymaking.

For *umnin*, this would not be enough. Craftsmen are always ready to attend to a nuisance in order to get it out of the way so they can go back to the exacting efforts of their profession. For a craftsman, to interrupt is no proof that his craft is not his most precious endeavor. Instead, he must drop his work—even in the middle of a creation, knowing he may have to start all over from scratch—in order to show his deference to the *Shema*. Moreover, he must show he is in no rush to return to his craft, and he does this by making a point of taking the time to append the *berachos* before and after *Shema* like he has all the time in the world, which is what one should have for one's primary interest. This is the way the *uman* prevents *Shema* from being treated as *arai*.

But do not think, concludes the *Rambam*, that he should descend from his tree. On the contrary, that would promote the impression that *Shema* could not possibly be incorporated within his lifestyle and assume prime status. He is to stay in his lifestyle, just taking the steps identified that show proper deference to *Shema* and its primacy, regardless of how little that lifestyle would seem to lend itself to *Shema*'s required honor.

Neither shall the worker take off more than the first paragraph from his work, again so he should not treat *Shema* as somehow unwelcome within his existing activities.

This approach answers all our questions on the *Rambam*.

In addition, they help us understand *Toraso umenaso*. As an *uman* is driven by the material and its demands, not by his needs, so too must the full-time Torah scholar be driven not by his spiritual ambitions but by the magnificent reality of the Torah and its need to be learned and understood.

So, too, we understand the mitzvah of *emunah*, which also comes from this same root word. It is the obligation to be driven by the reality of God, not by our desires to have a share in the spiritual treasures that may be yielded by any affiliation we may have with Him.

דף טז. (2)

חתן פטור מק"ש לילה הראשונה ועד מוצאי שבת וגו'.

A chassan is exempt from k'rias Shema on his wedding night and until Motza'ei Shabbos, etc.

1. According to the Mishnah, a *chassan* is *patur* from *k'rias Shema*. The Gemara quotes a *Beraisa* that derives this from the *pasuk* of *"b'shivtecha b'veisecha"*—*prat l'oseik b'mitzvah*; *"u'v'lechtecha va'derech"*—*prat l'chassan*. Although this *Beraisa* comes from a Gemara on *daf* 11a and appears to be the view of Beis Shammai, Beis Hillel does agree to the reading of *u'v'lechtecha va'derech*; he just adds that one can infer logically from the same *pasuk* that one who **is** obligated in *k'rias Shema* is required to do so *u'v'lechtecha va'derech*, i.e., as he is. The Gemara on the Mishnah in *Sukkah* (25a) derives from here the *p'tur* of a *shaliach mitzvah* from the mitzvah of *sukkah*. *Tosafos* understands this to mean that *k'rias Shema* is the source for *oseik b'mitzvah patur min ha'mitzvah* and applies the *p'tur* to all mitzvos, but avers that it is only while one is "actively" engaged in the mitzvah. Passive activity does not exempt. *Rambam paskens* that one who is distracted by his involvement in one mitzvah is exempt from another, but he does not distinguish between general *oseik* and *tirda d'mitzvah*, which is the basis for the *p'tur* of *chassan*. Why does the *Rambam* not make this distinction?
2. *Rambam* also does not distinguish between active and passive as *Tosafos* does. Why not?
3. Women are *patur* from *mitzvos asei she'ha'z'man grama*, yet no one suggests this is only when they are actively involved in their

p'tur-generating activities. Why is this different from the p'tur of an oseik b'mitzvah?

4. Rambam says a tarud b'mitzvah is patur from mitzvos and patur from k'rias Shema. K'rias Shema is a mitzvah. Why does the Rambam treat them as two separate things?

Yesod

Rambam holds the standard mitzvah-exemption that is applicable to a person engaged in a mitzvah is intuitive and needs no pasuk. But because k'rias Shema has an imperative of u'v'lechtecha va'derech—say k'rias Shema as you are (i.e., as part of your normal routine)—one might think that just as you have to say Shema in a tree if that's where you are, so too do you have to say Shema when you are preoccupied—if that's the way you are. The pasuk teaches that tarud tirda d'mitzvah is an exemption even from k'rias Shema (something that ordinary tirda is not!).

So no limud is needed to apply the standard oseik b'mitzvah patur min ha'mitzvah to other mitzvos. But if there would be another mitzvah whose observance is to be done amid one's normal routine, it would raise similar issues.

That mitzvah is sukkah.

Because sukkah is done amid our normal routine (teishvu k'ein taduru), I might think we're chayav even if we are engaged in other things, just as we sleep and eat at home even if we are engaged in other things. From k'rias Shema, we learn this is not required for a shelichus shel mitzvah.

This is why the Gemara earlier brought a case of sukkah as another dispute between Beis Hillel and Beis Shammai. This issue also comes down to the difference between maaseh Shamayim and maaseh adam.

דף טז:

מתני׳ רחץ לילה הראשון שמתה אשתו וגו׳.

Mishnah—[Rabban Gamliel] bathed on the first night following the death of his wife. Exclaimed his students, "Did not our Rabbi teach us that a mourner is forbidden to bathe?" Answered [Rabban Gamliel], "I am not like other men; I am fastidious [istenis]." And when his servant, Tavi, died, [Rabban Gamliel] accepted blessings of comfort over the loss. Asked his students, "Did not our Rabbi teach us that one may not accept condolences over the loss of a slave?" Answered [Rabban Gamliel], "Tavi, my servant, was not like other slaves. He was kosher."

1. Although this Mishnah follows a Mishnah about Rabban Gamliel holding himself different from the halachic standards applied to most men regarding *Shema* and their wedding nights, nevertheless, the topics here—bathing for mourners and accepting condolences on slaves—seem ill-suited for this *mesechta*. Why are they here?
2. If the purpose of the Mishnah is to teach us that an *istenis* is exempt from the prohibition against a mourner bathing, why not just say so?
3. The Gemara understands that the *istenis* would be excused only from a Rabbinic prohibition, and thus concludes that the first night following a relative's death must have a status of Rabbinic mourning and not Biblical mourning. But if that is so, this law could have been taught about any day of Rabbinic mourning (i.e., the entire rest of the seven days of *shivah*). Why does the Mishnah go out of its way to tell me the incident occurred on

the night after the first day? It can only have been to teach me (tangentially) that the first night is Rabbinic. Why is this such an important lesson for the Mishnah to go out of its way to teach me here?

Yesod

Rabban Gamliel lived in the period following the destruction of the Bayis Sheni, and faced a dangerously discouraged population.

According to Rav Nachman Cohen in the book *Esther's Plea* (Torah Lishmah Institute, 1999), Rabban Gamliel's dispute with Rabbi Yehoshua over *Maariv* being *reshus* or *chovah* was regarding this concern. As *Maariv* was introduced by Yaakov Avinu as a preface to *galus*, it was deemed to be a *chovah* only when the Jewish People are in *galus*. Rabbi Yehoshua argued it was a *reshus* because he held that God could not possibly be initiating a *galus*, as in his view Klal Yisrael did not have the fortitude to survive a major *galus*. Rabban Gamliel did not share the pessimistic view that we could not survive *galus*, and he brought to bear the full weight of his position in order to condemn Rabbi Yehoshua's stance.

Here, too, Rabban Gamliel faced off against despair, and it came from two groups. The Beis Hamikdash was seen as primarily representing either a place of *avodah* or a place of *hashra'as haShechinah*. The group that saw it as the latter held they had just lost a "wife," i.e., the *Shechinah*. How could they "pleasure bathe," i.e., study Torah with enjoyment ever again (just as we are required to refrain from pleasurable learning on Tishah B'Av)?

Rabban Gamliel responded viscerally. I bathed on the night after I lost my wife, he proclaimed. If you are an *istenis*—one who is in painful discomfort without the pleasurable activity (bathing or Torah study, according to *Rashi*) like I am, you may continue to study Torah with enjoyment.

The other group held that with the loss of *avodah*, they were like servants who had died.

Berachos 16b

We are so worthless, they lamented, that God would not even care enough about us to accept condolences on our loss! To them, Rabban Gamliel responded viscerally by accepting *tanchumin* over Tavi, his servant. When you are a "kosher," God does accept *tanchumin*.

With these techniques, he was able to launch Klal Yisrael on a path that has borne a legacy of fruitful accomplishment, in spite of the painfulness of the genuine *galus* it has been.

AND WITH THIS we understand why the Mishnah insisted on going out of its way to teach us that *aveilus laylah rishonah* is *d'Rabbanan*. *Laylah* represents the darkness associated with *galus*. The *aveilus* is the *aveilus* over the loss of the Beis Hamikdash. The *aveilus laylah rishonah* is the darkness that sets in after the bitter day of the *Churban*. The position of Rabbi Yehoshua and his group was that the period of history that threatened to commence would have been a *galus d'Oraisa* and could not be overcome. Hence, they promulgated a variety of enactments designed to confirm their belief that *galus* was not setting in. Illustrating their view, Rabbi Yehoshua was convinced that the emperor Hadrian would allow the rebuilding of the Bayis (see *Bereishis Rabbah* 64), and Rabbi Akiva believed that Bar Kochba was Mashiach. Rabban Gamliel's entire counterpoint was that it was not an unconquerable *galus* that was setting in. *Aveilus laylah rishonah* is only *d'Rabbanan*! Thus, it was a real *galus* commencing, and it would be tough, but ultimately it would be manageable, and the Jewish nation would emerge from it intact.

Endnotes

1 Or, more playfully, how much wood could a woodchuck chuck if a woodchuck could chuck wood?
2 *Bereishis Rabbah* 98:2.

Chapter Three
Mi She'meiso

Berachos 17b

דף יז:

נוֹשְׂאֵי הַמִּטָּה וְחִלּוּפֵיהֶן וְחִלּוּפֵי חִלּוּפֵיהֶן אֶת שֶׁלִּפְנֵי הַמִּטָּה וְאֶת שֶׁלְּאַחֲרֵי הַמִּטָּה וְגוֹ׳.

Mishnah—Pallbearers, their replacements, and their replacements' replacements are all exempt from *k'rias Shema*, [both] those ahead of the mitah and those behind the mitah...

Most Rishonim divide these pallbearers up into two groups—those whose services are required and those whose services are not required.

The difficulty with this is that, if so, why would the Mishnah bother to mention a different split—those in front and those behind—when either way it comes down to whether or not their services are required?

Rashi's girsa recognizes a split between those in front and those behind, and also a second split between those whose services are required and those whose services are not required. And he reads the second split as being a limitation or expansion upon the first.

In other words, those in front are exempt, but only to the extent their services are required. If their services turn out not to be required, they revert to being obligated in *k'rias Shema*. And those in back are obligated and remain so, even if their services are required!

Rashi explains this surprising halachah by presenting it from the angle of the individual's mitzvah to be involved in carrying the *mitah*. The ones in front have not yet performed their mitzvah, thus as long as they still anticipate doing it, they remain exempt. The ones behind have already done their mitzvah, thus, even if they are required again, they must decline the second opportunity in favor of their primary obligation of *k'rias Shema*.

דף יז:

The problem with this is that it seems to be ignoring the needs of the *meis*! The *meis* needs the ones in back to carry again, and yet they are not allowed to participate until they have completed *k'rias Shema*? It seems the needs of the meis are not being sufficiently respected.

The *Rambam* divides between those whose services are required and those whose services are not required, and in this, he says, there is no difference between those in front and those behind. **But, he says, this is not a division within pallbearers.** Pallbearers are just an example of a group whose services would be considered required. But, in fact, anyone whose services are required is exempt, even escorts pressed into impromptu carrying service. All other escorts (i.e., the ones not pressed into carrying) are men whose services are not required, so they are obligated in *k'rias Shema*.[1]

So now, at least, we are clear regarding three categories: Escorts whose services are required are exempt from *k'rias Shema*; escorts whose services are not required are obligated in *k'rias Shema*; and pallbearers whose services are required are exempt from *k'rias Shema*.

But what about pallbearers whose services are not required?

They remain exempt, says the *Rambam*. Their having been designated as pallbearers, as opposed to escorts, yields them a blanket exemption, whether or not their services in actual carrying are required. We see this in the *Rambam* from the fact that he uses the pallbearer as the example ("*k'gon*") of someone needed. If *Rambam's* only purpose was to tell us that all people are governed by the one question (of whether he is needed), the *Rambam* would not have had any purpose to give pallbearers (as a group) as an example. He could simply have said, "Anyone needed to carry the *mitah* is exempt; anyone not needed is obligated."

By mentioning pallbearers as an identified group, the *Rambam* is saying that anyone with the designation "pallbearer" has an automatic exemption, and that anyone else who had not been designated a "pallbearer" but turns out to be needed to do the same task the pallbearers had been designated to do also receives an exemption. But the difference between the designated pallbearer and the one playing the pallbearer's role is that the former is exempt whether or not his services are

Berachos 17b

required—he is exempt by definition—and the latter is exempt only once he finds himself pressed into service carrying the *mitah*.

But still, why, according to the *Rambam*, does the Mishnah bother to mention the split between ahead of the *mitah* and behind the *mitah* if the halachah is the same regardless?

To answer, let us look at some remaining unanswered questions. What happens with our pallbearer after he has completed his carrying? In other words, we might understand that a pallbearer has an automatic exemption built into his designation. But perhaps the entire exemption lasts only up until the pallbearer has completed his carrying duties, and right after that he must pick up on his diverted *k'rias Shema* obligation, like any ordinary escort? And, for that matter, what happens with our escort pressed into last-minute carrying service after his round of service ends?

To these questions, the *Rambam* provides the answers. Let us assume that the *Rambam* agrees with *Rashi*'s definition of *lifnei ha'mitah* as "yet to carry" and *l'achar ha'mitah* as "already discharged his duty of carrying." We can now assert that when the *Rambam* says, "whether they were *lifnei ha'mitah* or *l'achar ha'mitah*," he is referring exclusively to the pallbearers. They are the ones who maintain their official exemption before, during, and after their actual performance. What the *Rambam* is saying is that **anyone who gets called upon to carry becomes exempted for as long as he is carrying, in the same way that all officially designated pallbearers get exempted for as long as they are busy being officially designated pallbearers.**

Where does the *Rambam* know this? He knows it from the Mishnah. If we can assume that he had the *girsa* of the *Rif*, the Mishnah reads like this:

> *Pallbearers and all their officially designated replacements, whether they have performed actual service yet or not, [as well as] anyone else the mitah requires, are exempt [from the mitzvah of k'rias Shema]. Anyone the mitah does not require [and who is there only because of his own mitzvah obligation but not to*

shoulder an actual physical need of the meis] remains
obligated in the mitzvah of k'rias Shema.

Why distinguish between pallbearers whom the *mitah* requires and anyone else whom the *mitah* requires, wonders the *Rambam*, unless it is to inform you that the two categories yield different application levels of exemption? So the "official" people (the pallbearers and their designated replacements) get an exemption throughout their service (of being "official"), and the non-official carriers get the same exemption throughout *their* service (of carrying). The exemption is one and the same. But the two forms of service are in fact different, so the exemption will have two different durations.

Once we know how the *Rambam* is reading the Mishnah, we can see that he has no problem with our first question. The Mishnah needs to mention *lifnei* and *l'achar* to teach us how the exemption works for official carriers in contrast to how the exemption works for unofficial carriers! And he has no problem like the one we were bothered with in *Rashi*. According to the *Rambam*, there is no split between *lifnei* and *l'achar*—together those are a designation of the nature of the service of official carriers, in contrast to unofficial carriers who do not receive that designation. And the needs of the *meis* always generate an exemption of one kind or another. The only group that gets no exemption is the group of pure escorts, who provide no physical need of the *meis*.

THE PRECISE LANGUAGE in the *Rambam* bears out the truth of our explanation. When he starts out, he uses the present tense: "[If] they are **escorting** the *meis*, anyone for whom the *meis* **has** a need." But when he mentions the pallbearers and replacements, the *Rambam* shifts to past tense: "for example, the pallbearers and their replacements, whether they **were** before the *mitah* or after the *mitah*..." This can only be because his reference to before and after the *mitah* is to the pallbearers and replacements exclusively, in contrast to anyone else for whom the *meis* has a need, just as we are saying—that the official carriers' exemption extends to them whether or not they have already carried, while the other carriers' exemption ends as soon as their carrying is complete.

Berachos 17b

In closing, we can say that it is likely that *Rashi* would have learned like the *Rambam* as well, had he not been burdened with a *girsa* that did not allow for him to learn that way.

.דף יח

מתני׳ מי שמתו מוטל לפניו פטור מק״ש ומן התפלה ומן התפילין וגו׳.

Mishnah—One whose dead is before him is exempt from k'rias Shema, from prayer, from tefillin, and from all mitzvos in the Torah.

1. Does "before him" mean that the body is physically in his presence, or that the task of burying the person lies ahead of him in terms of time?
2. In general, when we say that one who is involved in a mitzvah is exempt from a mitzvah, does that mean he does not *have* to do the mitzvah, or does it mean he *should* not do the mitzvah?
3. If it just means that he does not have to do the mitzvah, but he can choose to do so voluntarily, does he get less reward for it than had he been obligated? And if it means he should not do it, and he does it anyway, does it count?
4. Is our case just a standard *ha'oseik b'mitzvah patur min ha'mitzvah*, or is it something unique to someone and his dead?
5. Our Mishnah implies that the mitzvah exemption is limited to a dead relative. The Gemara challenges this from a *Beraisa* that applies the same exemption to a *shomer*. We conclude that it does, in fact, apply to both cases. Nevertheless, it seems to not apply to one walking in a cemetery. The Gemara on *daf* 18a challenges this omission from a *Beraisa* that rules that one may not walk in a cemetery with tefillin showing and while learning from a *sefer*. How is this *Beraisa* a challenge? These cemetery rules are not saying the person is exempt from any mitzvah; it is only saying he may not perform these mitzvos in a cemetery!

Many mitzvos cannot be performed in a lavatory. Does that make a person in a bathroom *patur* from mitzvos?

--- *Yesod* ---

Our initial understanding of this Mishnah was that *mutal lefanav* was a way of saying that one who has the duty to bury a relative remains exempt from all mitzvos until the burial is complete. This would be a time-bound exemption from which there would be no escape.

This understanding was challenged by a *Beraisa* applying the exemption to a *shomer*. A *shomer*, unlike what we understood about the relative, has a way he can escape from the mitzvah exemption—he can simply walk out of the *shemirah* room and get a replacement! Why should he be treated any differently from one who finds himself in an *ashpah* (garbage dump) when a mitzvah moment such as *k'rias Shema* arrives—to whom we say he has no exemption and he must jump out of the *ashpah* and do his mitzvah?

This challenge could be deflected if we were to say that, for the sake of *kavod ha'meis*, we grant the *shomer* an exemption so he does not have to be troubled to find a replacement every time he needs to do another mitzvah.

But this deflection meets a challenge in the *Beraisa* of the cemetery. If the *shomer* can be included in the special exemption on account of *kavod ha'meis*, why is the same exemption not extended to one walking in a cemetery? Is it not possible he is there working on the needs of a *meis*? Until we included the *shomer*, we would not have asked this question, because we would assume the halachah obligates one to step out of the cemetery to do any mitzvah that cannot be done in the presence of dead bodies. But now that we see the *shomer* being exempted from mitzvos, why is the cemetery worker not granted the same exemption?

Here is the Gemara's answer: The cemetery laws are limited to the four-cubit area around the dead, as opposed to the relative and the *shomer*, whose exemptions apply even beyond the body's four cubits (for the *shomer*, they extend to the entire room; for the relative, they extend to the entire city).

דף יח.

But all three sets of laws (exemptions for the relative and the *shomer*, and restrictions for the worker) are merely proper protocols for how one needs to behave in a manner showing decency and respect around a corpse. There remains an entirely different halachah that legislates an actual prohibition against mocking a dead person. This is known as *lo'eg la'rash*, and it applies to one who learns within four *amos* of the dead. The way to read the *Beraisa* is as follows:

> One should not walk in a cemetery with tefillin on his head, while carrying a Sefer Torah, or while reading from a Sefer Torah. [These are proper protocols for conduct within four amos of a meis. It is left out of the Mishnah because the Mishnah was addressing protocols that apply even beyond four amos. However, you need to be aware of one more thing:] If you do this [last thing, i.e., learn from a Sefer Torah within four amos of a meis, in addition to breaching protocol], you are in violation of the prohibition of lo'eg la'rash.

This entire understanding of the Gemara is based on our contention that the *machlokes* on *daf* 3b between the two versions in Rav Abba bar Kahana is whether he was teaching simple standards of decency or the actual *lo'eg la'rash* prohibition. Like the first version, which makes the issue about standards, since *mili d'alma* are not disrespectful, they do not breach protocol. But like the second version in Rav Abba bar Kahana, that the issue here is *lo'eg la'rash*, all matters not relevant to the deceased must not be said in their vicinity, even *divrei Torah*. They all mock the dead person, who is not able to participate. (See *Beis Yosef, Yoreh Deah* 344, where a comparable distinction is suggested.)

Berachos 18b

דף יח:

מעשה בחסיד אחד שנתן דינר לעני בערב ראש השנה בשני בצורת וגו׳.

An incident occurred in which a certain chassid gave charity to a poor man on Erev Rosh Hashanah in a year of famine...

The Gemara brings a *pasuk* that suggests that the dead know nothing of what goes on in our world. To challenge that, it brings a *Beraisa* that suggests otherwise.

The *Beraisa* tells of a *maaseh b'chassid echad* who donated a *dinar* on Erev Rosh Hashanah to an *ani*. His wife found out about the charitable gift and was incensed. That night, the *chassid* went to sleep in a cemetery, where he overheard two spirits talking, one of them being that of a deceased young girl. The other spirit proposed to that of the girl that the two travel about and learn from the "other side" what fate was in store for the world in the year ahead. The girl demurred, claiming she could not go because she was buried in a sack made of *kanim* (reeds).

"But you go and tell me," she suggested.

With the *chassid* listening in, the spirit returned and reported that she had heard that anyone planting during the first rain that year would lose his crop to hail. The *chassid*, armed with this inside knowledge, planted instead during the second rain, and his crop was spared.

The next year, the *chassid* repeated his behavior. The girl again requested that the other spirit bring a report from the "other side," and this time the spirit revealed that whoever planted during the second rain would be wiped out by blight. The *chassid* planted during the first rain and was again spared.

דף יח:

His wife questioned him on his unlikely success, whereupon he told her what had been happening.

Shortly thereafter, a quarrel broke out between the wife of the *chassid* and the mother of the deceased young girl. In its course, the wife exclaimed, "Come and I will show you how your daughter is buried in a sack of reeds!"

From this outburst, the spirits realized that their stories were known in the land of the living, and they ceased their annual excursion. No longer could the *chassid* gain his inside information. So concludes the Talmudic passage.

My questions are as follows:

1. Why is it important to this story that the man was a *chassid*?
2. What was it about her husband's charitable gift on Erev Rosh Hashanah that upset the wife?
3. What made the *chassid* sleep in a cemetery the night after his wife got angry? Had he no friends with whom he could stay?
4. Why does a sack made of reeds prevent a spirit from traveling about?
5. What is the significance of the *chassid* getting rich off the spirits' inside information?
6. What is the takeaway message for us from this incident; and what is it doing in our Gemara?

Yesod

It is said that opposites attract. In marriage, if true, this would be so that the parties should find *sheleimus*, marrying an opposite in order to incorporate a quality they otherwise do not possess and thereby complete themselves.

If so, then it would make sense that a *chassid*—literally, one who is defined by the *middah* of *chessed*—would be married to a possessor of the *middah* of *din* (strict judgment or self-restraint).

So firstly, we can explain why the wife was so angered by her husband's act of *chessed* on Erev Rosh Hashanah. All year long, she lived in the shadow of her husband's attachment to *chessed*, all the while silently believing in the superior value of *din* and reviling the harm and shame caused by too much indulgent engagement in unbalanced *chessed*. Finally, Rosh Hashanah is upon them—the *Yom HaDin*! At least on the Great Day of Judgment, she anticipated some respite, when even her *chassid* husband would appreciate the value of *din*. But what does he do instead? He prepares for Judgment Day by doing a last-minute act of *chessed*!!

She is livid!

His response to her anger is one of saddened resistance: "Living a life without *chessed* is not living," he moans. And to punctuate his disgust with his wife's point of view, he goes to sleep in a place where people are in fact not living—the local cemetery!

But then an interesting thing happens. From the conversation he overhears between the dead spirits, he learns that *chessed* has a dark side too. A life of *din*, of self-control, teaches a soul responsibility, self-reliance, and independence. The deceased girl, buried in *kanim* (an extraction of the word *kinyan* [acquisition]), had apparently been raised to be a taker, an acquirer. Her spirit, unschooled in the trait of independence that would have come with an exposure to *din*, was not free to move about in the World of Truth, and she remained dependent on her spirit companion for news and information.

Discovering *chessed*'s dark side lands a striking blow on the *chassid*. He finds himself exploring the reaches of corrupted *chessed* and allows himself to take information that should not rightly have been his.

[It is worth noting at this point that the Vilna Gaon was once offered spectacular Torah insights that would be revealed to him by a spirit, and he turned it down, stating he did not want any Torah insights he had not earned with his own toil and effort!]

The *chassid* reinforces his lack of moral compunction about the ill-gotten fortune, eagerly revisiting the cemetery the next year and repeating his rotten activity.

Meanwhile, the wife is busy further corrupting her own *middas ha'din*. This she demonstrates by becoming quarrelsome, a rotten outgrowth of judgmentalism. To snipe at her opponent, she rips her for how she raised her now-deceased daughter.

"You taught her only to take," the wife lashes out at the mother. "Now she is eternally crippled!"

OUR STORY THUS far is a morality tale of the dangers of untempered *middos*, whether it be *chessed* or *din*.

But let us step back from that for a moment. What are we to make of the spirits' finding about what goes on on the "other side"? People are going to be harmed at random because they plant during the wrong rain? On Rosh Hashanah, don't we understand that individuals are judged one by one? What is the idea of blanket disasters being fated for the new year, disasters that presumably will wipe out worthy and unworthy alike?

Here we arrive at the biggest *chiddush* of all. What goes on "over the wall" is indeed random and ready to cause chaos. But that is only on the "other side," the "death side." A living soul, a *ben ish chai*, by seeing pattern and detecting meaning, invests the seeming chaos with significance, even causing the rest of reality to coalesce around the sequences he discovers and the significance he is organizing.

To illustrate, happenings in the life of a non-spiritually-oriented person not only appear to be random, they actually are—unless and until the perceiver decides he will relate to them as messages from God. Suddenly, they become messages from God. In an arrangement found elsewhere only in the world of quantum physics, it is the observer who determines objective reality.

The dead who have merit can traverse between the fates and remain connected to good fortune.

The wicked dead are not free and cannot "move" to escape their vicissitudes. The living can invest the fates with meaning, as they apply their significance to their relationship with God. The *chassid* of our story abandoned the true purpose of *chassidus*—using life to engage in a relationship with G-d by giving to others and emulating His giving—and began instead to practice a form of black magic, accepting benefit from celestial sources while bypassing and ignoring their Source. This, as an aside, will help explain why all black magic involves resorting to some connection to the world of the dead.

Berachos 18b

THE TRUE LESSON of *misah*, and of this *perek*, is for us to appreciate the concept of *chessed shel emes*—an apparent oxymoron. *Chessed* must never be used to enrich oneself at the cost of one's relationships, even if his intent is to enrich others at the same time. Pulling away into discipline and self-control is an indispensable part of true living. *Chessed* without that balance is akin to death.

דף כ.

מתני׳ נשים ועבדים וקטנים פטורין מק"ש ומן התפלין וגו׳.

Mishnah—Women, [gentile] slaves, and children are exempt from k'rias Shema and tefillin, and obligated in prayer, mezuzah, and bentching.

1. The Mishnah in *Berachos* (20a) says that women (along with Canaanite slaves and minors) are exempt from saying *k'rias Shema* and wearing tefillin. *Rashi* gives as the reason for *k'rias Shema* that it is *mitzvas asei she'ha'z'man grama*, citing the Mishnah in *Kiddushin* 29a. Tefillin, he adds, is also *mitzvas asei she'ha'z'man grama* because (in the opinion of our Mishnah) tefillin is restricted to daylight hours on weekdays. But in *Kiddushin*, in explaining the notion of *mitzvas asei she'ha'z'man grama*, *Rashi* says the idea is that time causes the onset of these mitzvos. Why does *Rashi* give different reasons in different places?

2. It is surprising that *Rashi* in *Berachos* feels the need to explain why tefillin should *also* be considered as *mitzvas asei she'ha'z'man grama*, when in *Kiddushin* 34a, tefillin are considered the **source** of the *p'tur* of *mitzvas asei she'ha'z'man grama*!

3. In explaining why *ketanim* are *patur* from *k'rias Shema*, *Rashi* explains it is because they are not always around when it is time for *k'rias Shema*. What kind of an exemption is that? If they are *chayav*, they are obligated to be around!

4. The Gemara asks: Isn't it obvious that women are *patur* from tefillin? They are *mitzvas asei she'ha'z'man grama*! The Gemara answers, "Yes, but tefillin are linked to mezuzah, in which

Berachos 20a

women are obligated." That might make me think women are obligated in tefillin just as they are obligated in mezuzah, so I need this Mishnah to inform me otherwise. But if that's the case, why, in fact, are women **not** obligated in tefillin? Aren't both tefillin and mezuzah about *kabbalas ol malchus Shamayim*? And while it is true that *k'rias Shema* is also about *kabbalas ol malchus Shamayim*, and women are exempt from that, the same question needs to be asked: Why are women exempt from the other mitzvos that emerge from the same source that obligates them in mezuzah?

Yesod

There are two reasons women are exempt from tefillin, and both reasons are related to their being *mitzvas asei she'ha'z'man grama*.

One reason is because women don't need tefillin. Men define themselves by what they do (e.g., I'm a lawyer, I'm an engineer, etc.), so they need a variety of actions that will define them as ones who serve Hashem. Among those actions are *talmud Torah*, *k'rias Shema*, and tefillin. All are defined by time, because time is the causative of action (I have to take a certain action at a certain time). Since tefillin is linked to *talmud Torah*, as soon as we discover that women are exempt from *talmud Torah*, we know they are exempt from tefillin; and knowing that women tend to define themselves not so much by what they do but rather by what they are, we understand their *p'tur* to extend to all positive mitzvos that are caused by time.

This halachah is cited in the *Rambam* (*Hilchos Avodah Zarah* 12:3), where it emerges as an adjunct to similar halachos showing how men and women differ in basic makeup, structure, and definition.

Another reason that women are *patur* from tefillin is because women do not have time to be obligated in tefillin; they are simply too busy. That is the reason behind our Mishnah, in which women's exemption from tefillin is linked to their exemption from *k'rias Shema*, which, in turn, is linked to the exemption of a *chassan* involved in marrying a *besulah*. Both are too preoccupied to be obligated in these mitzvos. This halachah is cited in *Hilchos K'rias Shema* (4:1) and in *Hilchos Tefillin* (4:13), where the exemption is linked to the preoccupation of anyone who is "*tarud v'nechpaz l'd'var mitzvah.*"

Why do we need a second exemption? That is the question of the Gemara when it asks "*p'shita!*"

The answer is that I might think it should apply even to women because even women need to be *mekabel ol malchus Shamayim*. Our Mishnah is teaching us that women do indeed need to be *mekabel ol malchus Shamayim*, but just as a *chassan*, who certainly needs to be *mekabel ol malchus Shamayim*, is exempt from it when he is preoccupied, women have the same exemption, and they are considered preoccupied all the time! So even if you could justify being *chayav* in *k'rias Shema* on the grounds of *ol malchus Shamayim* and not on the grounds of needing actions to stabilize and define themselves, they would still be exempt because of a *z'man grama* of the other type—that they cannot be buttonholed into time-bound obligations for which they have no time.

The proof that women have a connection to *ol malchus Shamayim* is the fact that they are obligated in mezuzah. Tefillin are indeed linked to mezuzah, but whereas tefillin are an action, mezuzah is a state of being of the house. Since women are defined by what they are and not by what they do, and living in a home is an expression of being, women are obligated in mezuzah—which represents that one's being at home is dedicated to G-d.

To put it in another way, the exemption from all *mitzvos asei she'ha'z'man grama* would have been derived from tefillin insofar as women do not need actions to condition them. But women might still have needed to put on tefillin anyway, not for the action aspect of it but for the *ol malchus Shamayim* aspect of it, if not for the fact that they are exempted from even **that** aspect by their being *tarud tirda d'mitzvah* (a constant condition, because that is who they are, not what they do), unlike the *chassan*, for whom the exemption of *tarud* is only for a limited time.

Now we can explain why *Rashi's* reason for the *p'tur* on *ketanim* is because they are not around. They too are too busy!

Berachos 20a

WITH THIS WE can explain another perplexing thing. Chazal tells us "*cheirus*" is *charus al ha'luchos*. If so, how can Pesach be *z'man cheiruseinu* when the *luchos* are not received until Shavuos?

The answer is that *cheirus* is a natural condition of who we are. As long as we are not owned by a slavemaster, we exist in a state of *cheirus*. But that only helps for one who defines himself by who he is. If one defines oneself by what one does, one will not relate to the *cheirus* he may already have until he has committed himself to actions by which he can define himself as a free man. Those actions are what is *charus al ha'luchos*, so *cheirus* becomes felt and perceived on Shavuos. But that's only for the men, who are defined by what they do! For the women, who are defined by what they are, the perception of *cheirus* came immediately upon the *geulah*—*z'man cheiruseinu* itself.

Indeed, this gives us an insight into the inclusion of *avadim Canaani'im* in our Mishnah. Like women, they should have a connection to *ol malchus Shamayim*, should be obligated in *k'rias Shema* and tefillin, and should have an even stronger reason than women to be obligated in these mitzvos because they need the actions for stabilization and self-definition. But they are *meshubad* to a master, and because of that, even if they did these actions, it would not express their connection to *ol malchus Shamayim*. And even if their master invited them to be *meshubad* to Hashem as well as to him, they are too preoccupied with serving their immediate master to undertake the obligation of service to a Higher Master.

Finally—*ketanim*. *Ketanim* who are not of the age of *chinuch* have no connection to *ol malchus Shamayim*. *Ketanim* of *chinuch* age could have a connection—that of being trained for it by their fathers. But they still cannot undertake this as an obligation, because they are too busy. This is reflected perfectly in the language of the *Rambam*, who says to be *mechanech* children but still calls them *patur* (unlike the other Rishonim, for whom *ketanim* whose father must teach them are called *chayav*; see *Tosafos*, s.v. *u'ketanim*).

דף כ:

מתני׳ בעל קרי מהרהר בלבו ואינו מברך לא לפניה
ולא לאחריה וגו׳.

Mishnah—A baal keri thinks [the words of k'rias Shema], and he says neither the berachos before it nor those after it. And [he recites Birkas Hamazon] after eating, but he does not say the berachos before eating. [Rabbi Yehudah says he says berachos both before and after Shema and eating.]

Gemara—Says Ravina: This suggests that thinking is akin to verbalizing, for if it is not, why [trouble yourself to] think [the words of k'rias Shema]? Responds the Gemara: Well, if you hold thinking is akin to verbalizing, why not say [the words of k'rias Shema] out loud instead? [Says Ravina:] It must be as it was done at Sinai.

Says Rav Chisda: This suggests that thinking is unlike verbalizing; for if it is, [once you are going to think them already,] why not just say the words [of k'rias Shema] aloud? Responds the Gemara: Well, if you hold thinking is unlike verbalizing, why [trouble yourself to] think [the words of k'rias Shema, when doing so accomplishes nothing]? Answers Rav Adda: It accomplishes the purpose of keeping you engaged when others are praying.

1. Ezra HaSofer was was the one who instituted a *takanah* placing restrictions against a *baal keri*. Why would the *baal keri* under *takanas Ezra* be allowed to do no more than think the words of *k'rias Shema* when he can fully recite the words of *bentching*,

Berachos 20b

and both are equally *d'Oraisa*? And if you will try to answer that *k'rias Shema* contains *divrei Torah* while *bentching* does not, then how will you explain why he cannot recite or even think *Birkas k'rias Shema* and *birchos ha'nehenin* at all, despite the fact that they contain no *divrei Torah*?

2. In general, why did Ezra need to make a *takanah* when the Torah already restricts a *baal keri* from learning Torah?
3. When the Gemara asks Ravina, "If *hirhur k'dibur*, why should one not say *k'rias Shema* aloud?" Ravina answers, "It must be as it was done at Sinai." When Rav Chisda asks that question, why does the Gemara not offer the same answer?
4. What is the answer, "It must be done as it was done at Sinai"? At Sinai, there **was** *dibbur*. How is that a rationale to explain why we **cannot** use *dibbur*?

Yesod

There are two mitzvos of learning Torah. One is to gain the knowledge and wisdom of Torah. The other is to reexperience the original Revelation at Sinai through our study of Torah.

The latter has a special requirement that the former does not have—to approach the study of Torah with fear, awe, trembling, and perspiration.

Sinai offered both.

The Torah's intention was that the two aspects of studying Torah should always come together. Anytime one is learning to gain Torah knowledge, he should be doing so with *eimah*, *yirah*, *resses*, and *zei'ah* so that he also is reexperiencing *kabbalas haTorah*.

As the actual experience of Sinai began to fade into the past, the aspect of reexperiencing Sinai became progressively more difficult. After a while, Klal Yisrael as a whole was unable to consistently climb to the level of *eimah*, *yirah*, *resses*, and *zei'ah* every time they sat down to learn. They stopped relating to learning as a means to experience Sinai and instead focused their efforts only on learning Torah for its wisdom.

Then came Ezra. The Gemara says Ezra was fitting to have had the Torah given through him. He decided to restore the aspect of learning Torah as a reexperience of Sinai. He felt the problem was that there was nothing forcing the people to rise to that level. After all, they could always learn Torah for its wisdom, even without purifying themselves.

So Ezra made a *takanah*. He reminded the Jews that they were expected to learn with *eimah*, *yirah*, *resses*, and *zei'ah*. For those unable to do so because of the *kalus rosh* associated with *keri*, they would be banned from learning Torah until they had purified themselves from *tumas keri*. Of course, Ezra did not ban them from learning Torah entirely. It remained permitted to learn Torah in a cerebral manner that supported only the wisdom aspect of Torah study. But one could no longer learn out loud unless he could do so with *eimah*, *yirah*, *resses*, and *zei'ah*, something a *baal keri* cannot do.

This plan worked. No longer able to engage verbally in their beloved Torah study without also reaching levels of purity, they learned how to maintain purity. *Takanas Ezra* was a success!

Later *batei din* decided to capitalize on this success, so they broadened the *takanah* and expanded it to include other *devarim she'b'kedushah*—e.g., *k'rias Shema*, *tefillah*, *bentching*, and *berachos*. Depending on the conditions presenting themselves, these *devarim she'b'kedushah* could be

- recited out loud by a *baal keri* only if they met the Biblical threshold (so, for example, the *baal keri* could *bentch* out loud if he had eaten *k'dei sevi'ah*);
- recited by a *baal keri* but not out loud (when they were Biblically mandated but contained *divrei Torah*—like *Shema*);
- not recited by a *baal keri* at all (when not Biblically mandated).

Soon people were maintaining purity in connection with all these activities, and the spiritual advancement of the community was very great.

But once again, as the inspiration of the days of Ezra had passed, the spiritual abilities of the people waned. They were still refraining from Torah study until they had gained purity, but they became more and more likely to content themselves with remaining impure and to simply refrain from studying. Because it was understood that this had never been Ezra's intention, it was easy for Rabbi Yehudah ben Beseirah to clarify that the *takanah* still stood for those still willing to learn in purity, but that no restriction against learning for wisdom applied to those who are not. And that is the way it remains until today.

ONCE THE *TAKANAH* was redefined, its extension to other *devarim she'b'kedushah* naturally slipped into disuse. Indeed, the nature of the extension had never been such that it could ever really stand alone.

The *machlokes* between Ravina and Rav Chisda is over whether the extension as made by the later *beis din* incorporated all the conditions of the original *takanas Ezra* or not.

Ravina held it did, and so just as *takanas Ezra* prohibited a *baal keri* from learning Torah out loud, so too the *takanas Ezra* extension prohibited a *baal keri* from reciting any *davar she'b'kedushah* out loud until after he visited a *mikveh*. But just like *takanas Ezra* was never intended to keep people from learning, so too the *takanas Ezra* extension was never intended to keep people from being *yotzei mitzvos*. So when *z'man k'rias Shema* arrived and a person found himself a *baal keri*, he was to think the *Shema* and thereby fulfill the mitzvah without speaking out *divrei Torah*. Clearly the Mishnah is telling us, states Ravina, that thinking is akin to speaking without it being considered speaking **out loud**; and thus the mitzvah can be fulfilled through *hirhur*, an activity silent enough not to violate *takanas Ezra*, as adopted by its extension. (It actually already works *b'dieved*—see 15b; the *beis din* was simply *mesaken* that it is to be used *l'chatchila* by a *baal keri*, who needs some way to be *yotzei* his mitzvah.)

Hence the Gemara asks: All fine and well; we like the idea of fulfilling a mitzvah without breaking the *takanah*. But why say such a big *chiddush* as *hirhur k'dibur*, when there is a non-*chiddush'dik* way to accomplish this task—to *whisper* the *Shema* (*yotzi b'sefasav*)! This is indisputably *dibbur*, yet it is not the "speaking out loud" that would break the *takanah*!

To this, Ravina answers: If you are not willing to be *mechadesh* a non-*dibbur* method for fulfilling a *dibbur*-based mitzvah, essentially you are looking to confirm some form of expression as being actual *dibbur*. Whispering is certainly a form of *dibbur*. But at Sinai, where things not only had to be said but had to also be effective at fostering an "experience," whispering would not have qualified as *dibbur*. Anything that would not qualify as *dibbur* to achieve the reexperiencing of Sinai (*k'd'ashkechan b'Sinai*) cannot qualify as *dibbur* for the purpose of overriding the restrictions laid by the extension of the Sinai-inspired *takanas Ezra*. The only kind of *dibbur* that would have qualified as Sinai *dibbur* would have been *dibbur* recited aloud, something not allowable to a *baal keri* under *takanas Ezra*. We are forced to concede to the innovation of *hirhur k'dibur*.

Rav Chisda held that just because the original *takanas Ezra* was based on Sinai, the extension need not follow Sinaitic definitions of *dibbur*. If the mandate to think the *Shema* was because of the need to be *yotzei*, the Mishnah would have told us to whisper instead. Whispering is *dibbur* that does not break the *takanah*, and it is not excluded by any need for "*ashkechan b'Sinai*." Obviously, the Mishnah is not giving us a methodology by which to be *yotzei* a mitzvah. The technology for that—whispering—was already available to us. Maybe Ezra did not want people kept from lesser forms of the great things he was trying to inspire, but the *Chachamim* of the extension did not attempt to draw all their conditions from the original *takanas Ezra*. A *baal keri* is restricted from *devarim she'b'kedushah*, even at the expense of his being *yotzei mitzvos*. He cannot speak them, even in a whisper. *Hirhur* is not *k'dibur*, but the *baal keri* still must be *meharher* in order to keep him from being blank-minded while everyone around him is doing a mitzvah.

Rav Chisda is actually *l'shitaso*. You see, he was the *bar plugta* of Rav Yosef on *daf* 15a–b. There, the Gemara had been discussing a Mishnah in which the *Tanna Kama* held that *b'dieved k'rias Shema* could be inaudible, and Rabbi Yose held it could not. Rav Yosef pondered the application of this *din* to other mitzvos. He started to say that by other mitzvos there was no debate that audibility was an absolute necessity. But after seeing a *Beraisa* that said that one could be *yotzei bentching b'dieved* with *hirhur*, he changed his position and adopted the view that by other mitzvos there was no debate and audibility was **not** required *b'dieved*. Rav Chisda, in contradistinction to Rav Yosef, did not apply that *Beraisa*

Berachos 20b

to the *sugya*. And thus, the lowest level of halachic acceptability known to Rav Chisda is *hotza'ah b'sefasav* (whispering), not *hirhur b'lev*, while Rav Yosef was able to drop it one step down to *hirhur b'lev*.

RAVINA, BY ENTERTAINING the possibility of a halachically valid *hirhur b'lev*, is simply adopting the position of Rav Yosef on *daf* 15, with Rav Chisda over here abiding by his own view over there.

Like whom should be the halachah?

All the Rishonim on *daf* 15 *pasken* like Rav Chisda's understanding of the *sugya*, and, as can be seen from *Tur* and *Shulchan Aruch* (*Orach Chaim* 158, 206), *b'dieved* one can be *yotzei* without hearing the words, but his lips must utter them. Therefore, they too *pasken* here like Rav Chisda and conclude that *hirhur* is not *k'dibur*.

But *Rif* explicitly *paskens* like Rav Yosef, and *Rambam* (*Hilchos Berachos* 1:7) says that with all *berachos, b'dieved* one is *yotzei* with *hirhur ha'lev*, a view that is true only according to Rav Yosef. So the *Rambam* will be able to *pasken* over here like Ravina and learn that *hirhur* is *k'dibur—b'dieved* for the rest of us, and *l'chatchila* for a *baal keri*.

But does he? Unlike *Tur* and *Shulchan Aruch*, *Rambam* never says explicitly that one **cannot** be *yotzei k'rias Shema b'hirhur*. But he doesn't say he can either. All he says is that *shemi'as ozen* is not required *b'dieved*. If he really holds that even *hotza'ah b'fiv* is not required *b'dieved*, don't you think he should have told us?

The answer is no. He *paskens* like Rabbi Yehudah, not like the *Tanna Kama*. Rabbi Yehudah holds the *takanas Ezra* was never extended to all *devarim she'b'kedushah*. It was extended only to *k'rias Shema*, so people wouldn't get confused with the *baal keri*'s restriction against Torah study.

But the Gemara still has to discuss *shitas Tanna Kama* so we will know how to *pasken* in general about *hirhur* as a mechanism.

Also, keep in mind that even *Rambam* held like Rav Chisda in the *sugya* on *daf* 15—as the basis for the requiring of *shemi'as ozen* by *sha'ar mitzvos*, despite *paskening* the *sugya* like Rav Yosef. See earlier *shiur* on הקורא את שמע ולא השמיע לאזנו יצא (pp. 90–94).

דף כב:

תנ"ר היה עומד בתפלה ומים שותתין על ברכיו פוסק
עד שיכלו המים וגו'.

The Rabbis taught: One standing in prayer who experiences urine discharging down his legs must interrupt his prayer until the discharge ends, after which he returns to his praying.

The Gemara in *Berachos* on 22b brings a *Beraisa* about one who had to interrupt his *Amidah* due to incontinence. The Gemara's conclusion is that if one interrupts for longer than it would have taken to start and finish the entire *Amidah*, he must go back and start over from the beginning.

But passages in *Rosh Hashanah* (34b), *Megillah* (18b), and ahead in *Berachos* (24b) make it clear that one who has interrupted his hearing of the shofar or his reading of *Hallel*, *Megillas Esther*, or *k'rias Shema* for longer than it takes to perform the entire respective task does not need to go back and start over from the beginning, and he is *yotzei* his mitzvah even if he just picked up where he had left off before the interruption and finished it.

From this, the *Sar m'Coucy* derives the following halachah: One who is engaged in performing any of the *devarim she'b'kedushah* and **is forced** to interrupt due to some cause that halachically prohibits him from proceeding (such as incontinence) must, if the delay is of sufficient length, go back and start over from the beginning when he is ready to resume. If, however, his interruption was **voluntary**, he may resume from where he left off.

Tosafos, *Rosh*, and *Tur* accept the approach of the *Sar m'Coucy*.[2] To underscore the fact that he accepts the approach of the *Sar m'Coucy*,

Berachos 22b

the *Tur* doesn't even bring this halachah in *Hilchos Tefillah* despite that being the case of the Gemara. He brings it in *Hilchos K'rias Shema*, as if to say the halachah is the same for all *devarim she'b'kedushah*.

Rif and *Rambam* disagree.[3] According to them, the halachah is unique to *tefillah*. Furthermore, it does not matter why you took the break. Any interruption in *Amidah* that lasts longer than the amount of time it takes to complete the entire *Amidah* will always require you to go back and start it from the beginning, while a similar interruption in any other mitzvah recital or activity longer than the time it takes to perform the recital or activity will require no more than picking up where you left off.

Shulchan Aruch is a little unusual.[4] He brings the halachah in *Hilchos K'rias Shema* like the *Tur* does, but he *paskens* like the *Rif* and the *Rambam*, so he says you do not have to go back to the beginning after a mid-*k'rias Shema* bout of incontinence, the scenario where—based on our Gemara—the other Rishonim would say you must. As a result, the *Rama* there in *siman* 65 parts ways with the *Mechaber* and rules you must go back to the beginning (of *k'rias Shema*, *tefillah*, or any other *davar she'b'kedushah*) after the urine discharge has ended.

1. According to the *Sar m'Coucy*, it makes sense that the Gemara on 22b was made to discuss a case of incontinence because that is the only type of case that will trigger the obligation to start over. But according to the *Rif*, the *Rambam*, and the *Shulchan Aruch*, it would have been enough for the case to just have been one of a person standing for *Shemoneh Esreh* and encountering an interruption of sufficient length. Why did we need to illustrate the case of an interruption with a scene as odd as a person urinating in the middle of his *Amidah*? Furthermore, there is little doubt that a person faced with uncontrollable incontinence in the middle of *Shemoneh Esreh* would be advised even halachically to stop and make his way to the bathroom. So even if the Gemara had wanted to choose a case of incontinence for some reason, it could have done so without the graphic imagery of the urine streaming down the man's legs! The *Shulchan Aruch*,

to address this, asserts that the purpose of the Gemara is to teach us a tangential lesson—that pants wet from urine will not be a cause of one's losing the prior recitation of whatever part of *Shema* he was up to when the accident began; and thus as soon as the stream ends he may resume. This might work for the *Shulchan Aruch*, but it cannot work for the *Rambam*, who brings the Gemara the way it was written—as a halachah in *Hilchos Tefillah*. There the law is that one *does* lose his prior recitation and must start again from the beginning anyway. Urination is just an added reason to declare his *tefillah* void; there is no evidence it would be acceptable in a case of delayed *k'rias Shema*, and thus it teaches us no new *chiddush l'halachah*. So why, according to the *Rambam*, do we have to be presented with such an odd and graphic case?

2. All opinions agree that the halachah is like Rav Yosef in *Megillah* (18b) that *k'dei ligmor es kula* is defined as meaning "from beginning to end." It is patently obvious that there cannot be such thing as a single streaming of urination that lasts as long as it takes to recite the entire *Shemoneh Esreh* from beginning to end. So how can the *Rambam* bring the case of *shaha k'dei ligmor es kula* where he does—as part of the halachah of *mayim shosesin al birkav*?

3. Also in *Megillah* 18b, how could Rav Yosef be in support of Rav Bibi in his saying that Shmuel is the one who said *halachah k'Rav Muna*, so as to say the halachah—being that we rule like Rav and not Shmuel in ritual matters—is **not** like Rav Muna (and therefore by *k'rias Megillah* we can say *chozer l'makom she'pasak*), when he himself was quoted earlier in the Gemara saying *halachah k'Rav Muna*—that if one paused in *k'rias Megillah k'dei ligmor es kula* he must be *chozer l'rosh*? (From this question, the *Sefas Emes* changes the *girsa* to remove Rav Yosef's earlier statement, but there is no evidence anywhere in the early Acharonim to suggest that the Rishonim did not have the *girsa* we have, so how do we explain it?)

Berachos 22b

4. In *Rosh Hashanah* (34b), Rabbi Yochanan says one who interrupted his hearing of *teki'as shofar* for more time than it would take to go through them all from beginning to end is *yotzei* his obligation without having started over from the beginning. This would be consistent with the halachah being—according to the *Rambam*—that for all *devarim she'b'kedushah* other than *tefillah*, one needs to be only *chozer l'makom she'pasak*. If so, then why, when he is asked by Rabbi Abahu what to do when he emerges from the alley in the incident brought next in the Gemara (in which Rabbi Abahu had stopped reciting *Shema* as he walked through a dirty alley), does Rabbi Yochanan tell him to be *chozer l'rosh*? The Gemara explains he was answering not based on what he holds, but rather *l'shitas* Rabbi Abahu. But let's think about that. Rabbi Abahu was reciting *k'rias Shema*, not *tefillah*. The halachah for *k'rias Shema* is *chozer l'makom she'pasak* and Rabbi Yochanan agrees. Now it is true that Rabbi Yochanan personally disagrees with Rabbi Abahu, **but their only point of disagreement is whether or not walking through a dirty alley demands an interruption in *k'rias Shema*.** About that issue, he could have spoken "*l'shitas* Rabbi Abahu." But on the matter of to where one should return when resuming, why can't Rabbi Yochanan tell Rabbi Abahu what he holds, which is *chozer l'makom she'pasak*?

Yesod

We have completely misunderstood this *Rambam*. Let us start by going back to Rabbi Yochanan.

The way the *Rambam* reads the Gemara, Rabbi Yochanan never held *chozer l'makom she'pasak* at all.

Rabbi Yochanan holds that when a person has been *shaha k'dei ligmor es kula*, whether by *tefillah* or by any other *davar she'b'kedushah*, he is *chozer l'rosh*, not *chozer l'makom she'pasak*. He was not merely citing his *rebbe* when he said that by *Hallel* and *Megillah* one must be *chozer*

דף כב:

l'rosh. And the reason he told Rabbi Abahu to go back to the beginning is because **that is his *shitah*!**

But how could that be? Didn't the Gemara in *Rosh Hashanah* say Rabbi Yochanan was quoting his *rebbe* and that he himself doesn't hold of *chozer l'rosh*? And didn't Rabbi Yochanan say that one who heard the shofar *b'serugin* is *yotzei* without having to go back to the beginning?

Yes, but if you'll notice, all Rabbi Yochanan said was that one who heard the shofar *b'serugin* is *yotzei b'dieved*. He never said one may *l'chatchilah* be *chozer l'makom she'pasak*, and if you read carefully, you'll see that the Gemara actually challenged the explanation that Rabbi Yochanan was merely quoting a halachah in the name of his *rebbe*. That was the challenge from his response to Rabbi Abahu. And while the Gemara did say that he was just addressing Rabbi Abahu *l'shitaso*, it is *Tosafos* who says conclusively that Rabbi Yochanan was indeed saying, "I don't hold of *chozer l'rosh*." *Rambam* would say we don't necessarily know what Rabbi Yochanan meant, and the Gemara was only saying it could get out of the challenge by claiming Rabbi Yochanan was speaking *l'shitas* Rabbi Abahu. Indeed, the story is brought differently in *Berachos* 24b than in *Rosh Hashanah*. There, the question asked by Rabbi Abahu was not "*mahu ligmor*" but rather, "*l'heichan ahader*."

What is the difference between these two versions? The difference is enormous. If Rabbi Abahu is asking "*l'heichan ahader*," he is indicating that he already knows he will be *mehader*. He is just asking, "to where"? If his question is "*mahu ligmor*," he is indicating he does not even know if he can complete the *Shema* because he does not know if he has lost it by going through the dirty alley or not. In the Gemara in *Rosh Hashanah*, the Gemara was trying to prove that Rabbi Yochanan holds *chozer l'rosh* and is in contradiction with his having said that one who hears shofar *b'serugin* is *yotzei* without having had to be *chozer l'rosh*. After dispelling Rabbi Yochanan's statement that one must be *chozer l'rosh* by *Hallel* and *Megillah* with the deflection that he was simply quoting his *rebbe*'s position, the Gemara next proceeded to cite his response to Rabbi Abahu. How could he have told Rabbi Abahu to be *chozer l'rosh* if he doesn't hold that way? The Gemara again deflects the proof. Rabbi Yochanan could have been telling Rabbi Abahu that, while in his personal view, the

Berachos 22b

answer would have been *"ligmor"*—and therefore *chozer l'makom she'pasak*—because walking through a dirty alley does not cancel a person's *Shema*, from the perspective of Rabbi Abahu, who holds reciting *Shema* while walking through a dirty alley is forbidden, the answer would have to be *"lo ligmor,"* and once it's *"lo ligmor"* because of a canceled *Shema*, it will have to be *chozer l'rosh*.

That's a valid deflection, but *al pi ha'emes*, Rabbi Yochanan could have been saying something else. He could have been saying, "I hold you have to be *chozer l'rosh* because as far as I am concerned, you would have been allowed to keep reciting *Shema*. Your choice to stop made you a voluntary *shaha k'dei ligmor es kula*, which, according to me invokes a halachah of *chozer l'rosh*."

From the Gemara in *Rosh Hashanah*, we have no way to know what Rabbi Yochanan really holds. But from the Gemara in *Berachos* 24b, we do. There, the story of his conversation with Rabbi Abahu was brought because the Gemara was trying to prove that Rabbi Yochanan could not possibly hold it is permissible to recite *Shema* while walking through a dirty alley. It cites his response to Rabbi Abahu (*chozer l'rosh*) as a way to prove that he must hold walking through a dirty alley cancels one's *Shema*.

The Gemara deflects the proof by saying he was addressing Rabbi Abahu *"l'shitaso."* But it is clear from the question of *"l'heichan chozer"* that Rabbi Abahu's *shitah* does not carry any doubt that his *Shema* is still valid. If so, what possible reason would Rabbi Yochanan have to respond with a view other than the one he actually holds?

Bishlama in *Rosh Hashanah*, where he had to respond to Rabbi Abahu's question that included doubt over whether his *Shema* was still valid at all, Rabbi Yochanan could have been saying, "I don't hold there was anything wrong with what you did, but that's because I hold you can say *Shema* in a dirty alley. But *l'shitasecha* that you cannot, my answer to you is that you have lost your *Shema* and you must be *chozer l'rosh*. I, for my part, might still hold that one who interrupts in such a way that he has not lost his *Shema* is *chozer l'makom she'pasak*." But in *Berachos*, the question, "Have I lost my *Shema*?" is not on the table. The only question Rabbi Abahu is asking is, "When I go back to my *Shema* after I

דף כב:

leave the dirty alley, to where in *Shema* do I go back (i.e., like whom do we *pasken* in the *machlokes* between Rav Chisda and Rav Hamnuna)?" What possible reason would Rabbi Yochanan have had—in that version of the story—not to answer *chozer l'makom she'pasak* if that's what he truly holds? It must be, concludes the *Rambam*, that Rabbi Yochanan actually holds *chozer l'rosh*.

So the *Rambam paskens* like Rabbi Yochanan straight up. He paskens *kara Megillah o shama tekios l'serugin yotzei* not because he holds *chozer l'makom she'pasak* on *devarim she'b'kedushah* other than *tefillah*, but because Rabbi Yochanan holds one is *yotzei* with *serugin b'dieved*. But *l'chatchila*? Go start over! And he holds *chozer l'rosh* by *tefillah* not because *tefillah* is different than anything else, but because he holds *chozer l'rosh* by all *devarim she'b'kedushah*!

But where does the *Rambam* say all this? He says it right in *Hilchos Tefillah* 4:13: "If one was standing in *Shemoneh Esreh*, and urine began streaming down his legs, he waits until the urine stops and then he continues from where he left off. And if he paused long enough to have completed an entire *Shemoneh Esreh*, he goes back to the beginning."

MOST READERS DON'T see this as a general rule of *chozer l'rosh*, but that is because they are reading it incorrectly. They read the *Rambam's* second clause ("And if he paused...") as modifying the case of the urine streaming, thus reading it as if it relates only to the case of the *Beraisa*. In fact, the clause cannot possibly modify that case, as the case of urination cannot possibly ever be as long as *k'dei ligmor es kula*. Rather, "And if he paused..." is a new general rule, setting up the idea that if one, rather than being compelled by a condition in which halachah forces him to stop, instead pauses (voluntarily, which is how *Rambam* translates "*shaha*") for longer than it takes to complete a whole *Amidah*, he must be *chozer l'rosh*. This applies *l'chatchila* to all *devarim she'b'kedushah*. In *Hilchos K'rias Shema* 2:12, *Rambam* merely adds that *b'dieved* if one was not *chozer l'rosh* but instead just kept reading straight ahead after his pause to the end, he is *yotzei* even if the pause was longer than *k'dei ligmor*. In *Hilchos Shofar* (3:5-6), *Megillah* (3:2), and by *Hallel* he says the same thing.

Berachos 22b

But what about Rav Muna? Doesn't Rav Muna say *chozer l'rosh* only to have the Gemara support Rav Bibi who says "*Ein halachah k'Rav Muna*" and thus reach a conclusion that the halachah is *chozer l'makom she'pasak*?

No! That is not what that Gemara is saying at all! If you notice, Rav Bibi never said "*Ein halachah k'Rav Muna*." What he said was that the statement "*halachah k'Rav Muna*" was the statement of Shmuel, not of Rav. This caused us to infer that "*ein halachah k'Rav Muna*" because the halachah in ritual matters tends to follow Rav over Shmuel.

But if you look at the source case in *Yevamos*, you see that it too presents a case where Shmuel follows the view of the minority lone opinion, and there the halachah is like Shmuel! Here too, then, it is fair to say that Rav Bibi is merely mentioning the fact that Rav Muna's halachah is the one championed by Shmuel, but he is not saying that the halachah is not like him. And thus, when Rav Yosef tells us to adopt the view of Rav Bibi, he is not contradicting what he said earlier. He consistently holds *chozer l'rosh*—the same way Rabbi Yochanan does and the same way the *Rambam* does.

The only remaining question is how do we explain what the *Rambam* says by dirty alleys. There he *paskens* that *chozer l'makom she'pasak*, regardless of how long the break was (*Hilchos K'rias Shema* 3:14).

We understand that if it is less than *k'dei ligmor* it should be *chozer l'makom she'pasak*. But if the break is *k'dei ligmor es kula*, and Rabbi Yochanan holds *chozer l'rosh*—as we see him explain to Rabbi Abahu—and *Rambam* holds like Rabbi Yochanan, shouldn't the halachah be *chozer l'rosh* if the pause was *k'dei ligmor es kula*?

This can be explained simply. It is true that Rabbi Yochanan holds *chozer l'rosh* after taking a long break during a walk through a *mavui metunaf* (dirty alley). But that is because he holds a person who takes a voluntary break is required to start over, while one who takes a halachically forced break (like the break halachically imposed due to incontinence) may pick up from where he left off; it's just that *mavui metunaf* is a case of a voluntary break because reciting *k'rias Shema* while walking through a dirty alley, according to Rabbi Yochanan, is *mutar*. So the halachah should be *chozer l'rosh*.

דף כב:

But the *Rambam* breaks with Rabbi Yochanan on one issue—the *heter* to recite *k'rias Shema* in a dirty alley. On that issue, the *Rambam paskens* like Rav Chisda (against Rabbi Yochanan) that it is *assur* to recite *k'rias Shema* in a dirty alley. As a result, pausing in a dirty alley according to the *Rambam* now has a status as a halachically forced pause—and then *Rambam* simply goes back to Rabbi Yochanan's opinion about forced pauses, that after such a pause—regardless of its length—one is *chozer l'makom she'pasak*, exactly as *Rambam* rules.

Berachos 23a

דף כג. (1)

ת״ר הנצרך לנקביו אל יתפלל וגו׳.

The Rabbis taught: One who feels a need to eliminate waste should not daven…

Rambam in *Hilchos Tefillah* (4:10) writes:

> One must not begin Shemoneh Esreh while needing to eliminate waste, and if he did so, his tefillah is an abomination and he must daven again. However, if he was able to hold it in for the amount of time it takes to walk a *parsah*, his tefillah is not an abomination. Nevertheless, he should not pray until he has checked himself very well.

This is based on two versions of a *Beraisa*, and one statement of Rav Shmuel bar Nachmani:

Version One

Tanu Rabanan—One who needs to relieve himself shall not daven. If he does, his prayer is an abomination.

Said Rav Zvid—This was said only regarding one who could not restrain himself. But if he could restrain himself, his prayer is a valid prayer.

How long [need one be able to restrain himself in order to be permitted to daven—*Rashi*]? Said Rav Sheishes, the length of time it would take to walk a *parsah*.

Version Two

Tanu Rabanan—One who needs to relieve himself shall not daven. If he does, his prayer is an abomination. When was this said? When he is unable to restrain himself, but if he is able to restrain himself, his prayer is a valid prayer.

דף כג.

And for how long [need one be able to restrain himself in order for his prayer to be valid—*Rambam*]? Said Rav Zvid, the length of time it would take to walk a *parsah*.

Rav Shmuel Bar Nachmani

One who needs to relieve himself, behold this one shall not daven, because it says, "Prepare, Israel, before encountering your G-d."

THE WAY THE *Rambam* understands this, the reason for not praying given in the opening *Beraisa* is not because you have to relieve yourself. If that were true, the status of the prayer would be irrelevant at best, and misleading or even wrong at worst. Think about it: If there is a *hakpadah* against beginning a prayer while in a state of needing relief, what possible difference could there be if you could restrain yourself for a *parsah*? What if your *tefillah* turns out to last longer than a *k'dei hiluch parsah*? It must be that the reason for not praying is that one cannot begin a prayer that is not a prayer but an abomination (similar to *"ein zeh mevarech ela mena'eitz"*). Therefore, we get the immediate qualification that a prayer begun by a person capable of restraining himself a *k'dei hiluch parsah* is not an abomination. That prayer does not have the *issur* based on the stated reason. Nevertheless, adds the *Rambam*, there remains a second reason not to daven—one should not begin even a *tefillah* that is a valid *tefillah* and not an abomination when one is in a condition of having to relieve himself.

Actually, the *Rambam* is agreeing with *Rashi*. One who feels an urge to relieve himself may not daven, and if he does, he will have to daven over unless the urge was one he was able to restrain the length of time to walk a *parsah*. And even if he feels no urge, he should still not daven without first checking himself to see if he could relieve himself anyway.

IN OTHER WORDS, "able to restrain himself for a *parsah*" could be informing us of one of two things because it could be talking about one of two people. It could either be talking about one who is able to hold it in and feels no urge, or one who is able to hold it in despite an urge.

Let's pick one and see if it will work. Let's try the first possibility:

Berachos 23a

One who is able to hold it in and feels no urge, his *tefillah* is not an abomination. This approach leads to a series of questions:

1. *Rambam* already said one cannot daven if he needs to relieve himself. Why does he repeat himself at the end of the halachah and say *l'chatchila* one should not daven until he checks himself?
2. We could answer the first question by distinguishing between those with an urge and those without, but all the sources the Gemara brings begin with those with urges. Where would *Rambam* get his last halachah?
3. If *Rambam* agrees with *Rashi*, why does he say that *ad parsah* is the standard for not having to repeat davening when *Rashi* calls it the standard for being allowed to daven in the first place? And if he doesn't agree with *Rashi*, how does he learn?
4. What is the difference between the versions?

Yesod

There is a *machlokes* between the two versions.

What is the *machlokes* between the two versions? The *machlokes* is whether "*ad parsah*" is talking about a person who feels an urge or about a person who feels no urge.

According to the first version, the *Beraisa* told us in an unqualified way that one who feels an urge may not daven. Rav Zvid is just advising us that the status of "abomination" applies only to one who begins to pray while feeling he has an urge he cannot restrain, which will limit the halachah of when he has to repeat his prayer. However, by saying this, he is leaving it patently obvious that anyone who feels an urge is banned from praying—both those whose urge will yield an abomination and those whose urge is mild enough that it will yield a prayer. Neither may begin davening. Rav Sheishes is addressing a different issue. The *Beraisa* already ruled that anyone with an urge is banned from davening. People without an urge may daven. But that does not mean they will not start to feel an urge mid-prayer. Rav Sheishes is simply informing us that a person who wishes to invoke the *heter* of "I feel no urge" must be one who knows in himself that whenever he does feel an urge, he can hold it *k'dei hiluch parsah*.

According to the second version, the *Beraisa* qualified what it told us about people who feel urges. The ban is only on those who cannot restrain themselves. No one can restrain themselves forever, so we need to know how much the threshold for restraint on people with urges is; Rav Zvid tells us they have to be able to hold it in for a *k'dei hiluch parsah*. The *heter* would be "I can restrain my urge a *k'dei hiluch parsah*." But there is no *Beraisa* implication or Rav Sheishes telling me there is a *heter* called "I feel no urge." The *Beraisa* and the *k'dei hiluch parsah* were not addressing him! They were focused on the status of the *tefillah* of one who davens with urges. But *avada*, one should not infer that there is anyone who can daven without checking himself, urge or not, to see if he has anything that would cross the *parsah* threshold.

The *Rambam paskens* like both versions *l'chumrah*. So he begins:

No one with an urge should daven (like the first *Beraisa*).

Then, for one who did, he says it's an abomination and he must daven over, unless it was an urge he was able to restrain himself from *k'dei hiluch parsah*. (This is like the second version, the version that, on its own, would actually have let the latter guy daven *l'chatchila*, urge and all. That *kula* of the second version the *Rambam* rejects. The first version would have accepted his prayer *b'dieved* even if he could hold it in only less than a *parsah*, as long as he could hold it in through *Shemoneh Esreh*. That's the *kula* of the first version that the *Rambam* rejects.)

Finally (and here he rejects the other *kula* of the first version), [despite the fact that I've just introduced the first version that permits a person without an urge to daven, we need to be *machmir* like the second version, and] *l'chatchila*, even a person who feels no urge should not daven until he checks himself (like the second version—the first version would say he does not have to check himself at all as long as he knows he can restrain himself *k'dei hiluch parsah*).

דף כג. (2)

תנו רבנן הנכנס לבית הכסא חולץ תפיליו בריחוק ד׳ אמות ונכנס אמר רב אחא בר רב הונא אמר רב ששת לא שנו אלא בית הכסא קבוע אבל בית הכסא עראי חולץ ונפנה לאלתר.

The Rabbis taught: One about to enter a bathroom must remove his tefillin at a distance of four amos, and then he may enter. Rav Acha bar Rav Huna quoted Rav Sheishes as saying the above is taught only with regard to an established bathroom; but with an undesignated space, one may proceed directly from removing his tefillin to relieving himself.

If a bathroom is such an affront to tefillin that they must be removed four *amos* away, why should this halachah apply only when one is planning to enter the bathroom? Why should one not be equally required to remove his tefillin anytime he is walking **within** four *amos* of a bathroom—even if he is just walking by the bathroom with no plans to enter?

And if you should answer that what is demeaning to the tefillin is not the bathroom so much as the act of voiding, then why does the halachah distinguish between a *kisei kavu'a* and a *kisei arai* when both are about to be used for an act of voiding?

THE POINT HERE is not that either a bathroom or the act of voiding is demeaning to tefillin. Rather, what is demeaning is when a human being does not recognize the vast difference between what he is while garbed in tefillin and what he is while relieving those urges he shares in common with the animal. Of course, we know we cannot relieve ourselves while wearing tefillin, but we may fail to recognize that in shifting from wearing tefillin to eliminating, we actually shift into a different level of our humanity. It is a vastly different person displaying the glory of God's sign than the one satisfying his gross physical needs. In order to remind us of that gap, the halachah requires us that when we are heading to the bathroom to engage in elimination of wastes, we are to remove the tefillin at a distance of four *amos* away as if to say we are going to need to depressurize, as if we had been an airplane just flying at 30,000 feet and are now on a rapid descent in anticipation of becoming earthbound. By this means, the halachah makes us aware that our higher self and our lower self are not all one and the same thing.

Clearly, this is not necessary when we are merely walking past a bathroom with no intention of making use of it.

OK, but then why does this requirement not apply to a *beis ha'kisei arai*?

THE TALMUD TELLS us in *Yoma* 19b that a person should make his Torah study "*kavu'a*" and the pursuit of his livelihood "*arai*." Pursuing a livelihood, like going to the bathroom, is done for the purpose of satisfying our physical needs. What we see from this Gemara is that the proper balance between our spiritual side and our physical side is attained when the former is "*kavu'a*" and the latter is "*arai*." So long as the bathroom we are about to use is a *beis ha'kisei arai*, the right balance is met, so there is no fear that we will forget that we are great spiritual beings who must at times attend to the needs of the physical bodies in which we are encased.

But as soon as we start establishing and dedicating special spaces for our gross physical functions and assigning them the term "*kavu'a*," that is when we become at risk. A *makom midrash* (place of learning) is what should be "*kavu'a*" in our lives. But a bathroom? *Kavua*? It is specifically when we are heading to a *beis ha'kisei* "*kavu'a*" that we must take the special measure of creating a four-*amah* buffer zone, so we can demonstrably remind ourselves that our tefillin-wearing self is our elevated self, while our body-function self—as *kavu'a* as it might become in our lives—remains a projection of our lowest common denominator, the *tzad bahami* that may be a part of us but must never be allowed to define or dominate us.

דף כד. (1)

בעי מיניה רב יוסף בריה דרב נחוניא מרב יהודה שנים שישנים במטה אחת מהו שזה יחזיר פניו ויקרא ק"ש וגו'.

Rav Yosef son of Rav Nechunya asked Rav Yehudah: If two people are lying in one bed, is it permitted for one to turn to one side and recited Shema and the other to turn to the other side and say Shema? [Rav Yehudah] responded: Thus says Shmuel: [One may keep a pair of tefillin on his bed] even if his wife is [present in the bed] with him.

Rav Yosef challenges: "**Even**" if it is his wife who is present in bed with him, and other people go without saying? On the contrary, his wife is like [an extension of] his own body; another person is not like his body!

A question is raised: [Beraisa—] Two people lying in one bed, this one can turn aside and recite *Shema*, and that one can turn aside and recite *Shema*. [Another Beraisa—] One person lying in bed with his children and family members at his side cannot recite *Shema* unless a garment [or fabric] intervenes between them. (But if the children are minors, it is allowed.) At least Rav Yosef can explain that the first *Beraisa* is talking about his wife being the one present with him, while the second *Beraisa* is talking about another person. But how will Shmuel explain [the *Beraisa* that does not allow *Shema*]?

Shmuel would respond: And is Rav Yosef's position any better? [A *Beraisa* states:] One lying in a bed surrounded by his household members may not say *Shema* unless a blanket or garment intervenes! Rav Yosef has no choice but to say [that saying *Shema* with a] wife [also present in the bed] is the subject of a Tannaic dispute. So, too, do I say that [wife and/or others] is a Tannaic dispute.

1. *Rosh* states that one should be strict with regard to saying *Shema* while in a bed in which his wife is also present, because the dispute remains unresolved. How can he say the dispute remains unresolved when both parties to the dispute—Shmuel and Rav Yosef—agree that one *can* say *Shema* when next to one's wife? They argue only about saying *Shema* while in a bed in which someone else is also present, for example, another family member. The only opinion restricting *Shema* in the presence of one's wife is an outside *Beraisa* that neither opinion holds of!
2. Why does the Gemara set up Rav Yosef's comment as a "*maskif lah*" challenge when it should be written up as just an ordinary *machlokes* Shmuel versus Rav Yosef?
3. Why are we bringing a quote from Shmuel ("*v'afilu ishto imo*") that he said by tefillin—where the issue was proper respect for tefillin and the "*afilu ishto*" meant as opposed to him being alone in the bed—to a question in *k'rias Shema*, where the issue is untoward thoughts and "*afilu ishto*" means as opposed to individuals other than his wife?
4. We just had a refutation (*tiyuvta*) of Shmuel, mitigated only because of an overriding need to protect the tefillin. How can we bring Shmuel's debunked statement to answer a question here?

Yesod

In order to understand what is going on here, we need to take a step back.

Having just learned that there exists a conflict between being a *baal keri* and accepting the *ol malchus Shamayim*, and seeing that played out in one stated contradiction between saying *Shema* and walking in filthy alleys and another between wearing tefillin and being in a lavatory, Rav Yosef son of Rav Nechunya on *daf* 23b wonders about a possible conflict regarding someone lying in a bed upon which there also lies a pair of tefillin.

Berachos 24a

He clarifies for us that he knows there is no issue of shame (*bizayon*) to the tefillin, but he suspects there may be an incompatibility issue. So he asks Rav Yehudah.

In answer, Rav Yehudah cites for him Shmuel's statement: "*mutar afilu ishto imo.*" Now this, of course, does not necessarily answer Rav Yosef son of Rav Nechunya's question. It only answers him if Rav Yosef son of Rav Nechunya's question is grounded in the assumption that the presence of the person's wife in the bed as well makes things worse, to which Shmuel would then be saying no, it is permitted to have tefillin on the bed even in the event that the person's wife is also present. But Rav Yosef son of Rav Nechunya might hold of a *sevara* that would maintain that *ishto imo* would actually be better. And then how does the statement from Shmuel—who obviously doesn't hold that way—answer Rav Yosef's question?

Well, what might that *sevara* be?

I SUGGEST RAV Yosef son of Rav Nechunya's *sevara* is as follows: Tefillin is a symbol (*os*) of the *k'rias Shema* recitation, extending the message of *k'rias Shema* across the entire rest of the day. What is the message of *k'rias Shema*? It is the need to accept upon ourselves the responsibility of God's dominion (*kabbalas ol malchus Shamayim*). But, as we have learned elsewhere (see pages 72-75), the alter ego of *kabbalas ol malchus Shamayim* is the receiving of the Divine Presence (*kabbalas p'nei haShechinah*). The reason why Shabbos is exempt from tefillin is precisely this reason—with the *kabbalas p'nei haShechinah* that it brings, Shabbos already serves as a sufficiently effective symbol such that we can dispense with the need for the *os* of tefillin.

Now, we know that a man and wife channel the *Shechinah* between them (*ish v'ishto Shechinah sheruyah beneihem*), so their presence on a bed presents no conflict with tefillin being on the same bed. But a man who is lying **alone** on a bed, symbolizing a man without his completion and unable to channel the Divine Presence, may appear to be a contradiction to what tefillin represents, and is therefore, conjectures Rav Yosef son of Rav Nuchunya, an affront to the tefillin when in their presence.

So what is Rav Yehudah's answer to Rav Yosef son of Rav Nechunya?

Rav Yehudah answers by saying that both Shmuel—who held the issue was worse with *ishto imo* (the *sevara* being that too much physicality is a *setirah* to the *kedushah* of tefillin—otherwise why would the tefillin "object" to a situation of mitzvah?) and nevertheless *paskens* it's *mutar afilu ishto imo*—**and** the *Beraisa*—that overrules Shmuel but is untroubled by the lesser level of physicality of one man lying on the bed alone (without the added suggestion of physicality represented by the presence of one's wife)—both agree that it is *mutar* for a lone man to sleep on a bed with tefillin near him. And if there existed the kind of affront that is of concern to Rav Yosef son of Rav Nechunya, continues Rav Yehudah, neither Shmuel nor the *Beraisa* would have permitted that.

Indeed, Rava's willingness to permit *ishto imo* for the sake of protecting the tefillin is a further boost to the premise that *ishto imo* actually carries a strong case for being *mutar* through Rav Yosef son of Rav Nechunya's reasoning. *Ishto imo* is the *os* of tefillin lived out! And it is why Rava made such a show of it being *halachah l'maaseh*.

So that brings Rav Yosef son of Rav Nechunya to his next question. If you are willing to permit the *os* even without the lived-out form being present, are you willing to permit the **actual** *kabbalas ol malchus Shamayim*—*k'rias Shema* itself—while a man is in bed in physical contact with his wife? Man and wife might be the lived-out version of the *os*, but even the finest *os* is still just a symbol of the real thing—it is only a *mashal*. So is it allowed for a man to be *mekabel ol malchus Shamayim*—the real thing—while feeling connected to his wife—who is only the *mashal* for the *Shechinah*?

Actually connecting with his wife is certainly a contradiction to connecting to Hashem; its intense physicality overtakes its signature role in realizing *Shechinah sheruyah beneihem*, so face-to-face (i.e., *ervah*-to-*ervah*) is out. But back-to-back physical contact (i.e., not connect**ing**, but simply being physically connect**ed**), is that sufficiently unassuming, or is it still a contradiction to the notion of reciting *k'rias Shema*?

To that, Rav Yehudah answers again with his quote from Shmuel (by tefillin). You see, says Rav Yehudah, Shmuel does not consider "physicality" per se a reason to block *kabbalas ol malchus Shamayim*. Now the

Berachos 24a

Beraisa does, but that is only for *expressive* physicality, not for ordinary physicality. So the issue you are asking about, Rav Yosef son of Rav Nechunya—*k'rias Shema* while one is in contact with his human sense of physicality—must be permitted too. (This is why the second Gemara doesn't say **mutar** *afilu ishto imo*, so you would recognize this is just a partial quote from his earlier statement.)

On hearing this response-and-conclusion from Rav Yehudah, Rav Yosef erupts. "What are you talking about, Rav Yehudah? You can't conclude from Shmuel's statement in tefillin that physicality between any two people is compatible with saying *k'rias Shema*! Don't you understand? The issue is *hirhur taavah*, not challenges to the *kedushah* of *kabbalas p'nei haShechinah*! Shmuel's *afilu ishto imo* may have been saying the *hirhur* factor of a person's own wife is low enough to allow tefillin to be placed on the same bed, but it certainly would not be that low a factor when the man is lying on a bed together with other people, for example family members!"

The proof to our explanation of Rav Yosef son of Rav Nechunya's issue is the existence of the immediate next *sugya*—that of *agavos*. As we demonstrate in our *shiur* on that *sugya*, it is clear that the entire discussion about *agavos* centers on the issue of reciting *k'rias Shema* while in physical contact with *agavos*, specifically whether buttocks are too physical for connection with them to be compatible with *k'rias Shema*. That is an extension of precisely the issue being raised here by Rav Yosef son of Rav Nechunya, as understood by Rav Yehudah—to whom he had posed the question.

Only after this discussion ends does the Gemara proceed to its next topic—an examination of which items constitute **non**-physical experiential *ervah* (both visual and aural).

So, first of all, we now understand why this was a *"maskif lah"* from Rav Yosef. An ordinary *machlokes* would look like this: Rav Yosef son of Rav Nechunya asks a question, (Rav Yehudah *amar*) Shmuel answers it one way, and Rav Yosef challenges that answer and instead answers it another way. Here, what happened was Rav Yosef son of Rav Nechunya asked a question; (Rav Yehudah *amar* Shmuel) answered it in accordance with his understanding of the questioner's presumptions about the issue; Rav Yosef came along and offered an alternative answer to the question, **but to do so he attacked Rav Yehudah's entire understanding of the question.** Rav Yehudah had answered the question—using a statement of Shmuel—understanding the question as one of possible spiritual incompatibility. Rav Yosef says that cannot be the answer **because that was not the question.** The question was a question of *hirhur aveirah* undermining the mitzvah performance, argues Rav Yosef. That is a *"maskif lah,"* not an ordinary alternative answer.

But now we also understand how, at least according to Rav Yehudah's understanding of the question, we could bring a discredited statement made by Shmuel about an unrelated issue. It is because we are using the fact that even Shmuel **could have said what he said** as the proof we need to answer our question.

And now we can appreciate why the *Rosh* might be uncomfortable relying on everyone's agreement that reciting *k'rias Shema afilu ishto imo* is *mutar*. No one actually ever made that statement in connection with reciting *k'rias Shema*! Shmuel said it only with regard to tefillin. Rav Yehudah extended it to *k'rias Shema*, but only under the assumption that the issue being questioned was one of spiritual incompatibility. But in attacking Rav Yehudah, Rav Yosef claims the question is really about *hirhurim* compromising the mitzvah. Under **that** presumption, we have no basis to extend *shitas* Shmuel to *k'rias Shema afilu ishto imo*. And without a resolution of the actual *machlokes* between Rav Yehudah and Rav Yosef, we truly do not know what the halachah is regarding reciting *k'rias Shema* in bed while one's wife is also present in the same bed, and the *Rosh* is right to caution us to be *machmir*, especially when there are *Beraisos* that forbid the practice!

We have thus answered all four of our original questions.

דף כד. (2)

אמר מר זה מחזיר פניו וקורא ק"ש והא איכא
עגבות וגו'.

The Master said: This one can turn away [from the other] and recite k'rias Shema [and so can the other]. But what about the agavos?...

1. The Gemara concludes that it is permissible to say *Shema* in a bed, unclothed, back-to-back with another person. The question is asked regarding the *agavos* (buttocks) that are touching (*Rashi*)—isn't that a problem? We see from the fact that it is not considered a problem that Rav Huna must be right when he says *agavos* do not carry with them a designation of *ervah*. The Gemara next tries to bring a proof from a Mishnah in *Challah* that teaches that a woman can say a *berachah* when unclothed sitting on the ground, as she can conceal her *ervah*, while the man in a similar position cannot. The first question is: Who needs a Mishnah to tell me basic anatomical truths about the difference between men's and women's bodies? Isn't it self-evident what a woman can conceal and a man cannot?

2. The proof to Rav Huna is said to be from the fact that the Mishnah is not concerned about the exposed *agavos* of the seated woman. The proof is deflected by Rav Nachman bar Yitzchak, who learns the case to be about a woman whose lower *panim* is "*tuchos b'karka*," so that there is no *agavos* exposure. But one can ask: Her lower *panim* was already flush against the ground when we were learning the Mishnah *before* we brought Rav Nachman bar Yitzchak; how is there any difference between the original way we learned the Mishnah and Rav Nachman bar

Yitzchak's way? And if you will answer that in Rav Nachman bar Yitzchak's view her entire lower half is buried in sand up to her torso, thus completely covering both her front *and* her backside—a position that would cover even a **man's** *ervah*—so why would the Mishnah allow only a woman to say a *berachah* while seated that way?

3. Even without Rav Nachman bar Yitzchak, the Mishnah itself is difficult to understand in terms of *metzi'us*. What kind of *agavos* exposure is there when a person is sitting on the ground? How was it ever a proof to Rav Huna?

4. Because of the difficulty explaining Rav Nachman bar Yitzchak, the Vilna Gaon learns a different *mehalach* in the Gemara. He learns that the Gemara concludes not with a **failure** to bring a proof to Rav Huna, but rather with a valid proof. A sitting woman can conceal her lower *panim* but not her *agavos*, and so we see that *agavos* are not *ervah*. Rav Nachman bar Yitzchak only adds a further point—that until she is seated "*tuchos b'karka*" her *ervah* is not considered concealed. This *mehalach* is difficult for a number of reasons. For one thing, the Vilna Gaon is forced to change the *girsa* from "*leima mesayei'a lei*" to "*mesayei'a lei.*" For another, it is unusual for the Gemara to bring a second "*mesayei'a lei*" right after a first one, especially when the first one goes unchallenged. Also, what would have made Rav Nachman bar Yitzchak assume that the "*b'karka*" of the Mishnah did **not** mean "*tuchos b'karka*"—what else could it have meant? And why does the Gemara feel Rav Nachman's input into how to properly conceal front-side *ervah* has anything to do with the *sugya* of *agavos*?

5. Really, how can anyone genuinely argue that *agavos* are not an *ervah*? Isn't it self-evident that the sight of bare *agavos* produces *hirhurim*? Why else is there an instinct to cover them the same way other curvaceous portions of the body get covered? Isn't it clear that *agavos* are part of the shapeliness the Torah refers to as *yefas to'ar*—certainly more so than the *panim shel matah*? Indeed, despite our Gemara, the *Shulchan Aruch* and the *Eliyah*

Berachos 24a

Rabbah come out *l'halachah* that *agavos* **do** have a *din ervah*. How could Rav Huna be saying that *agavos* are not an *ervah*?

6. The Gemara's question, as we saw in *Rashi*, was from *agavos* **touching**. Why are we bringing in Rav Huna, whose issue was the *ervah* of **seeing** exposed *agavos*?

Yesod

I would like to suggest another approach in the Gemara, using the *chiluk* made by the Vilna Gaon, but taking it in a different direction.

The Vilna Gaon distinguishes between "*yosheves...b'karka*" and "*tuchos b'karka*." I think this difference recognizes that the normal way a person sits on the ground is actually not with his bottom flat on the ground but rather with his legs tucked beneath his body. This mode of sitting will not guarantee full concealment of the *panim shel matah*, so when the Mishnah tells us a woman is able to conceal her lower *panim*, Rav Nachman bar Yitzchak rightly points out that the only kind of "*yosheves b'karka*" that will enable the complete concealment of the *ervah* is the sitting on the ground that is done directly on one's posterior, with legs out in front of the body—a position known as "*tuchos b'karka*."

So far, so good. But I believe the issue here is not one of exposure of the *agavos*.

The *ervah* issue in halachah actually comprises two concerns—(1) exposure to *ervah*, and (2) contact with—or touching—*ervah*. The two concerns address two different problems. Being **exposed** to *ervah* leads to *hirhurim*—distracting images that will disrupt the *berachah* or *tefillah* in which one is trying to engage. On the other hand, being **in contact** with *ervah* means being too closely linked to that part of the body (ours or someone else's) that stands at the polar opposite of contact with *Shamayim*. The *ervah* comprises the earthliest part of our existence, and contact with it must be avoided during activities that demand *kedushah* the same way contact with a corpse must be avoided by one who wishes to engage in activities that demand *taharah*.

The question in our Gemara, as *Rashi* tells us, has to do with contact with *agavos*. The proof to Rav Huna, then, must logically be a proof to his view on contact with *agavos*. Using the Vilna Gaon's *chiluk*, it is easy to see the proof the Mishnah in *Challah* appears to afford:

"A woman can say a *berachah* unclothed and seated on the ground." Isn't the normal way to sit on the ground the way that has one's legs tucked up under one's bottom? And if the woman is unclothed, isn't there a concern that, in this position, her heels will be in direct contact with her *agavos*? It must be proof that *agavos* are not an *ervah* problem—**meaning they are not a contact-with-*ervah* problem**. Let us say this is a proof to Rav Huna, who claims there is no contact-with-*ervah* problem with *agavos* (he may hold *m'sevara* that the *agavos* are not involved in the procreative process and are thus no more indicative of our earthly nature than the fleshy parts of our arms or legs).

To this, Rav Nachman bar Yitzchak responds that there is no proof from the Mishnah. The Mishnah only permits a woman to recite *berachos* in an unclothed state **when she is sitting "*tuchos b'karka*"**—with her *agavos* directly in contact with the ground and not with her feet. The Mishnah never permitted her to say a *berachah* while in contact with her *agavos*, thus we have no proof that *agavos* are free of *ervah*-contact concerns.

It turns out that neither Rav Huna nor the Gemara were ever even discussing the issue of **visual exposure** to *agavos*, where all would no doubt agree that they cause *hirhurim* and therefore have a *din ervah*, which is why *Shulchan Aruch* and *Eliyah Rabbah* are not contradicting our Gemara when they point that out.

And now we understand why a Mishnah was needed to teach us about men's anatomy. The Mishnah is not telling us that men cannot conceal their *ervah*. Indeed, maybe they can! The point is that even if they would conceal it from view by sitting in a way that their legs conceal the *gid*, nevertheless, their legs are still in contact with the concealed *gid* as it extends out from the body, and thus men remain prohibited from saying *berachos*, though not due to *ervah* visibility, but rather due to contact with their own *ervah*.

It is only in the *sugya* coming up further down the *amud* that the Gemara first takes on the issue of visual exposure to *ervah*. For now, the only issue is *ervah* contact.

דף כה. (1)

אמר רב פפא פי חזיר כצואה עוברת דמי וגו׳.

Rav Papa said: A pig's snout is comparable to passing excrement.

Gemara: Isn't that obvious?

Answer: Its point is that this is so even if the pig has just emerged from a cleansing river.

Rav Yehudah said: If there is a doubt about the presence of excrement, we assume it is present and we are forbidden from reciting Shema. If there is a doubt about the presence of urine, we assume it is not present and we are permitted to say Shema.

Another Version—

Rav Yehudah said: If there is a doubt about the presence of excrement in a house, we assume it is not present and we may say Shema. If there is a doubt about the presence of excrement in a landfill dump, we assume it is present and we may not say Shema. If there is a doubt about the presence of urine, we assume it is not present—even in a landfill dump—and we may say Shema. And in this, he follows Rav Hamnuna, who follows Rav Yonasan, who notes that in one place the Torah insinuates that it does not require the covering of waste while in another it **commands** the covering of waste. To explain this, Rav Yonasan avers that the former is addressing urine while the latter excrement. Accordingly, says Rav Hamnuna, the presence of urine [other than the actual urination stream] is restricted only Rabbinically, and when the Rabbis issued their restriction, they did so only against the **known** presence of urine. They made no enactment against the **possible** presence of urine.

The question to ask here is: We have a rule already in place called *safek d'Rabbanan l'kula* telling us that all questionable cases regarding Rabbinic restriction are to be decided leniently. The Gemara is addressing the leniency we find by urine. Why does it say that the leniency we can adopt regarding *safek mei raglayim* is due to the fact that the Rabbinic restriction never extended to cases of *safek* urine, when even if they had made no such distinction, it would have been permitted anyway because of *safek d'Rabbanan l'kula*?

Another question: Why is the discussion of *safek* human waste introduced with the statement by Rav Papa about a pig's snout?

I'D LIKE TO suggest there is a difference between a *safek* in fact and a *safek* in halachah. With a *safek* in **fact**, the reality is definitely in existence. It is one of two possibilities, but its nature is just hidden from us. The urine is either there or it is not there. In that case, since we don't know what to do, we turn to the Torah, and the Torah tells us to decide stringently if it is a *d'Oraisa* (because, after all, if something were *safek* poison, you wouldn't eat it even if the chance were minute), and leniently if it is a *d'Rabbanan*.

With a *safek* in **halachah**, there is no certainty of any reality. We do not know if any halachah has been established at all. And even if it has, until we have a ruling, we never know if a particular case is covered by that ruling until it is so ruled. With this kind of *safek*, we are not able to turn to our standard *safek* approach, because maybe the halachah, whose parameters we do not know, has overridden the standard approach!

ACCORDING TO THE first version in Rav Yehudah, the issue was a *safek metzi'us* (fact): Is there excrement and/or urine or is there not? Excrement is *d'Oraisa*, so we are strict. Urine is *d'Rabbanan*, so we are lenient.

But according to the second version, we are clearly not dealing with a *safek b'metzi'us*. If we were, how could we be lenient with excrement—a *d'Oraisa*—just because we are in a house? Even if the probability in a

Berachos 25a

house is smaller, do we not avoid taking even small risks when a *d'Oraisa* is at stake?

According to the second version, the whole question is a *safek* in halachah. We cannot apply *safek d'Rabbanan l'kula*. But we can understand the *gezeirah* the rabbis made to include urine. Urine is very different from excrement. While excrement is all waste, urine is considered by some experts to be perfectly clean and sterile. It is the product of filtered blood processed by kidneys designed to rid the body of toxins. It could be called "processed water" more aptly than "waste water."

EVEN IN THE Mishnah, urine shows it has great theoretical value. In its discussion about the components of the *ketores*, the Mishnah says that *mei raglayim* would actually have been a fine ingredient to add pungency to the mix, just that the objectionable nature of its origin disqualifies it.

SO LET'S GO back to our second version above. How could Rav Yehudah justify not being concerned about the possibility of excrement being in the house? Isn't it a *safek d'Oraisa*? The answer is that now that we know we are dealing with a *safek* in halachah, we can take a look at the matter from a halachic prespective. We have a halachic precedent that tells us we do not have to check something if the item is not normally brought there. That is the rule of *makom she'ein machnisin bo chametz*. If there is a place where *chametz* is not introduced, it does not need to be checked. And even though *bedikas chametz* is *d'Rabbanan*, *chametz* itself is a serious *d'Oraisa*, and the *Chachamim* would not have taken liberties in the search they enacted if the principles upon which it was based were not sound, *d'Oraisa*-compatible principles.

Rav Yehudah simply holds that a house with regard to human waste is the equivalent of a *makom she'ein machnisin bo chametz*, giving us halachic license to assume none is ever present unless and until we see it. A landfill dump, in contrast, is considered a *makom she'machnisin bo tzo'ah*, telling us we are halachically obligated to assume *tzo'ah* is there unless and until we have proven to the contrary (not because of any probability of its presence, but purely by halachic dictate). But with regard to urine, it is considered a *makom she'ein machnisin bo mei raglayim*. Unless and until we know it to be present, the assumption can be made that it is not there. If it **is** known and present (either in a dump or at home), urine will be a Rabbinical barrier to *k'rias Shema*, for the same reason it was declared ineligible for inclusion in the Temple incense.

AND NOW WE can see why the Gemara introduced this *sugya* with the case of the pig's snout.

The Gemara was setting up the idea that even if something can be clean of *tzo'ah* from a standpoint of *metzi'us*, it can still be considered *tzo'ah* from the standpoint of halachah, which is the entire basis for the approach of the second version of Rav Yehudah, the version embraced by halachah.

AS PROOF, IF you notice you will see that the *machlokes* between the *makshan* ("Isn't that obvious?") and the *tartzan* ("It is so even if the pig has just emerged from a cleansing river") by Rav Papa is an exact parallel of the *machlokes* between the first version in Rav Yehudah and the second: Are we to look at borderline *tzo'ah* questions as questions of *metzi'us* or as questions of halachah?

Berachos 25a

דף כה. (2)

צואה אפילו כחרס אסורה וגו׳.

[In the presence of] human waste—even if it is as dry and brittle as pottery—it is forbidden [to recite k'rias Shema]...

1. The Gemara here tells us one is not allowed to recite *k'rias Shema* in the presence of human waste (*tzo'ah*). This is based on a *pasuk* that requires our military to maintain a clean camp out of respect for the presence of the *Shechinah*. Our ancient adversaries seem to have had a special fixation on human waste. Pharaoh maintained his image as a god by pretending to have no need of excretion; a popular Moabite worship was Baal Peor, which called for defecation in front of the idol. Is there some lesson to be learned from the contrast between the Torah's perspective on *tzo'ah* and our enemies' obsession with it?

2. The Gemara says once *tzo'ah* has dried beyond the dryness of pottery, the restriction against reciting *k'rias Shema* is lifted. There is a *machlokes* Amora'im whether that point has been reached when the *tzo'ah* can be **thrown** without breaking (*nifreches*), or when the *tzo'ah* can be **rolled** without breaking. What is the issue?

3. On that Gemara, there is a *machlokes* Rishonim. *Rashi* says the *chumrah* position is the one that holds the *tzo'ah* must be able to be *rolled* and stay intact. *Rabbeinu Yonah* holds the *chumrah* position is the one that holds the *tzo'ah* must be able to be *thrown* and remain intact. What is the significance of this *machlokes*?

4. The word "*karpas*" has two possible meanings. One possibility is to see it as related to "*chur karpas u'techeiles*" from *Megillas*

דף כה.

Esther. The other is to see it as a backward rendition of *"samech perech,"* telling us that six hundred thousand souls performed difficult labor. What is at the root of this duality?

Yesod

The *Perishah*, having declared that a *machlokes* in the Gemara cannot possibly exist over the *metzi'us* of whether a a piece of rolled *tzo'ah* or a piece of thrown *tzo'ah* takes longer to break, explains that the *machlokes* between *Rashi* and *Rabbeinu Yonah* has to be about the definition of the word *"nifreches."*

Rashi holds *"nifreches"* means "broken apart." Thus, he holds rolling is a bigger *chumrah*. A piece of drying *tzo'ah* is far more likely to break apart upon being thrown than it is upon the gentler process of being rolled. To have to wait to say *k'rias Shema* until a rolled *tzo'ah* is brittle enough to break apart is going to require a lot more dryness than to have it break being thrown.

Rabbeinu Yonah holds *"nifreches"* means "crushed." So he holds the bigger *chumrah* is throwing, as a piece of *tzo'ah* encountering a lot of ground resistance is much more likely to be crushed than one encountering mostly air.

This becomes relevant to the Haggadah when we realize that the word *"nifreches"* is related to the phrase *"avodas perech"* that we translated earlier as "difficult labor." Based on the *Perishah*, then, we will be able to explain the *machlokes* between the two possible meanings of the word *"karpas."*

IF *"NIFRECHES"* MEANS "broken apart," *avodas perech* will be a reference to the hard, physical work the B'nei Yisrael were made to endure, as in the term "backbreaking labor." The word *"karpas,"* will derive from the word *"karpas"* in the *Megillah*. *"Karpas"* there means cotton, one of the choice fabrics spread out at Achashveirosh's party. But harvesting cotton is known to be a backbreaking, labor-intensive operation, requiring slave labor, as was seen in the early American South. It is clear that such a term could easily earn a second life as a reference to whatever backbreaking work the Israelites were made to undergo, and—with

Berachos 25a

ancient Egypt well-known for its cotton production—may well have been the exact kind of labor that broke our ancestors' bodies.

If, however, *"nifreches"* means "crushed," *avodas perech* will refer not to an assault on the body, but rather to an assault on the spirit, as in the phrase, "their spirit was crushed." The chief way this was accomplished was by Pharaoh dispiriting the Israelites by forcing the men to do women's work and the women to do men's work. Rav Yochanan Zweig, *shlita*, explains that this notion is indicated in the abbreviation *"samech perech,"* in the fact that it presents the phrase in reverse (*"karpas"* instead of *"saprach"*), a hint to the spirit-crushing "reversal" of gender roles.

It now becomes clear why this entire discussion is linked to *k'rias Shema*. Mitzrayim was a place that could not host the Divine Presence, primarily because the Egyptians were too caught up imagining themselves as divine beings. *K'rias Shema* is the antithesis of Mitzrayim, because it is all about *kabbalas p'nei haShechinah*, an adjunct to *kabbalas ol malchus Shamayim*. Rather than an Egyptian viewpoint, which attempts either to deny human waste or make it a sacrament, *yetzias Mitzrayim* implanted a Torah viewpoint, seeing *tzo'ah* as a necessary part of human existence but one that can and must be managed and controlled in order to create an atmosphere conducive to the *Shechinah* living among and within us.

דף כה. (3)

קטנים לא אסרה תורה אלא כנגד עמוד בלבד הא נפול לארעא שרי ורבנן הוא דגזרו בהו וגו׳.

The Torah prohibition against reciting k'rias Shema opposite urine covers the urine stream only. Once it has fallen to the ground, the Torah permits it. It is the Rabbis who continue to forbid it, and only when its presence is definite, not questionable.

So when urine is definitely present, until what point does reciting Shema in its presence remain prohibited?

Said Rav Yehudah, quoting Shmuel: As long as it is wet.

And so said Rabbah bar Rav Huna, quoting Rabbi Yochanan: As long as it is wet.

And so said Ulla: As long as it is wet.

Geniva said in the name of Rav: As long as the outline of its stain can still be seen.

Rav Yosef said: O Master, please forgive Geniva! If by excrement, Rav Yehudah quotes Rav as saying that once its surface has dried it is permitted, is there any doubt that Rav will permit urine once it has dried?

Rava rules: Excrement dry as pottery is prohibited; urine as long as it is wet.

A challenge is raised from a Beraisa: "Urine remains prohibited as long as it is wet; if it got absorbed [in the ground] or evaporated [from on top of rocks], it is permitted." If absorption is being compared to evaporation, just as evaporation leaves no stain, must we not conclude that the absorption must be of the type that leaves no stain—ein rishuman nikar? Apparently, urine remains prohibited even after it is no longer wet!

The Gemara responds: That may be how you will read the seifa, but how will you read the reisha: "Urine remains prohibited as long as it is wet" implies that once it is dry it is permitted even if a stain remains. This Beraisa cannot be buttonholed either way.

A different Beraisa appears to anticipate the machlokes Rav and Shmuel: "If urine spilled from a vessel, one is not allowed to say Shema opposite the vessel. As far as the urine itself, if it has been absorbed, it is permitted; if not, it is prohibited. Rabbi Yose says, as long as it is wet." "Absorbed" here cannot mean that it is has dried, with "not absorbed" meaning it is still wet, for then what is Rabbi Yose adding by saying "as long as it is wet"? Once it has dried it is permitted? Tanna Kama already said that! It must be that "absorbed" means it remains prohibited until **no stain** is left [like Rav], and Rabbi Yose is permitting Shema in front of urine that has dried even if a stain is still there [like Shmuel]!

No, responds the Gemara. All agree that it is prohibited only as long as it is wet, and that once it has dried it is permitted, even if the stain can still be seen. The difference between them will be found only where the urine is wet enough to wet another thing. [Rashi comments: Tanna Kama will require that it be wet enough to wet another thing, and Rabbi Yose will be stringent.]

When the *Beraisa* featuring *Tanna Kama* and Rabbi Yose was first brought, we thought *Tanna Kama* was requiring no stain (like Rav) and Rabbi Yose was requiring only dryness, even if the stain could still be seen (like Shmuel). In response we said there is no difference between the two Tanna'im in the ordinary case of urine. All agree it is prohibited only as long as it remains wet, and having a stain in sight is OK. The difference between them is found only in a case of urine that is wet enough to wet something else.

What does this mean? If it means that while they **don't** argue about how dry *ordinary wet* urine must get, but they **do** argue about how dry *sopping wet* urine must get, why is *Tanna Kama* suddenly the *meikil*? Let *Tanna Kama* say sopping wet urine must become super dry (no stain), and let Rabbi Yose say it is enough to be plain dry, and have Rabbi Yose continue to be the *meikil*!

And even if you can show me some reason why *Tanna Kama* must now be lenient and Rabbi Yose strict, why does *Rashi* use the phrase, "*Tanna Kama* will require *tofei'ach al m'nas l'hafti'ach*"? Does it mean he'll require the urine to be sopping wet before he'll declare an *issur*? That's not true; we just said all agree that ordinary urine is prohibited until it dries. Does it mean he'll require it to be sopping wet before he's willing to be *matir* even with a stain still in sight? That's not true; he just agreed ordinary urine is *mutar* when it has dried even if *rishuman nikar*. Does it mean he'll require *ein rishuman nikar* (super dry) for a urine patch that is sopping wet? Then *Rashi's* phrase should have been "*Tanna Kama* will require super dry by sopping wet urine," not "*Tanna Kama* will require sopping wet urine"! And, anyway, that would leave Rabbi Yose as the *meikil*, which *Rashi* says is not the case. So what does *Rashi* mean?

Furthermore, in the *Beraisa*, the word "*nivle'u*" meant one of two things: super dry or plain dry. So how can the *Rambam* (in *Hilchos K'rias Shema* 3:7) say that "*nivle'u*" encompasses two possibilities: wet and sopping wet? Doesn't "*nivle'u*" mean the urine has dried?

And another question: At the Gemara's end, how dry does sopping wet urine have to get for it to be *mutar*? If it has to get to super dry, how does it make sense that a wetter start has to get to a super-dry finish? From a wetter starting point, it took an awful lot of drying just to get to plain dry. Why isn't that good enough?

Finally, if the *machlokes Tanna Kama* and Rabbi Yose is over *tofei'ach al menas l'hafti'ach*, the Gemara should say: *Tofei'ach al m'nas l'hafti'ach ika beineihu* ("sopping wet" is the difference between them). If instead

Berachos 25a

what the Gemara meant to say was that it is **in** the case of *tofei'ach al menas l'hafti'ach* that you will find the difference between them, the phrase should be *b'tofei'ach al menas l'hafti'ach pligi* (in a "sopping wet" case they argue).

What kind of a phrase is *b'tofei'ach al menas l'hafti'ach ika beineihu*?

--- *Yesod* ---

In a previous chapter on *tzo'ah*, we had noted that there were two *issurim*—an *issur d'Oraisa* that applies to moist *tzo'ah*, and an *issur d'Rabbanan* that continues to apply even to dry *tzo'ah* until it reaches enough dryness to be considered dirt.

We were also advised, at the outset of our Gemara, that the Torah has only a limited *issur* on *mei raglayim*—that *"mei raglayim eino assur m'd'Oraisa ela kilu'ach bilvad*—[Reciting sacred matters in the presence of] urine is Torah-prohibited only before an actual stream [from a urinating person]."

Rambam brings the *din* of *tzo'ah d'Oraisa* in *Hilchos K'rias Shema* 3:6. He then says *v'chein mei raglayim*. **This *"mei raglayim"* in the *Rambam* is the *din* of *mei raglayim d'Oraisa*.** It is *assur* only *b'kilu'ach*—when originating from a urinating person—and it remains *assur* until it is absorbed in the earth. This is logical. Urine in midstream doesn't stop being *mei raglayim* when it is cascading through the air. So too, it doesn't stop being *mei raglayim* when it is lying pooled on the ground. It stops being *mei raglayim* when it gets absorbed into the ground to the point that we now have "wet ground" and no longer "distinct *mei raglayim*." When all of it is absorbed, we have no more *issur d'Oraisa*. If it lands on a non-absorbent surface, the urine remains *assur m'd'Oraisa* until it evaporates to the point that it is no longer wet (a stain remaining behind presents no problem—for the *d'Oraisa* we are only interested in what bears the definition *"mei raglayim"*). This is the position of all opinions.

The split between *Tanna Kama* and *Rabbi Yose* occurs in the *issur d'Rabbanan* that parallels dry *tzo'ah* in the laws of *mei raglayim*. There remains an *issur d'Rabbanan* even after *mei raglayim* are absorbed and the *issur d'Oraisa* has passed. This is because even after they are no longer defined *min haTorah* as *mei raglayim*, they remain offensive to human sensibilities, and one cannot properly concentrate on *k'rias Shema* in their presence. In this, we find a *machlokes Tanna Kama* and Rabbi Yose. While both agree there is an *issur d'Rabbanan* that kicks in after *nivle'u*, *Tanna Kama* will not declare this *issur* unless it is *tofei'ach al menas l'hafti'ach*. Rabbi Yose is *machmir* and will declare it even at regular *tofei'ach*.

You can hear it in the *lashon* of the Gemara: *B'tofei'ach al menas l'hafti'ach ika beineihu*—In a case of sopping wet absorbed urine we will discover an *ika beineihu*, that the *Tanna Kama* considers that to be the **only** case of an *issur d'Rabbanan* and Rabbi Yose will **not** consider it the only case of an *issur d'Rabbanan*.

This is *Rashi*—*Tanna Kama* requires *tofei'ach al menas l'hafti'ach* **after absorption in the earth** in order to have a new *issur d'Rabbanan*, and Rabbi Yose is *machmir*, declaring a post-absorption *issur d'Rabbanan* even if the wet ground is just *tofei'ach*.

The basis of their *machlokes* is their difference over what is the cause of the new *issur*. Both agree it is because of its offensiveness to human sensibilities. But Rabbi Yose claims the sensibility is the offensive awareness that this material just came out of a human being's animal-like orifice. *Tanna Kama* disagrees and claims it is the fear he harbors that this offensive material will splash onto him! Thus, Rabbi Yose will be *machmir* and declare the *issur* in the face of any detectible wetness, while *Tanna Kama* will require the material to be capable of re-wetting another thing before he will declare the *issur*.

The *Rambam* in 3:6 is dealing with the *d'Oraisa*, so he says *"v'chein mei raglayim."* It is *assur b'kilu'ach* and remains so as long as it retains its identity as that original *mei raglayim*. But you will notice he does not say when that *issur* stops (i.e., at the point of absorption). This is because it may still go on, if only *m'd'Rabbanan*. In 3:7, after dealing with the *issur tzo'ah m'd'Rabbanan*, he *paskens* like *Tanna Kama* and states the condition under which we would go on and face an *issur mei raglayim m'd'Rabbanan* after *nivle'u* ends the *issur d'Oraisa*. That condition is *tofei'ach al menas l'hafti'ach*—sufficient wetness that it would wet the hand.

Berachos 25a

So everyone agrees that as long as the urine is wet it is *assur*, because that is the *issur d'Oraisa* that lasts until *nivle'u* or *yavshu*.

Like the *Tanna Kama*, at *nivle'u* or *yavshu* the *issur* is over, unless it is sopping wet ("*martivin ha'yad*" in the language of the *Rambam*) after *nivle'u*, in which case it is still *assur* albeit now only *m'd'Rabbanan*.

Like Rabbi Yose, as long as it is wet prior to *nivle'u* the urine is *assur*—*d'Oraisa*—and plain dry is enough dryness to make it *mutar* after it has been *nivle'u*. But wetness after *nivle'u*, while not a problem *m'd'Oraisa*, will remain *assur m'd'Rabbanan* (since it is wet after *nivle'u* rather than plain dry) even if it is not sopping wet.

Now we can go back and understand the first *Beraisa*. We can now explain that it is referring exclusively to cases that remain on the *d'Oraisa* level. They are *assur* as long as they are *matpichin*—unabsorbed wet—and they are *mutar* once they are evaporated or dry-absorbed (the *nivle'u* that is *dumia* to *yavshu*). And neither requires *ein rishuman nikar* (super dry).

We also understand the *Beraisa* with the *machlokes*. That one is about the *issur mei raglayim m'd'Rabbanan*. That is why its case is given as "spilled urine." Spilled urine cannot be *assur d'Oraisa*, because it is disembodied from the person whose body produced it; it cannot be called *kilu'ach*. *Tanna Kama* says *nivle'u mutar lo nivle'u assur*, which is true for a *nivle'u* that is no wetter than *tofei'ach*. But in that same case, Rabbi Yose would declare even *nivle'u* to be *assur*, therefore he just says *kol z'man she'matpichin assur*—to which all agree—and *rishuman nikar shari*, which is his way of saying if it is dry after absorption it will be *mutar*, but not all *nivle'u* is **mutar** as a blanket statement. Where it is still wet, still *tofei'ach*, it remains *assur*, albeit *m'd'Rabbanan*.

If the case had been "*nivle'u aval adayin tofei'ach al menas l'haftiach*—absorbed but still wet enough to wet something else," *Tanna Kama* would have left out *nivle'u mutar*, because it would now be *assur* once again—*m'd'Rabbanan*.

TO SUPPORT MY idea of the split between the *d'Oraisa* and *d'Rabbanan* levels of the *issur* of *mei raglayim*, just look at the *pitum ha'ketores*. There, in describing the need for a pungent substance, the Mishnah says, "*Mei raglayim* would be good for this purpose, but we cannot bring in *mei raglayim* because of the *kavod*." I was always bothered—if urine is recognized as being an effective medium for honoring God, should it not be considered *prima facie* a thing of *kavod*?

Now the answer is clear. God would have been fine with the introduction of urine to the *ketores*. It would come from vessels, not from a *kilu'ach*, so it would be perfectly fine *m'd'Oraisa*. But because it would trigger our human sensibilities, it cannot be used despite its suitability. It is our own sense of *kavod* that would be assailed.

דף כה: (1)

ירד לטבול אם יכול לעלות כו׳ ואם לאו יתכסה במים ויקרא. והרי לבו רואה את הערוה וגו׳.

If one had [already] descended [into the mikveh] to immerse when the time for reciting k'rias Shema arrived, if he is able to emerge, dress, and recite Shema prior to sunrise, he should do so; and if not, he could cover himself with the water and recite. But is his heart not still able to see his ervah?...

1. The *Rambam* in *Hilchos K'rias Shema* 3:16 says the solution to the *issur* of saying *k'rias Shema* facing another person's *ervah* is to look away from it. Then, in 3:17, he says:

   וכשם שהוא אסור לקרות כנגד ערות אחרים כך הוא אסור לקרות כנגד ערותו.

   Just as he is not allowed to recite *k'rias Shema* facing others' nakedness, **so too** he is not allowed to recite it facing his own.

   This would suggest that he can solve this problem too by looking away from his own *ervah*. So why does the *Rambam* go on to say:

   לא יקרא כשהוא ערום עד שיכסה ערותו.

   He shall not recite [Shema] when he is naked until he covers his ervah.

   Why must he cover his nakedness? Let him just look away!

2. Furthermore, earlier in 2:7, the *Rambam* says that even if one sets out to be covered in water, it can't be in clear water, because the *ervah* can be seen in the water. So what? Just look away!

3. What is the idea of "*libo ro'eh es ha'ervah*—his heart sees the *ervah*." Hearts don't see!
4. At the end of 3:17, when dismissing one who says *k'rias Shema* under a blanket pressed against his neck, the *Rambam* describes him as "he's like one who reads without a belt." He should say, "like one who reads naked"!
5. We are told that only cloudy water can be an adequate cover, because cloudy water is like being buried in sand (*ar'ah semichta*). But then we are told we can create cloudy water by stirring up bottom dirt with our feet. How is a little swirling dirt the equivalent of being buried in sand?
6. Why does the *Rambam* in 2:7 first say, "be covered in water that is standing there," and then change his language to "be covered...in his place"?
7. *Rama* says the only problem is "his heart seeing the *ervah*," not "his eyes seeing [it]." And thus one would have no halachic issue reciting *k'rias Shema* while standing in clear water up to his waist. Why does the *Rambam* not make this distinction?
8. If all that has to be covered for the recitation of *k'rias Shema* is the *ervah*, why does *Tanna Kama* in the *Beraisa* on 25b say that in clear water one must sit up to his neck?

Yesod

The Gemara in *Menachos* (43b) tells us that David HaMelech once saw himself naked in a bathhouse and fretted that he was disconnected from all mitzvos (no tzitzis, no tefillin, no mezuzah, no permissible Torah study). When he remembered his *bris*, he felt relieved.

One can ask: If David HaMelech "saw" himself naked, why did he have to "remember" that he had a *bris*?

It must be that a person can see something with his eyes, but until he pays attention to what he is seeing, it is not considered that he is seeing it. This paying of attention is what we call "the seeing of the heart," as the heart is always used to denote the seat of awareness (e.g., "*Sim lev*—Pay attention!").

Berachos 25b

When it comes to another person's *ervah*, the entire awareness I have of it is a function of my seeing it. As soon as I look away, I have no more awareness. With my own *ervah*, however, this is not enough. Even if I am looking away from my *ervah*, I may still be aware of it (my heart might be still "seeing" it).

If so, how can I ever say *k'rias Shema*? Aren't I always aware of my nakedness?

No. I am aware of my nakedness only when I feel connected to it, such as when I have no clothes on. In truth, we are always naked underneath our clothes, but as long as we are covered with clothes, we feel dressed, not naked. But sometimes a covering is not enough. For example, if I am completely covered, though only by a loose blanket, I will still feel I am naked under the blanket. Feeling naked, even if all my *ervah* is covered, is what is known as the problem of "one's heart seeing one's *ervah*."

The solution to this problem is to do something or be wearing something that distracts my mind from awareness of my nakedness. One way to do this is to don a *chagurah* (belt). This act of wanting to distinguish between my thinking parts (brain and heart) and my *ervah* parts is an act significant enough to distract myself from *ervah*-overawareness. Of course, without a physical covering, my *ervah* still provokes too much awareness of it in me, so a *chagurah*, which both girds the waist **and** drapes over the *ervah*, is a complete solution.

What if I try to use water? Water is a covering, but it is transparent. If my friend's *ervah* is underwater, I can look away. Or he can stir up dirt and make it cloudy. But what if it is my own *ervah* under the water? The feeling of being naked in water is a feeling of freedom that keeps me in touch with my nakedness and not disconnected from it. With what we are saying, it is not enough to look away, as I will still have an awareness of my naked state under the water—*harei libo ro'eh es ha'ervah*! To this, the Gemara answers: "*mayim akurim shanu*—dirty waters are different." If one is standing in dirty water, one's attention shifts from the feeling of freedom one has in water to the feeling of potential suffocation one could have by being buried in sand or dirt. It becomes the psychological equivalent of *ar'ah semichta*, and *k'rias Shema* can be recited. And even

דף כה:

a little stirring of dirt is enough to trigger that internal psychological shift.

Now the whole *Rambam* makes sense. If I have gone down into a *mikveh* just before *netz ha'chamah*, I have two problems: 1) I am naked, and 2) I am in a *mikveh*, which is the halachic equivalent of a bathhouse. If I can emerge from the *mikveh* room and get dressed all before *netz ha'chamah*, I have resolved both problems, and I should do that rather than tarry and miss the ideal *z'man* for *k'rias Shema*. But what if I cannot do all that in time?

The *Rambam* says to just cover yourself up while standing right there in the water. At this point, the *Rambam* is not yet addressing the question of what materials you might be using to cover yourself with. His point here is that catching the ideal *z'man* for *Shema* will outrank even the requirement to vacate a *beis ha'merchatz* (bathhouse).

But wait! Being covered while in the water—whether by a robe (even a belted one) or by the very water itself—creates a new problem. The freedom of the water is going to leave you feeling naked underneath—*harei libo ro'eh es ha'ervah*! Thus the *Rambam* interrupts the halachah of *z'man netz* outranking *beis ha'merchatz* to give us a list of waters that exacerbate our self-awareness and must be avoided when using this approach. Foul-smelling water reminds us of the rot, which is a function of our physical existence. *Mei mishreh* (work water) makes us aware that we must work to feed our bodies, keeping us connected to our physical side. And clear water makes us feel free in our nakedness (even with a belt—the feeling of freedom stirred by the free movement of the water around our lower parts under the robe is stronger than the sense of self-control invoked by the brain/body separation). But dirty water is fine, because it evokes *ar'ah semichta* rather than freedom, and even a slight stirring of dirt is all it takes to pull that mental trigger (just think about the difference between swimming in a pool and swimming in the ocean). Anyway, once you have worked out the *libo ro'eh es ha'ervah* problem, concludes the *Rambam*, you can say *k'rias Shema* "in his place," without having to exit the bathhouse that is a *mikveh*.

Up to this point, we have answered questions 1, 2, 3, 5, and 6.

Berachos 25b

Now let us explain why (in 3:17) the *Rambam* compares one who recites *k'rias Shema* under a blanket completely loose below his neck to one who is saying *Shema* without a belt, as opposed to comparing him to one who is saying *Shema* naked:

Saying *Shema* naked and saying *Shema* without a belt address two different *k'rias Shema* concerns. Saying *Shema* naked is a concern that my eyes will connect with my *ervah*. Saying *Shema* without a belt is a concern that my thoughts (heart) will connect with ("see") my *ervah*. Being under a loose blanket is not like saying *Shema* naked. There is no concern that my eyes will connect with my *ervah*. The only concern is that the feeling of freedom underneath the loose blanket will keep me aware of my *ervah*—the same way I would feel if I were wearing a loose-fitting robe with no belt. And, as we have just learned, it is the same way I would feel if covered—either by water or by even a belted robe—while standing in the water of a *mikveh*.

By telling us one sits in clear water up to one's neck and recites *Shema*, *Tanna Kama* is not telling us one **must** sit up to one's neck. He is saying, since I do not hold of the problem of *libo ro'eh es ha'ervah*, one may even sit in clear water up to one's neck, as the water counts as a covering, the heart has no eyes, and the one reciting the *Shema* can avoid looking down through the clear water at his *ervah*! The *Rama*, who disagrees with the *Tanna Kama*'s position about *libo ro'eh es ha'ervah* not being a problem, but fundamentally agrees with his *definition* of *libo ro'eh es ha'ervah*, can allow a person to recite *Shema* sitting in clear water up to his waist. The water counts as a covering; the heart is not in the same space as the *ervah*, and the person can avert his gaze.

We, of course, don't *pasken* like the *Tanna Kama*. But whereas *Rama paskens* against him in halachah but not in definitions, the *Rambam paskens* against the *Tanna Kama*'s very definition of *libo ro'eh es ha'ervah*. The *Rambam* holds it is awareness of the heart that is the issue; thus even in water up to one's waist, and—as we've seen—even covered in a robe with a belt while in the water, one is not permitted to recite *k'rias Shema* until he stirs up some dirt and changes his heart's focus.

With this, we have answered all of our questions.

דף כה: (2)

אמר רבא צואה בעששית מותר לקרות ק"ש כנגדה ערוה בעששית אסור לקרות ק"ש כנגדה וגו'.

*Rava said: In the presence of tzo'ah covered by glass, one is allowed to recite Shema; but in the presence of ervah covered by glass, one is not allowed to recite Shema. Tzo'ah is allowed because the Torah says, "And you shall cover your tzo'ah," and it is covered. Ervah is not allowed because there the Torah says, "You shall **not see** an object's nakedness." And when it is covered by glass, it can still be seen.*

Said Abaye: If there is a small bit of *tzo'ah*, you can nullify it with spit. Rava said: It must be thick spit.

Said Rava: If *tzo'ah* is in a hole, you can cover it with your shoe and say *Shema*. Asked Mar the son of Ravina—What is the law if the *tzo'ah* is stuck to your shoe? Answered the Gemara: *Teiku* [We do not know—Eliyahu HaNavi will come and give us the answer.]

1. Rava contradicts himself. The reason, it would seem, that Rava requires thick spit is because without the extra thickness, the *tzo'ah* can still be seen. But didn't he just teach us that if *tzo'ah* is covered by glass, *Shema* can be said despite the *tzo'ah* being visible, because the Torah merely requires that it be covered? So what is wrong with a see-through covering of thin spit?

2. The Rishonim all say, "*teiku d'issura l'chumrah,*" and that even though the question of *tzo'ah devukah* is not answered by the Gemara, the halachah will be stringent as this is a matter of an *issur d'Oraisa*. How is it an *issur d'Oraisa*? The Torah's mandate regarding *tzo'ah* is "Cover it." This is a *mitzvas asei*, not a *lav*.

Berachos 25b

Since when do we call failure to carry out a positive commandment an *"issur"*?

3. *Rava's* case is stated as *tzo'ah* in a hole. If having the shoe be simply in contact with the *tzo'ah* is *mutar* and the only question is when the *tzo'ah* is **attached** to the shoe, why can't we have a normal case where a person wishes to say *Shema* while his shoe is in contact with *tzo'ah*? The halachah can then be that if the *tzo'ah* is just touching the shoe it is *mutar*, but if it is stuck on so much that if you lift the shoe the *tzo'ah* will remain attached, saying *Shema* is *assur*. Why do we need that the *tzo'ah* be in a hole? It must be like *Rabbeinu Manoach* explains—that *tzo'ah b'guma* means it is separated from the shoe by the air space in the hole, and *Rava* is trying to tell us that even contact touching is *assur*. So how can *Raavad* and *Rabbeinu Yonah* say contact touching is *mutar*? How do they explain *Rava's* case being about a hole?

4. But on the other hand, if even simple contact touching is *assur*, how could the *Gemara* not know if stuck-on *tzo'ah* is *assur*? That should be obviously *assur*!

5. Why must you place *davka* your shoe over the hole? If you place your foot over the hole, is the *tzo'ah* not covered?

6. How can this be a *"teiku"*? *Eliyahu* does not come to *pasken halachah*, as *Torah lo ba'shamayim hi*. All he can teach us is facts that had remained hidden from us. *Tzo'ah devukah* is a *sh'eilah* of halachah, not of *metzius*. How can that be left as a *"teiku"*?

7. *Rabbeinu Yonah* cites the *Rambam* as ruling that, "If the shoe is in contact with the *tzo'ah* it is *assur* [to say *Shema*]." That seems to be the *Rambam's* position. But why does the *Rambam* not explicitly say so? Why does he only say, "If *tzo'ah* is in a hole, stand with your shoe over the hole and say *Shema*, provided your shoe is not in contact with the *tzo'ah*." Why does he not spell out, "But if the shoe is in contact with the *tzo'ah*, [saying *k'rias Shema*] is *assur*"?

8. Why is the question of *tzo'ah b'guma* prefaced by the issue of *tzo'ah* and *ervah* under glass?

Yesod

We are mistaken. This is properly a *teiku*, because it **is** a *sh'eilah* of *metzi'us*.

As far as the obligation to cover *tzo'ah* before reciting *Shema*, covering the hole with either your foot or your shoe fulfills that obligation. But there is another issue here.

In the previous chapter, we noted that a person can have his *ervah* completely covered by water (or a loose blanket), and he might still not be allowed to recite *Shema* because of an astonishing *din* called *libo ro'eh es ha'ervah*. We explained this *din* to mean that if a person is still in a state of active awareness of his nakedness, even after being covered, the covering is not enough.

Here we have a case where, despite the Torah's mandating only that *tzo'ah* must be covered, we find that covering *tzo'ah* is not enough.

What could make covering *tzo'ah* not be enough, where, and why? The answer is found in a case where *tzo'ah* is in contact with your foot or shoe. Here, even if it is satisfactorily covered, **if you have a feeling of revulsion toward the *tzo'ah* connected to you, it is forbidden to recite *k'rias Shema*.** But why? Isn't it covered? Yes, it is covered. But there is the other *din* called "*Lo yireh b'cha ervas davar*—Do not have a disgusting thing in your active awareness [at the time of reciting *k'rias Shema*]." Just as awareness of one's nakedness prevents one from saying *Shema* even where the nakedness is covered and unseen, so too does awareness of *tzo'ah* in a way that causes disgust prevent one from saying *Shema*, even where it is technically covered.

The actual halachah is that where there is no contact and the only issue is *v'chisisa es tzei'asecha*, reciting *Shema* is *mutar* whether the *tzo'ah* is covered in the hole with your foot or with your shoe. But when there is contact with the *tzo'ah*—by your foot or by your shoe—we have an issue even though the *tzo'ah* is covered. Could one be considered repulsed by the contact with the *tzo'ah*? If so, it is *assur* because of *lo yirah b'cha ervas davar*. But we don't know exactly when it is that people's revulsion to being in contact with *tzo'ah* rises to the level of *ervas davar*. So it is a

Berachos 25b

teiku. But it is a *teiku d'issura*, the *issur* of *lo yireh b'cha ervas davar*, thus we *pasken l'chumrah* and it is *assur*.

Now we can understand the *Rambam*. We asked why he does not spell out explicitly that contact with *tzo'ah* makes saying *Shema assur*, when it is clear by inference that this is what he holds. The answer is that while he indeed holds that contact with *tzo'ah* makes saying *Shema assur*, that *issur* for now is due only to the *teiku d'issura*. When Eliyahu HaNavi comes, he will reveal to us to what extent people's revulsion actually reaches. Since the halachos in the *Rambam's Yad Hachazakah* are for all time, the *Rambam* cannot state unequivocally that contact with *tzo'ah* makes *Shema assur* when Eliyahu might someday reveal information that causes us to conclude it is not. All *Rambam* can say for sure is that if there is **no** contact, covering the *tzo'ah* makes *Shema mutar*.

So why does the *Rambam* say only that he may cover the hole with his shoe? Can he not use his foot alone just as well?

He can use his foot. But if the *Rambam* would have said he should cover the hole with his foot, and then gone on to say this is only so long as there is no contact with the *tzo'ah*, we would have concluded that it is only contact between *tzo'ah* and the **foot** that carries a problem of disgust, but *tzo'ah* on the shoe would be OK. But the *Rambam* knows from the Gemara that the *teiku* was *davka* about contact between *tzo'ah* and the person's shoe, suggesting that the Gemara already assumes there is definite revulsion from *tzo'ah* on one's foot.

So instead, the *Rambam*, in the interest of simplicity, chooses to follow the approach of the *Ra'ah*—that "shoe" is the proper way to refer to the foot, as the foot is generally encased in a shoe. And then he teaches us that the shoe/foot may be used to cover *tzo'ah* without contact, but not with contact—the foot because there is definite revulsion and an active *issur* of *ervas davar*, and the shoe because someday we will learn that there might be a similar *ervas davar* there as well, and for now *teiku d'issura l'chumrah*.

Now we can explain Rava. Rava does not contradict himself at all. *Tzo'ah* covered by glass avoids the secondary problem of *ervas davar* due to revulsion, because no one is repulsed by *tzo'ah* that cannot touch him. But see-through saliva covering *tzo'ah* is different. While the *tzo'ah* may indeed be covered—enough for Abaye to declare it *mutar*—a person is still liable to be repulsed by it even after it is covered, says Rava, since he can see it and nothing in its covering can preclude it from getting on him. This *tzo'ah* is *assur* for the secondary reason of *ervas davar*—disgust. The only solution is thick spit, because a person is not disgusted by what he cannot see.

Now it is beautifully clear how the *sugyos* are strung together. First Rava sets up for us the existence of two fundamental Torah issues—covering of *tzo'ah*, and making sure that seeing *ervah* is blocked. But just prior to this we had a *sugya* of *libo ro'eh es ha'ervah* that taught us that not seeing *ervah* means more than just not seeing it; it means making sure we are not actively aware of it. So now Rava goes on to teach us that covering *tzo'ah* means more than just covering it. It means making sure it is covered in such a way that it does not disgust us.

Then he takes it one step further and asserts that active awareness of disgust of any kind is the exact same problem as *ervas davar*. The Torah, when it gives *ervas davar* as a legitimate reason for divorcing one's wife, is talking not just about nakedness, but about any shameless behavior that repulses us. So too, teaches Rava, *ervas davar* can be about active awareness of any **substance** that disgusts us, sometimes including covered *tzo'ah*.

Berachos 25b

דף כה: (3)

ולא יתכסה לא במים הרעים ולא במי משרה עד שיתן לתוכן מים וגו׳.

One may not cover himself with foul water or with flax water, until he pours in water.

*And how much water could be added that would make the problem disappear? Rather, here is how the Mishnah must be read: One may not cover himself with foul water nor with flax water **at all**. And [one may not say Shema in the proximity of] mei raglayim [urine] until he pours in water.*

In a Beraisa, the Rabbis taught: How much water must he pour in? A drop. Rabbi Zakkai said: A revi'is.

Rav Nachman said: Their argument is [in a case where the water was introduced] at the end [i.e., water is poured into already-collected urine]. But at the beginning—a drop.

Rav Yosef said: Their argument is [in a case where the water was introduced] at the beginning [i.e., water is waiting in a vessel into which the urine will be produced]. But at the end—all agree, a revi'is.

Rav Yosef said to his attendant: Bring me a revi'is of water, like Rabbi Zakkai.

1. The Gemara, faced with a Mishnah telling us to pour water without disclosing how much, changes the Mishnah to say that no amount of water will re-qualify foul water or flax water. Why should this be true? Wouldn't a *rov* (majority) of clean water

certainly nullify a *mi'ut* (minority) of dirty water? Why should we say one may not cover himself with these dirty waters **at all**?
2. Indeed, why does it even bother the Gemara that the Mishnah did not specify the amount of water? Wouldn't the answer automatically default to *rov*?
3. The question of "How much water could be added that would make the problem disappear?" seems to be taken by the Gemara as a rhetorical question. That is certainly how *Rashi* learned it. But why could it not have been understood as a genuine question—seeking to know if a *rov* (the *d'Oraisa* standard) is enough or if it needs a higher standard *m'd'Rabbanan*, like *bitul b'shishim* in *taaruvos*?
4. Changing the Mishnah brings *mei raglayim* into the Mishnah. That may fit into the end of the Mishnah (How far must one distance oneself from them and from *tzo'ah*?), but the end of the Mishnah would have been just as good with the phrase "distance oneself from them" referring to the foul water and the flax water, and that would have been a better fit than having to justify why we want to equate a *d'Rabbanan (mei raglayim)* with a *d'Oraisa (tzo'ah)*. The real problem is—What is the issue of distance from *tzo'ah* and *mei raglayim* doing in this Mishnah at all? Distance required from problematic substances was not the topic of the Mishnah, and especially if "from them" is no longer even referring to the foul water and the flax water!
5. The *Rambam paskens* like Rabbi Zakkai that a *revi'is* is required—both for *t'chila* (when the water comes first) and for *sof* (when the water comes last).⁵ Why does the *Rambam* choose *shitas* Rabbi Zakkai over *shitas* Rabbanan when the regular rule is *yachid v'rabim halachah k'rabim*?
6. Why does Rav Yosef say to his attendant, "Bring me a *revi'is* of water like Rabbi Zakkai"? For *lib'sof*, it isn't only Rabbi Zakkai; it's the *shitah* of all opinions. Why leave it for *Rashi* to point out the most important detail—that it's talking about *l'chatchila* (where indeed only Rabbi Zakkai says *revi'is* and not Rabbanan)?

7. The *Rambam* states definitively that an additional *revi'is* is required for each additional urination. *Rashba* says only one *revi'is* of water is required no matter how many urinations are being neutralized. How does *Rambam* know he's right?

Yesod

We are reading the *Rambam* wrong. The reason he gives for one not being allowed to say *Shema* while standing in foul water is "*she'reichan ra*—because it has a bad smell." The reason he gives for one not being allowed to say *Shema* while standing in clear water (*mayim tz'lulin*) is "*mipnei she'ervaso nireis ba'hen*—because his *ervah* is exposed in such water."

Into which category does the *Rambam* place flax water?

While everyone assumes the *Rambam* classifies flax water together with foul water, as another example of "*reichan ra*," the *Rambam*, when read correctly, clearly says otherwise:

ולא יתכסה לא במים רעים שריחן רע
ולא במי המשרה ולא במים צלולין מפני שערוותו
נראית בהן.

What the *Rambam* actually says is that the problem with flax water is that one's *ervah* is exposed while standing in it, just like in clear water (the point evidently being that while flax water has some cloudiness, it is not cloudy enough to prevent the *ervah* from being exposed).

If so, it makes sense to the *Rambam* how the Gemara knows that its opening question: *kama maya rami v'azil* is rhetorical. There is no amount of added water that can make clear water unclear! It is obviously a rhetorical statement.

And so the Mishnah **has** to be a *chesori mechsora*.

But that is all about flax water. What about foul water? There, the question *kama maya rami v'azil* could have been genuine. How much water, the Gemara may have been asking, is needed to be *mevatel* a non-kosher smell? Is *bitul b'rov* enough, or do you need the olfactory equivalent of *bitul b'shishim*? But, explains the Gemara, because the

Mishnah linked foul water to flax water—which no amount of water can help—the Mishnah is evidently telling us that one cannot fix foul water just as one cannot fix flax water.

But lest we think *bitul* of objectionable materials can never help for *k'rias Shema*, the Mishnah advises us that in a different scenario—not *yitchaseh*—*bitul* will help. And what is that case? Saying *Shema* in proximity to *mei raglayim*. *Mei raglayim* will be amenable to *bitul* where flax water and foul water were not.

What kind of *bitul*? There are two possible kinds: Real and symbolic. Real *bitul* is the only type that can nullify on a Torah level, but the rabbis can decide to allow a symbolic *bitul* where the whole *issur* was only Rabbinic in the first place.

Rov and *shishim* are both types of real *bitul* (one is Torah-level real and one is real to our human senses). Here is where we run into our *Beraisa*. Rabbanan say the *bitul* can be done by a minimal drop (*kol she'hu*) of water. Rabbi Zakkai says it can be done only by a *revi'is* of water. Are these *shitos* suggesting the *bitul* for urine is real *bitul* or symbolic *bitul*?

That's where we come to the *machlokes* Rav Nachman and Rav Yosef. But first, we need to understand one thing—the difference between *l'chatchila* and *l'b'sof*.

L'chatchila means you want to be *mevatel* the urine you are about to produce. Water put in place *m't'chila* will accomplish that. But in that scenario, the water will be handling only one urination—*mei raglayim shel pa'am achas*.

L'b'sof means you have standing urine you wish to be *mevatel*. In that discussion, no assumption can be made that there is only *pa'am achas* of the *mei raglayim*.

So in hearing out Rav Nachman and Rav Yosef, the word "*l'chatchila*" must be seen as a code word for the desire to be *mevatel mei raglayim shel pa'am achas*, while "*l'b'sof*" must be seen as a code word for the attempt to be *mevatel mei raglayim shel afilu kamah pa'amim*.

Again, Rabbanan say *bitul* can be done with a *kol she'hu*. Rabbi Zakkai argues and requires a *revi'is*.

Berachos 25b

Rav Nachman pins this argument to a case of multiple urinations. By a single urination, he claims, *kol she'hu* will suffice according to everybody.

Does Rav Nachman hold *bitul* of urine is real or symbolic? It has to be symbolic. Like his Rabbanan, a *kol she'hu* will suffice both *t'chila* and *sof*. In *t'chila* it could be symbolic or it could have been real—as in *rishon rishon misbatel* (see *Rashi*). But from *sof*, we see it could only be symbolic, as how could a single drop of water dropped into a much larger amount of urine ever be *mevatel* the larger amount except symbolically? And like his Rabbi Zakkai, since he allows one *revi'is* to be *mevatel* an unrestricted number of urinations, the *bitul* cannot be other than symbolic.

How about Rav Yosef? Like his Rabbanan, only a single urination (*t'chila*) could rely on *kol she'hu*. That suggests that, *l'shitas* Rabbanan, *bitul* by urine is real—using the principle of *rishon rishon misbatel*. For multiple urinations (*l'b'sof*) then, Rabbanan will require *revi'is* because that is real *bitul* for *l'b'sof*, Chazal having assessed that one *revi'is* of water volume will physically nullify (*al pi din Torah*) one instance of urination (making it obvious, in turn, that one additional *revi'is* will be required per additional *pa'am*).

Although Rabbi Zakkai too requires *revi'is*, he does so not because he views *revi'is* as the Chazal-determined real *bitul*. *L'shitas* Rabbi Zakkai, says Rav Yosef, *revi'is* is symbolic, and he will require *revi'is* by *sof* the same way he requires it by *t'chila*—symbolic *bitul*, whether for a lot of urine or for a little.

So, like Rav Nachman, *bitul* of urine is symbolic. Like Rav Yosef, *bitul* of urine is real according to Rabbanan and symbolic according to Rabbi Zakkai.

Should we hold like Rav Nachman or like Rav Yosef?

The *Rambam* sees that on this question the Gemara clearly sides with Rav Yosef, as seen by the fact that it bothers to tell a story that addresses a concern only Rav Yosef would have. You see, if Rav Yosef calls to his attendant and asks for a *revi'is* as he is about to urinate, a Talmid or other onlooker could draw one of two conclusions:

דף כה:

1. *Bitul* of urine is real, like the *Rabbanan*, and Rav Yosef is asking for a *revi'is* because one *revi'is* is the real *mevatel* of one *pa'am* of *mei raglayim* (and even though *Rabbanan* themselves in that case would call for a *kol she'hu*, Rav Yosef might reject *rishon rishon misbatel* but still agree to the notion that *bitul* of urine is real).
2. *Bitul* of urine is symbolic, like Rabbi Zakkai, and Rav Yosef is asking for a *revi'is* because a *revi'is* is the arbitrary amount established by Chazal (who get to establish that arbitrary amount because they were the ones who declared urine *assur* in the first place).

To clarify which intention he has, Rav Yosef is forced to ask not just for a *revi'is*, but for a *revi'is* of water **like Rabbi Zakkai**, meaning, the symbolic *revi'is*—as opposed to a *revi'is* of water like *Rabbanan*, which would be the *revi'is* required for real *bitul*.

But now that *Rambam* knows the Gemara has chosen Rav Yosef's understanding of the *machlokes* Rabbanan v'Rabbi Zakkai over Rav Nachman's, he still is aware that in halachah we are bound by the principle *yachid v'rabim halachah k'rabim*. Rabbi Zakkai holds the *bitul* is symbolic; Rabbanan hold the *bitul* is real. We will have to *pasken* that the *bitul* is real.

Where does that leave us? By *sof*, it unquestionably means one *revi'is* per *pa'am* of urination. By *t'chila*, it might have meant *rishon rishon misbatel*, like the *Beraisa*, but we see that Rav Yosef picks up from the *Beraisa* only that Rabbanan "could" hold *kol she'hu* if one holds of *rishon rishon misbatel*, but since the Mishnah says it *stam—ad she'yatil l'sochan mayim*—and does not specify *kama yatil l'sochan mayim kol she'hu* like the *Beraisa* does, it is enough to say that Rabbanan "could" also dismiss *rishon rishon misbatel* as a valid real *bitul* method and just accept *revi'is* as their standard for real *bitul*.

So the *Rambam*, taking his cue from the Gemara, *paskens* like Rav Yosef in his understanding of the *machlokes* Rabbanan v'Rabbi Zakkai, and then *paskens* like Rav Yosef's Rabbanan *k'neged* Rav Yosef's Rabbi Zakkai, thus rendering the halachah "*revi'is, bein b't'chila bein b'sof*," and an additional *revi'is* in *l'b'sof* for every additional *pa'am* of *mei raglayim*.

Berachos 25b

[A hint to this *p'shat* is the Gemara saying "*aval b't'chila kol she'hu*" in Rav Nachman's agreement case as opposed to "*aval l'b'sof **divrei ha'kol revi'is**"* in Rav Yosef's agreement case. This is because in Rav Nachman's, all "could" hold of *kol she'hu*—if *rishon rishon misbatel* is accepted—but in Rav Yosef's, all **do** hold of *revi'is*.]

דף כה: (4)

ת״ר גרף של רעי ועביט של מי רגלים אסור לקרות
קריאת שמע כנגדן וגו׳.

[Chachamim:]It is forbidden to recite k'rias Shema opposite a chamber pot.

Rabban Shimon ben Gamliel says: If it is behind the bed it is permitted; and if not, you can move four amos away, and then it is permitted.

Rabbi Shimon ben Elazar says: Moving four amos away does not help inside a house. You must cover it or remove it.

1. *Rif* brings Rava, who says the halachah is not like Rabbi Shimon ben Elazar. That may be a fine way to tell me what the halachah is not, but how does this statement help us understand what the halachah **is**? Who do we *pasken* like—the *Chachamim* or Rabban Shimon ben Gamliel?
2. *Rit"z Geius paskens* like Rabbi Shimon ben Elazar, going *l'chumrah*, according to *Rabbeinu Yonah*, and saying the entire house is like *daled amos*. *Rabbeinu Yonah* is very troubled that *Rit"z Geius* would ignore Rava, who is the *basra'ah*. He suggests that maybe it is because the Gemara itself highlighted Rabbi Shimon ben Elazar by pointing out how it is he who holds one's entire house is like *daled amos*. But didn't the Gemara know that and yet still brought Rava? So how in fact can *Rit"z Geius* bypass Rava *l'halachah*?
3. *Rashi* says he doesn't know where to find the source suggesting that Rabbi Shimon ben Elazar is the one who holds one's entire

house is like *daled amos*. *Rabbeinu Chananel* claims its source is *Eruvin* 22a, where Rabbi Shimon ben Elazar says one may carry on Shabbos within the entirety of an enclosed open-air space used for living. *Rabbeinu Yonah* denies that, for if that were the source of our halachah, since it is a source no one disputes in *Eruvin*, how could Rava rule against it here? Also, how do we explain the fact that *Rashi* doesn't know the source of Rabbi Shimon ben Elazar's halachah?

4. *Rabbeinu Yonah* concludes that we must go with Rava, that the halachah is not like Rabbi Shimon ben Elazar, and that the halachah is instead like Rabban Shimon ben Gamliel. But how can the halachah not be like the *Chachamim*? Don't we say *yachid v'rabim halachah k'rabim*?

5. *Rif* omits the Gemara's query about what's considered a proper covering if a *geref shel re'i* is placed underneath a bed. *Rosh* claims this is because *Rif paskens* like *Chachamim* and therefore has no need to follow a discussion that has relevance only to Rabban Shimon ben Gamliel or Rabbi Shimon ben Elazar. But it would seem the *Chachamim* were merely denying the *heterim* of *achar ha'mitah* and *richuk daled amos*. Why should *Rif* assume they were eliminating the *heter* of covering up the *geref* (which is the point of the discussion of a bed 4–9 *tefachim* high)?

6. What really is the problem with reciting *k'rias Shema* before a clean *beis ha'kisei* when it no longer contains *tzo'ah* and should not be a problem of *v'chisisa es tzei'asecha*?

Yesod

In addition to the Biblical restriction against reciting *k'rias Shema* in the presence of *tzo'ah*, the rabbis added several similar restrictions of their own. For one thing, they prohibited reciting *k'rias Shema* in any presence of *mei raglayim*, something the Torah included only *b'kilu'ach*. Another thing they prohibited was reciting *k'rias Shema* in or facing an active lavatory or chamber pot (*beis ha'kisei*). This latter restriction is meant to underscore the notion that just as the act of eliminating waste

דף כה:

is best connected to a place—a *makom*—because it is transformative and *Avos* 5:17 teaches us how things that have the power to transform us do so best in a designated *makom*, so too is *k'rias Shema* designed to be, if not a transformative act itself, an activity intended to raise our consciousness daily of the need to constantly transform ourselves toward achieving ever higher spiritual plateaus. And even though *k'rias Shema* does not have a designated place per se, its place is surely **not** going to be in the same place as the one in which purely physical transformation takes place—or while we are actively cognizant of such a place. Those places are not compatible because we must never risk confusing physical transformation with spiritual transformation. Both are crucial and necessary, but the former can never be a substitute for the latter.

The explanation of this Rabbinic restriction is profound. *Shema* and *tzo'ah* are Biblically incompatible because our receiving of the Divine Presence is itself incompatible with cognizance of our lowly and waste-producing physical nature.

OK, that's between us and God.

But there is also an incompatibility within ourselves—the contrast between our spiritual side and our material side. While we don't hesitate to admit that both need renewal, the renewal process of the one must proceed completely independent of the renewal process of the other. Conflicts that rage exclusively within separate sides of our own nature are covered not by Biblical law but by Rabbinic law.

Because *beis ha'kisei* represents the transformative power of the physical, special care had to be taken by the Sages to ensure we don't ascribe **spiritually** transformative energy to things like a good workout, a hot shower, or a good night's sleep. By separating *Shema*—the clarion for *aliyah ruchani*—from *beis ha'kisei*—the symbol of bodily rejuvenation—they keep the two distinct types of transformation separate in our thinking.

This leads us to our Gemara. From Abba Binyamin on 5b, we saw that *lifnei ha'mitah* would mean any part of the room where from that vantage point, the bed stands between it and the wall. Thus *achar ha'mitah* would have to refer to a space between the bed and the wall, blocked off from the rest of the room by the bed. The blockage by the bed represents some obscuring of the importance of the *beis ha'kisei*—from within itself, not from any action I might be taking—as, for example, a workout session that involves minimal equipment in an uncelebrated venue. Another potentially mitigating factor might be some action that I might take, such as distance that I place between myself and the *beis ha'kisei*, representing a step taken by me to diminish the value of the physical renewal activity in my own eyes (limiting my refreshing eight-hour sleep nights to only Shabbos night, for instance).

In our *Beraisa*, on 25b, we find what ought to be a three-way *machlokes* between the Rabbanan, Rabban Shimon ben Gamliel, and Rabbi Shimon ben Elazar. Rabbanan would say: A *beis ha'kisei* with walls is defined by its walls. But a *beis ha'kisei* without walls—the kind of *beis ha'kisei* where simple cognizance creates the incompatibility—is *assur* if it is in my field of vision, whether it is obscured by a *chatzitzah* (here meaning a physical barrier that falls short of being a halachic wall) or not, and regardless of whether I am near it or distant from it. Rabban Shimon ben Gamliel would agree that distance **on its own** doesn't help, and so it is *assur* anywhere in my field of vision without a *chatzitzah*; but *chatzitzah* enables distance to help, so with a *chatzitzah* I can count on my ability to compartmentalize. Therefore, as long as I put some distance between it and me it is *mutar*, even if I can still see it. (The *chatzitzah* suggests the *beis ha'kisei*'s footprint is already somewhat diminished on its own—that plus my creating distance will remove the incompatibility.) Rabbi Shimon ben Elazar would say: Distance is actually all you need. The only problem is that being four *amos* away but still being under one roof with the *geref shel re'i* is not considered to be establishing distance. So practically, outside of my house, all I need to do is walk four *amos* away; but inside my house I will have to totally remove it from my field of vision.

A schematic of such a three-way *machlokes* would look like this:

- *Chachamim*—Field-of-vision awareness of an unwalled *beis ha'kisei*, even if tempered—from the *beis ha'kisei* side (*achar*

ha'mitah), from the observer's side (*richuk daled amos*), or even from both—is incompatible with *k'rias Shema*.
- Rabban Shimon ben Gamliel—If tempered from both sides together (both *achar ha'mitah* and *richuk daled amos*), incompatibility of awareness is lifted.
- Rabbi Shimon ben Elazar—If tempered even from the observer's side only (*richuk daled amos*), incompatibility is lifted, but that works only outdoors, as *richuk daled amos* does not qualify when done under the same roof as the *beis ha'kisei*.

As it is, however, as proven by the second *Beraisa*, our schematic changes:
- *Chachamim*—All direct vision awareness of an unwalled *beis ha'kisei* is incompatible, even if tempered.
- Rabban Shimon ben Gamliel—If tempered (from either side), this incompatibility is lifted.
- Rabbi Shimon ben Elazar—Tempering being done from the side of the observer, when done under the same roof, does not qualify as tempering. So while I am not even addressing *achar ha'mitah*, know that *richuk daled amos* will work outside of the house only.

If we would have stuck with the first schematic, we would have had a *rabim* versus two *daas yachids*—the *rabim* holding no tempering helps, one *yachid* holding two-sided tempering helps, and a second *yachid* holding even one-sided tempering can help. That would count as a *yachid v'rabim*, and the halachah would have to be *k'rabim*—like the *Chachamim*.

But once we adopt the second schematic, we no longer have a situation of *yachid v'rabim*. Rabban Shimon ben Gamliel and Rabbi Shimon ben Elazar both agree that tempering—even one-sided tempering—helps. It is now a "*rabim* (two *yechidim*) *v'rabim*," and we are not bound to *pasken* like the majority *rabim*. So the halachah can follow the view of the two Rabbi Shimons.

Does it? Let's see the *Rambam*:

> *Hilchos K'rias Shema 3:2*—One should not recite the Shema in a bathhouse [*beis ha'merchatz*] or latrine [*beis*

> ha'kisei], even if there is no actual physical waste in it, nor in a graveyard or next to a corpse. If he distances himself four cubits [richuk daled amos] from the grave or the corpse, he is permitted to recite it.
>
> Anyone who recites [the Shema] in an improper place must recite the Shema again.
>
> Hilchos K'rias Shema 3:12—It is forbidden to recite the Shema in front of [k'neged] a cesspool or chamber pot, even if it is empty and has no foul smell, as it is similar to a latrine.

At first, the *Rambam* seems difficult to understand. In 3:12, he says one cannot say *Shema k'neged* a chamber pot because it is considered a *beis ha'kisei*. But where did he ever mention any restrictions about a *beis ha'kisei* other than that it is prohibited to say *Shema* **inside** one?

And even if we can answer that question, it seems he must not *pasken* like the two Rabbi Shimons, because he limits the application of, "If he distances himself four cubits...he is permitted to recite it," to the cases of grave and corpse, but not *beis ha'merchatz* or *beis ha'kisei*.

HOWEVER, WE CAN answer our first question in a way that can address our second. The *issur* of *k'rias Shema* **k'neged** *beis ha'kisei* can actually be found hidden in the following *Rambam*:

> Hilchos K'rias Shema 3:3—The Shema may be recited facing [l'neged], but not inside, a latrine that has been newly built, but not used as of yet.

If *Shema* may be recited *l'neged* a **newly built** latrine, obviously the *Shema* may **not** be recited *l'neged* a used latrine (or chamber pot). Clearly, then, Halachah 3:2 was simply discussing walled latrines and 3:3 unwalled latrines.

OK, but what about the law of distance? Didn't 3:2 indicate the *heter* of *daled amos* is to be applied only to *kever* and *meis* and nothing else? No—not at all. The law of *daled amos* was **irrelevant** to *beis ha'merchatz* and *beis ha'kisei* because both are walled facilities, and walled facilities do not *need* a law of *daled amos*. It is enough to be outside the walls.

What you do see from this halachah is that in any such case in which you might need distance, distance is effective. What such case—besides the *kever* and the *meis*—might that be? That would be an open, unwalled latrine, about which we say in 3:3 that it is *mutar k'negdo* only when it is brand new, directly implying that it is forbidden when it is not. The halachah is clear. One may not recite *k'rias Shema* while facing a used, unwalled *beis ha'kisei*, **but with a distance of *daled amos*, one may**.

And 3:3 **must** be talking about an unwalled latrine because we just learned in 3:2 that for a walled latrine, *k'negdo* is *mutar* even if it were **used**. *K'negdo* of such a walled latrine **new**, then, would **certainly** be *mutar*, and the *Rambam* would have no reason to restate that in 3:3.

So we can safely conclude that the *Rambam paskens* that distancing oneself from a used chamber pot (or any open latrine) is effective, even if it remains within one's field of vision. With this statement, he is already clearly not *paskening* like the *Chachamim*.

Is he *paskening*, then, like Rabban Shimon ben Gamliel or like Rabbi Shimon ben Elazar?

Well, wait a minute. Were those two arguing? I thought we said they were the two Rabbi Shimons—in complete agreement that even tempering from one side would be enough to permit reciting *k'rias Shema* in front of an open chamber pot. And, anyway, if you tell me they argue, doesn't that revert us back to two separate *daas yachids* versus a *rabim*, and we would have to *pasken* like the *Chachamim*?

Our answer will show that Rabban Shimon ben Gamliel and Rabbi Shimon ben Elazar do argue, and that it is possible for those two to argue and nevertheless still allow us to *pasken* against the *Chachamim*.

That is because they both agree and disagree.

They agree—against *shitas Chachamim*—that a tempering, even from one side, of the power of the *geref* or the *avit* (the two varieties of chamber pot) can relax the restriction against reciting *k'rias Shema k'neged* a chamber pot. Neither holds you need two-sided tempering.

But they disagree over which side the one-sided tempering can come from.

According to Rabban Shimon ben Gamliel, the tempering can come from either side. So *achar ha'mitah* (blockage by the bed) can work

Berachos 25b

immediately (*miyad*, meaning with no *richuk daled amos*) and *lifnei ha'mitah* (no blockage) can work with *richuk daled amos*.

But it is clear from Rabbi Shimon ben Elazar that—while he eliminates the option of *richuk daled amos* working inside the house—if he agreed with Rabban Shimon ben Gamliel in every other way, he would have no reason to say, as he does, "*Lo yikra ad she'yotzi'eim o she'yanicheim tachas ha'mitah.*" One cannot recite *Shema* unless he removes or covers the chamber pot? Why not? Why can't he just put it **behind** the bed (*achar ha'mitah*)? That way, even though there is no *richuk* (since *richuk* in a house is not an option), there is still blockage, and one tempering is enough!

It must be, concludes the *Rambam*, that Rabbi Shimon ben Elazar argues on Rabban Shimon ben Gamliel and holds that the one-sided tempering can work only where it comes from the side of the observer (*richuk daled amos*), and not where it comes from the side of the object itself (blockage by the bed).

The *Rambam*, then, *paskens* like Rabbi Shimon ben Elazar, which is why he writes that the only *tikkun* for the *kever* and the *meis*—which we know to extend to the open latrine—is distancing oneself *daled amos*. So while he writes in 3:12 that it is *assur* to recite *k'rias Shema k'neged* a chamber pot, nevertheless since he goes on to say that a chamber pot is like a latrine, and we know it is a type of latrine that has no walls, and we know an unwalled latrine is like a *kever* or a *meis*, we automatically know that just as one is permitted to recite *k'rias Shema* facing a *kever* after he distances himself *daled amos* away from it, and just as he is permitted to recite *k'rias Shema* near a *meis* after he distances himself *daled amos* away from it, so too will he be permitted to say *k'rias Shema* facing a *geref shel re'i* or an *avit shel mei raglayim* after he distances himself *daled amos* away from it. The only caveat is that this cannot be effective indoors, as the entire house in which one finds the *geref* or *avit* is to be considered as one single large *daled amos*.

The only problem that remains is this: If the *Rambam paskens* like Rabbi Shimon ben Elazar, why don't we find any mention in the *Rambam* of the law of one's entire house being like one's *daled amos*? It seems he is *paskening* only the part of Rabbi Shimon ben Elazar that declares *chatzitzah* ineffective but not the part that places limitations on *daled amos*!

That is correct, and it comes from Rava.

You see, when Rav (supported by Bali in the name of Rav Yaakov the son of Shmuel's daughter) and Rava had their *machlokes*, it was not about the issue of allowing *heterim* for the *issur* of reciting *k'rias Shema* opposite a *geref shel re'i*. On that issue, as we've shown, *Rambam* clearly establishes from the Gemara that we *pasken* like Rabbi Shimon ben Elazar, avoiding the issue of *yachid v'rabim halachah k'rabim* by establishing that Rabban Shimon ben Gamliel and Rabbi Shimon ben Elazar agree that a single mitigating factor can ease the *issur* of *geref shel re'i*. (I actually think this may be why the Gemara first brings the last *Beraisa* with reversed *shitos*—as a way of hinting to us that in what counts at this point, they share their view in common.)

Rav and Rava propose their argument after the Gemara debates a new issue—the height of a bed and its resultant ability to act as a covering to the *geref shel re'i*!

Essentially, Rav Yosef sets up the following challenge: Accepting that we *pasken* like Rabbi Shimon ben Elazar against *Chachamim* that a *heter* can be had, we still have the following issue: According to Rabbi Shimon ben Elazar, we can only use *richuk daled amos* and then only outside the house. Says Rav Yosef, if the only avenue I have available to me inside the house is sliding the *geref shel re'i* under the bed to cover it, I'll need to have clarity on what kind of bed height offers such a covering. Three *tefachim* or less I know is a height that will make the chamber pot be considered covered, because three *tefachim* and less is considered *lavud* and it is as if the chamber pot is buried in the ground. Ten *tefachim* and above I know is a separate *reshus* and will not render the *geref* covered. What is the status of a bed with a height between three *tefachim* and ten *tefachim*? Rav Huna says to Rav Yosef that he does not know. When Abaye chimes in that ten *tefachim* really is an ineffective covering, the Gemara realizes we have a problem. To Rav, this remains a problem, because he *paskens* like Rabbi Shimon ben Elazar **on this issue as well**. But Rava comes and says, "Not to worry—on this issue, the halachah is not like Rabbi Shimon ben Elazar."

Berachos 25b

In other words, the halachah is still like Rabbi Shimon ben Elazar in the matter that *richuk daled amos* **is a legitimate** *heter* **for reciting** *k'rias Shema k'neged* **an unwalled** *beis ha'kisei*, **but the halachah is not like Rabbi Shimon ben Elazar in the matter of one's whole entire house being like a single** *daled amos*. So since we have the option indoors of just moving four *amos* away, it becomes unimportant how we view a bed height between three and ten *tefachim* tall.

And now we know why *Rashi* says he does not know the source for this *shitah* (single *daled amos*) of Rabbi Shimon ben Elazar when there seems to be a source in *Eruvin* 22a. That can't be the source. For if *Eruvin* 22a were indeed the source for this *shitah*, Rava could not declare that the halachah is not like Rabbi Shimon ben Elazar, as no one disputes the source brought in *Eruvin*. Since Rava **is** willing to declare the halachah not to be like Rabbi Shimon ben Elazar in this matter, Rava **must** hold its source is elsewhere, and *Rashi* does not know where that would be. Anyway, it matters little, because the halachah is not like him.

And now we can show that our other questions are answered as well. *Rif* can bring Rava, who says the halachah is not like Rabbi Shimon ben Elazar, because that only means the halachah is not like Rabbi Shimon ben Elazar **in the matter of one's whole house being like** *daled amos*. But in the matter of *heter daled amos* for reciting *Shema* opposite a chamber pot, the halachah is indeed like Rabbi Shimon ben Elazar, which is exactly how *Rit"z Geius* paskened. The halachah does not have to abide by *yachid v'rabim halachah k'rabim* and follow *Chachamim*, because Rabbi Shimon ben Elazar and Rabban Shimon ben Gamliel make up their own *rabim* on the issue they agree on in their dispute with *Chachamim*—that a single mitigating factor is enough to create a *heter* in the *issur* of saying *Shema* opposite a *geref shel re"i*. *Rabbeinu Yonah* is not wrong when he says we have to follow Rava and he is not wrong when he says the halachah is like Rabban Shimon ben Gamliel—it's just that following Rava and following Rabbi Shimon ben Elazar on the Gemara's **primary** issue are not mutually exclusive—and indeed for that issue Rabbi Shimon ben Elazar and Rabban Shimon ben Gamliel are in agreement! And *Rif* omits the rules of bed heights not because he *paskens* like *Chachamim*. He doesn't! He *paskens* like Rabbi Shimon ben

Elazar on the Gemara's primary issue. But once you *pasken* like Rava (and against Rabbi Shimon ben Elazar) on the Gemara's **secondary** issue, the need for the bed height rules over here fades quickly into irrelevancy.

The *Rosh* is compelled to say what he says in the *Rif* because the *Rosh*—despite his use of the language of *beis ha'kisei*—really holds like the *Tur*, that there actually *is* no problem with reciting *k'rias Shema* in front of a clean *beis ha'kisei*, and the only issue here is that a *geref shel re"i* will remain saturated with *tzo'ah* and create a problem of *v'chisisa es tzei'asecha*. It is for this reason that the Acharonim are busy adding *heterim* in cases where *tzo'ah* does not get absorbed in the chamber pot's walls—such as by a glass or stainless-steel container. This may be *shitas haRosh*, but it is not the *shitah* of the *Rambam*, *Rif*, or *Rit"z Geius*, who all hold **the problem with a *beis ha'kisei* is not what it contains but what it represents**, and none of whom, tellingly, make exceptions for chamber pots made of glass or other non-porous materials.

דף כה: (5)

רב אחאי איעסק ליה לבריה וגו׳.

Rav Achai made a match between his son and the daughter of Rav Yitzchak bar Shmuel bar Marta. They were unable to consummate the marriage. [Rav Achai] went to investigate and found a Sefer Torah lying in the room. He declared, "Had I not been here, you would have endangered my son's life!" for a Beraisa taught:

In a room that contains a Sefer Torah or a pair of tefillin, one may not engage in marital relations until it is removed or placed within a container, and that container placed within another container [k'li b'toch k'li]."

Said Abaye: This was taught only in regard to a container that is not the items' own container [kilyan]. But with kilyan, even ten coverings are all considered like one covering.

Said Rava: A garment draped over a [closed] bookcase with doors is considered like a k'li b'toch k'li.

Said Rabbi Yehoshua ben Levi: A Sefer Torah requires a ten-tefachim-high partition.

Mar Zutra visited the home of Rav Ashi. He noticed, in the room of Mar, the son of Rav Ashi, a Sefer Torah sitting behind a ten-tefachim-high partition. He said to him, "Like whom is this being practiced, like Rabbi Yehoshua ben Levi? When does Rabbi Yehoshua's law apply? It applies only when one has no other available room [to hold the Sefer Torah]. But Mar has another available room!" Responded Mar bar Rav Ashi, "I did not know."

דף כה:

It is difficult to understand the purpose and flow of this Gemara. The Gemara had previously been discussing reciting *k'rias Shema* in the vicinity of chamber pots, not engaging in marital relations in the vicinity of tefillin and *Sifrei Torah*. Why the sudden shift? One would expect the ensuing story to be an illustration of the current topic, not a shift into a new one.

Furthermore, there is an abrupt shift within this brief section, as it switches from containers to partitions. What is the point of the change of language and the whole fairly unsmooth text progression?

Looking into the issue, we find a more serious problem. Requiring *k'li b'toch k'li* implies that a single container is not enough; two are needed. Then, Abaye eliminates *kilyan*, implying that *kilyan* does not count as a halachically valid container. Yet the halachah (*Orach Chaim* 40:2) tells us that the combination of one *kilyan* and one standard *k'li* is enough to permit relations in the same room. How can this be? If we are discounting the halachically invalid *kilyan*, why do we not still require *k'li b'toch k'li*?

And why does Abaye start out saying "container" and then switch to "covering"?

Yesod

There are two ways to protect yourself in a situation in which you wish to decrease your exposure. One is to **make yourself invisible**. The other is to **create a diversionary vision** of yourself enough that whoever sees you will see what they imagine you to be instead of what you are.

By way of illustration, the Israeli Air Force in 1967 flew their jets beneath Egyptian radar in order to **make their presence invisible** as they streaked toward their bombing targets in the preemptive strike that kicked off the Six Day War. In 1976, on the other hand, when Israeli commandos raided Entebbe, they could not be invisible when they conducted the raid, so instead they emerged toward the targeted airport in vehicles bearing flags and markings of the Ugandan army, so the guards and soldiers **would see what they thought** were Ugandans and not Israelis.

Berachos 25b

THE DIFFERENCE BETWEEN *kilyan* and *k'li she'eino kilyan* is the above difference. When a *k'li she'eino kilyan* (an itinerant container) is used to cover something, it **makes it invisible**. It is a grocery sack that completely hides what it contains. A *kilyan* container, on the other hand, **creates a diversionary appearance** by expressing the image of its contents according to what the contents (or their owner) wishes to express.

SO LET US use tefillin as an example. Say you are approaching TSA airport security with a pair of tefillin, and you don't want them attracting undue attention and possibly being subjected to invasive scrutiny. One option you have is to conceal the tefillin in a paper bag and hope no agent will ask about the bag's contents. Another option is to carry them in a decorative velvet bag that gives off the impression of something precious and sacred within, in the hopes that the agent will keep his hands off in fear of being insensitive to a religious icon.

THE GEMARA IN *Shabbos* 113a says, "*Mai mani? Mechabdusi*—What is my clothing? The expression of my honor." But clothing is also called simply *keilim* (articles, *Taanis* 29b and elsewhere), where the reference is more to their strict functionality. The latter cover a person and protect him by blocking his body's visibility. The former—parallel to our *kilyan*—protect a person by projecting an image designed to deflect an observer from some aspect of his true reality he is seeking to shield.

    A *Sefer Torah* must be in a separate *reshus* (domain) from the marital relations being conducted. A container (*k'li*) can do that. But the first *k'li* placed over the uncovered *Sefer Torah* is not the one that can do that. That initial *k'li* provides it with **protection**, not with a separate *reshus*. It takes a second container—*k'li b'toch k'li*—to provide the separate *reshus*.

    Enter Abaye. He says this is only true for *itinerant* containers—purely protective containers that are not *kilyan*. But designer *keilim* (what he calls *kilyan*) have a different purpose—not to **hide the article** but to **express what it purports to project**.

    This has two consequences. The first consequence is that, unlike in the case of a standard *k'li*, a second one of these will not provide a separate *reshus*. It will only add more image projection. In Abaye's words: Even ten [expressive] garments are all like one [expressive] garment. Whereby in the case of functional *keilim*, the second one provides a new *reshus*, here in the case of *kilyan*, even the tenth one continues only to project the image of its wearer.

(This, of course, answers our question of why Abaye switches from the language of "container" to the language of "covering." It is a term that more aptly represents the Gemara in *Shabbos* and its reference to clothing as an expression of honor.)

The second consequence is that two (additional) itinerant *keilim* are not required. This is because the first *k'li* (the *kilyan*)—in addition to projecting expression—provides protection (albeit through the alternative method of deflection, mentioned above) thus enabling the second *k'li* to provide a separate *reshus*, so long as it is not another designer *k'li*. In other words, while the case of *keilim she'einan kilyan* requires two *keilim she'einan kilyan* to get to a separate *reshus*, the case of *kilyan* requires only one *k'li she'eino kilyan* to get to a separate *reshus*.

This is what the *Rabbeinu Yonah* means to say, according to the *Taz*. As the *Taz* reads it, *Rabbeinu Yonah* is saying, "You might think Abaye is saying the requirement is *k'li b'toch k'li* and *kilyan* doesn't count so you need two *keilim she'einan kilyan* in addition to the *kilyan*. He isn't saying that. He is saying the requirement is *reshus acheres*. With *keilim she'einan kilyan*, you get *reshus acheres* by the second *k'li she'eino kilyan*. But by *keilim* that are *kilyan*, while you can't get *reshus acheres* with another *k'li* that is *kilyan*, because even after ten such *keilim* they are all still performing the same original function, you can get *reshus acheres* with the first *k'li she'eino kilyan*, thanks to the protection provided by the *kilyan*."

WITH THIS, WE can explain the *hemshech* in the Gemara beautifully. The subject of the previous Gemara was not *Sefer Torah* or tefillin, true. But it was *reshus acheres*. *Reshus acheres* became critical in Rabbi Shimon ben Elazar's *shitah* that the only option available for a *geref shel re'i* in one's home is to have it be put in a *reshus acheres*.

Berachos 25b

Like Rava, who rejects Rabbi Shimon ben Elazar's *shitah*, the pressure is off, because all you have to do is step away four *amos*.

But Abaye might very well disagree with Rava, hold like Rav, and maintain *halachah k'Rabbi Shimon ben Elazar*. So he needs to emphatically make us aware of the status of things that may be protected but might not be considered to be in a separate *reshus*.

A three-*tefach*-high bed is considered *lavud*, so any *geref* underneath such a bed is definitely considered to be in a *reshus acheres*. A ten-*tefach*-high bed, at the other extreme, presents a ceiling over the *geref* so high that the ceiling itself is in its **own** separate *reshus* and the *geref* remains in the same *reshus* as the rest of the house. What about between three and ten *tefachim*, about which Rav Huna told Rav Yosef, "I don't know"?

The Gemara brings the case of the *Sefer Torah*, starting with the story of Rav Achai, to address this.

IN THE CASE of the *Sefer Torah*, we find a case where something requires the kind of covering that affords it "separate *reshus*" status. "*Ad she'yanichem k'li b'toch k'li*" is parallel to "*ad she'yanichem tachas ha'mitah*." And just as *tachas ha'mitah* is only definite for three *tefachim* and below, so too is *k'li b'toch k'li* only definite for *k'li she'eino kilyan*. As Abaye rolls out the case of *kilyan*, it soon leads us to the case of Mar Zutra—the case of a *Sefer Torah* sitting behind a *mechitzah* in a place where another room for it exists. There, **like the designer container that we call *kilyan*, the mechitzah does not serve as a strictly functional partition**. Pure functionality would have meant moving the *Sefer Torah* to its own room. No, this *mechitzah* was *expressive*. And in such a case it is not considered a separate *reshus*, teaches Mar Zutra. Similarly, in the earlier case of the chamber pot, the halachah will depend on the same factor. If the 3–10 *tefachim* space was storing the chamber pot by functional necessity (i.e., there was no other place it could have been protected), the pot would be considered to be in a *reshus acheres* just like a *Sefer Torah* with no other place to be stored. But if the *geref* were underneath the 3–10 *tefachim* bed **by *design* rather than necessity**, we will not consider it as being in a separate *reshus* and **k'rias Shema will be prohibited**—according to Abaye—from being recited anywhere in that house.

דף כה:

This has very practical halachic ramifications in the halachos of *geref shel re'i* even according to Rava. Like Rava, as we have said, it is sufficient to move four *amos* away from an odorless chamber pot. But let's say a person is bedridden or confined to a chair that is within four *amos* of a chamber pot and cannot move away—but the chamber pot is underneath a bed or chair of between three and ten *tefachim* in height! Prior to this insight, we would be forced to rule on the side of *chumrah* (especially since the *issur* of *geref shel re'i*, according to many Rishonim, is the *d'Oraisa* of *tzo'ah*), as we understood the matter of Rav Yosef's question to be unresolved. **Now we can assert that the question is resolved: The status of *reshus acheres* will depend on whether the bedpan is under the bed because a) it has nowhere else to be placed, or b) it is aesthetically preferable to keep it there.** If the former, it will be considered *reshus acheres* and *k'rias Shema* will be *mutar*. If the latter, it will be considered to be in the same four *amos* as the person and *k'rias Shema* will be *assur*.

It turns out the entire *hemshech* of the Gemara is all simply a carefully woven set of halachic material and relevant episodes arranged to teach us the answer to Rav Yosef's question.

A SMALL DETAIL at the end of the *sugya* supports my contention. What was it that Mar bar Rav Ashi was said to have commented when he heard the halachah from Mar Zutra? He said, "I didn't know."

You're in good company, Mar bar Rav Ashi. The halachah was the same as the one Rav Huna told Rav Yosef he didn't know either.

Berachos 26a

דף כו. (1)

In the previous lesson, we concluded that—according to the *Rambam*—Rava agrees that the halachah of distancing oneself from a chamber pot follows Rabbi Shimon ben Elazar. This means that as long as one creates a distance between himself and the *geref* of four *amos* or more, he may recite *k'rias Shema* in its proximity.

What Rava means by his statement, "The halachah is not like Rabbi Shimon ben Elazar," is that the halachah is not like Rabbi Shimon ben Elazar's **other** claim—that one's house is considered to be one large *daled amos*.

Rejecting Rabbi Shimon ben Elazar's claim on the unsuitability of the whole house—as we explained—makes it less crucial that we clarify the rules of what constitutes a "buried" chamber pot under a bed. After all, why bother to "bury" a chamber pot if all you need to do is move four *amos* away from it?

So when Rav Huna answered Rav Yosef's questions about buried chamber pots under the bed by saying "I don't know," it is clear he simply doesn't care enough to know—because, evidently, he agrees with Rava that the halachah is like Rabbi Shimon ben Elazar in accepting *four amos*, and not like Rabbi Shimon ben Elazar when he disallows the house on the grounds that it is considered like one large "four *amos*."

All of this leads us to our Gemara on 26a.

Rava quotes his source and mentor Rav Huna to limit the ruling one notch.

> לא שנו אלא לאחוריו אבל לפניו מרחיק מלא עיניו וכן לתפלה.

> *All that we just taught is as regards distancing oneself* **behind** *the geref [or other open tzo'ah or mei raglayim] or to its side. But* **facing** *it—four amos is not enough. It must be out of eyeshot. [This is true for k'rias Shema] and for tefillah.*

דף כו.

What appears to happen next is that the Gemara challenges this limitation from Rav Chisda. Rav Chisda says one can daven facing a bathroom (obviously an open one, for a walled one would go without saying). The Gemara seems to deflect this challenge by applying Rav Chisda's ruling to a bathroom emptied of *tzo'ah*. The deflection is scuttled by Rav Yosef bar Chanina's assertion that an emptied bathroom is the same as a *tzo'ah*-filled bathroom. So we are back to our challenge as it is found in Rav Chisda's ruling. So it seems.

The Gemara apparently proceeds to answer the Rav Chisda challenge by assigning Rav Chisda's *din* to a **new** bathroom. A brand-new bathroom is not a bathroom at all—**that's** the place to apply the *heter* of Rav Chisda! So when it comes to real bathrooms, Rava and Rav Huna are still cleared to place limitations on daveners who are facing them.

The Gemara attacks the premise of this answer from Ravina. "Not a bathroom at all? But Ravina is *mesupak* that maybe a bathroom becomes a bathroom by designation (*hazmanah*) alone!" So a brand-new bathroom **is** being considered as a possible bathroom and Rav Chisda is nevertheless allowing us to daven while facing it! The challenge is back on!

So, finally, it seems, the Gemara fires its winning salvo. "Ravina was *mesupak* only about *hazmanah* insofar as davening **inside** a room designated to be a bathroom. But to daven **facing** one, Ravina was never *mesupak*." So davening **facing** a bathroom is Rav Chisda's rule and Rava *amar* Rav Huna is home free to apply restrictions on *k'negdo*.

Then Rava adds one more halachah: Persian bathrooms are not bathrooms, because the waste material does not stay in them. So they would not be subject to the limitation just taught.

FROM THE APPARENT flow of the Gemara, it would seem the halachah should be like Rava *amar* Rav Huna—that facing an open bathroom or *tzo'ah* should be incompatible with reciting *k'rias Shema* or davening, and should be like Rava that Persian bathrooms are not bathrooms. But that is not how the *Rambam* rules.

203

Berachos 26a

He says that the *heter* of *daled amos*—wherever it applies—works without limitation (see previous chapter), and nowhere does he bring the *din* of Persian bathrooms.

1. Why does the *Rambam* reject the halachos as they seemingly emerge from a straightforward Gemara?
2. When the Gemara brought Rabbi Yosef bar Chanina, what was the Gemara thinking? Why should it matter that a bathroom without *tzo'ah* is as much a bathroom as a bathroom with *tzo'ah*? All that does is define a bathroom. But so what? Our issue was not about davening facing a bathroom—our issue was about davening facing *tzo'ah*! Even if a clean bathroom is called a bathroom, it is still a bathroom without *tzo'ah*. So the only issue here is not a person facing *tzo'ah*, it's a person facing a bathroom. Whoever said there is a halachic problem with davening facing a bathroom? That is nowhere in the Mishnah!
3. The *Rambam* states categorically that davening inside a new bathroom is forbidden. The *Raavad* does not understand this ruling, as, according to the Gemara, it was a *safek* to Ravina, *hazmanah* is at most a *d'Rabbanan*, and *safek d'Rabbanan* is *l'kula*. What makes *Rambam* rule as strictly as he does?

Yesod

The *Rambam* knows that davening inside a new bathroom is assur from a *hava amina* in the Gemara. When the Gemara tried to answer the question on Rav Chisda from Rabbi Yosef bar Chanina, it did so by saying Rav Chisda said his *din* by a new bathroom while Rabbi Yosef bar Chanina said his *din* by an existing bathroom. The

Gemara later changed this (after discovering this wouldn't help Rav Chisda—he would still have a problem from Ravina's *safek*) back to saying that Rav Chisda was discussing davening **facing** a bathroom.

Let's think. Now, at this point in the Gemara, that we are back to saying that Rav Chisda is discussing a person facing a bathroom, must we still assume Rav Chisda's case remains only about facing a **new** bathroom? Or can we say that new bathroom versus old bathroom is

דף כו.

not the issue anymore; the issue is davening facing a bathroom versus davening inside a bathroom. And there is no *kashya* from Rabbi Yosef bar Chanina, because he could be said to have been talking only about davening **inside** a bathroom when he equated an emptied bathroom with a full one. What we would say is that just like Ravina differentiated between "inside" and "facing," so too could Rabbi Yosef bar Chanina be differentiating between "inside" and "facing," and the *kashya* from Rabbi Yosef bar Chanina on Rav Chisda actually disappears.

But one thing the *Rambam* notices about *shitas* Rav Chisda is that the Gemara did not dismiss its *hava amina* (that the issue was new versus old) on the grounds that if Rav Chisda is indeed talking about a new bathroom, why would he limit himself to the smaller *chiddush* that davening is permitted facing a new bathroom, when he could have said a much greater *chiddush* that davening is permitted even **inside** a new bathroom? It must be, concludes the *Rambam*, that the Gemara knew already in the *hava amina* that Rav Chisda was never *matir* davening inside a new bathroom. The most he ever was going to be *matir* was davening facing a new bathroom. As long as we thought Ravina was *mesupak* even about davening **facing** a bathroom with *hazmanah*, we thought we still had a clash between Rav Chisda and Ravina. So the Gemara limited the scope of Ravina's *safek*. In limiting Ravina, we retain two options:

1. Continue with the notion that Rav Chisda is talking about new bathrooms, and learn Rav Chisda by "facing new" and Ravina by "inside new."
2. Go back to the earlier notion that Rav Chisda is "facing an old bathroom" and limit Rabbi Yosef bar Chanina to "inside an old bathroom."

Much more logical is to take Option 2)—Rav Chisda holds davening facing an old bathroom is *mutar*; davening facing a new bathroom is *mutar mi'kol she'kein*; Rav Chisda holds davening inside a new bathroom is *assur* (although Ravina is *mesupak*, and so like him it might be *mutar*); Rabbi Yosef bar Chanina holds davening inside an emptied bathroom is as bad as davening inside a *tzo'ah*-filled one; Rabbi Yosef bar Chanina

Berachos 26a

takes no position on davening facing a bathroom; and we don't know what Rabbi Yosef bar Chanina would say about davening inside a new bathroom.

But wait a minute—why are we suddenly so concerned with what Rav Chisda actually holds? Isn't the whole purpose of our Gemara to present the halachah of *l'fanav marchik m'lo einav*? Wasn't Rav Chisda cited only as a pesky problem for Rav Huna? Isn't it enough just to neutralize Rav Chisda—not to understand him?

Yes, that is the approach of Rava. But Rava quickly finds himself engaged in a *machlokes* with a strong foe—the *stama d'Gemara*, which disagrees with his approach entirely.

COME SEE HOW the *Rambam* learns a Gemara:

> *Rava:* Mishnah says harchakah is daled amos, but that's only from the sides and back of the tzo'ah. Harchakah required in front is unlimited [m'lo einav]!
>
> *Gemara:* What do you mean? Rav Chisda doesn't hold that way! He paskens you can daven facing a bathroom. Sure, we could've said he meant only an empty bathroom, but from Rabbi Yosef bar Chanina it is clear that an empty bathroom has the same halachah as a tzo'ah-filled bathroom. And Rav Chisda permits it! So evidently he holds the four amos din of the Mishnah is enough even in front of tzo'ah!
>
> *Rava:* Rav Chisda is talking about a new bathroom, which isn't a bathroom at all! It certainly isn't tzo'ah. But for tzo'ah, which happens to be the topic of our Mishnah? There is no limit to the harchakah required when standing face-to-face with tzo'ah.
>
> *Gemara:* You can't say a new bathroom is not a bathroom. Ravina thought about assering one based on hazmanah alone! No, Rav Chisda is definitely talking about every kind of bathroom, and he holds mutar *l'hispallel k'negdo*!

*Rava: Yes, I **can** say a new bathroom is not a bathroom. What Ravina thought about assering from hazmanah alone was davening **inside** a new bathroom. K'neged [facing] a real bathroom, it is certainly assur to daven.*

Gemara: You, Rava, just admitted that a chiluk can be made between "facing" and "inside." So apply that to Rabbi Yosef bar Chanina. Let's propose Rabbi Yosef bar Chanina says his din equating an emptied bathroom to a tzo'ah-filled one only with regard to davening inside a bathroom. And then let's propose he would have no problem with davening facing a bathroom that was free of actual tzo'ah [and maybe even one filled with tzo'ah, and maybe even tzo'ah itself, as long as you have daled amos, just like the simple reading of the Mishnah], as we wanted to say initially in Rav Chisda.

*Rava: I disagree. Rav Chisda is referring to chadti—a new bathroom only. Ravina is safek machmir on davening inside a chadti. On old [regular] bathrooms, the din is with Rabbi Yosef bar Chanina who equates emptied ones with tzo'ah-filled ones, both for davening inside them **and for davening facing them**. I only make one exception, and that is for Persian bathrooms, because of the clean way they are constructed. End of Gemara.*

The way the *Rambam* reads it, the Gemara does not end up with a rebuff to the challenges against Rava. The Gemara ends up with a firm, unresolved *machlokes* between Rava and the *stama d'Gemara*, for whom the existence of Rav Chisda makes it impossible to learn the way Rava wants. And the *Rambam paskens* like the *stama d'Gemara*, which compels him to *pasken* like Rav Chisda, thus there is no *m'lo einav* or other *k'negdo* restrictions on bathrooms, just on actual waste matter, no davening inside a new bathroom, and no need for an "exception" for Persian bathrooms. If it means davening *k'neged* them, it is already *mutar* to daven *k'neged* much worse ones than those. And if it means

Berachos 26a

davening inside them, if we can't even daven inside a brand-new bathroom, we certainly can't daven inside a Persian bathroom.

This way, the entire *Rambam* is *m'yushav*, *b'ezras Hashem*.

דף כו. (2)

מתני׳ זב שראה קרי וגו׳.

The Mishnah on 26a at the end of the third *perek* gives us three cases in which *Tanna Kama* and Rabbi Yehudah argue:

1. *Zav she'ra'ah keri*—A man was a *zav*, in the middle of waiting seven days to be able to purify himself in a *mikveh*, when he became a *baal keri*.
2. *Niddah she'paltah shichvas zera*—A woman was a *niddah*, in the middle of waiting seven days to be able to purify herself in a mikveh, when she became a *baalas keri*.
3. *Ha'meshameshes she'ra'asah niddah*—A woman was a *baalas keri* (from *tashmish ha'mitah*) and—before being able to purify herself in a *mikveh*—became a *niddah*.

In all three cases, *Tanna Kama* is *mechayev* a *tevilah* for the *keri* despite its inability to render the subject completely *tahor* due to the overlapping *tumah*; and Rabbi Yehudah exempts.

THE GEMARA GOES on to ask whether Rabbi Yehudah would exempt even in a case of *baal keri she'ra'ah zivah*. Would this be different since the *baal keri* status came first? The Gemara answers that Rabbi Yehudah's position would be the same, and that we see this from Case #3 in the Mishnah, where the woman's *keri* status preceded her *niddah* status and that did not change Rabbi Yehudah's position. The Gemara then goes on to cite a *Beraisa* formulating this theory explicitly:

תני רבי חייא בהדיא בעל קרי שראה זיבה צריך
טבילה ורבי יהודה פוטר.

Berachos 26a

> *Rabbi Chiya taught explicitly: A baal keri who then became a zav requires tevilah. Rabbi Yehudah exempts him.*

The Gemara is puzzling. From the fact that Rabbi Yehudah calls his position an exemption (*p'tur*), it seems he is allowing the *baal keri* to learn Torah, daven, and recite *k'rias Shema* and *berachos* without *tevilah*. But *Rashi* on 21a seems incompatible with this thinking. According to *Rashi*, the reason Rabbi Yehudah exempts is because the *tevilah* will be entirely ineffective. This gives the impression that the *keri* status cannot be repaired as long as other *tumah* overlaps it, and that he remains a *baal keri*—unable to learn, daven, or speak holy things—until it is removed! How can we understand Rabbi Yehudah in light of *Rashi*? According to *Rashi*, shouldn't Rabbi Yehudah have said *"chayav v'eino yachol"*? Why *"patur"*? Furthermore, why did the Gemara not already know about Case #3 when it asked its initial question, and what does the Gemara gain by bringing the additional source of Rabbi Chiya's *Beraisa*?

--- *Yesod* ---

Let's analyze the Gemara's whole question. What difference does it make whether the *tumas keri* comes first or the *tumas zivah* (or *niddah*) comes first? Aren't both of them cases of overlap?

The difference must be this issue of *"chayav v'eino yachol."* If all we have from Rabbi Yehudah is a case of *zav she'ra'ah keri*, we can say that the pre-existence of the *tumas zivah* cancels not the *tevilah* but the *tumas keri* itself, which is only *tamei* as a result of *takanas Ezra*, and it could easily be said that where no immediate solution exists, Ezra never imposed a status of *tamei*! But if this were the case, Rabbi Yehudah could learn *"patur"* only by *zav she'ra'ah keri*, where the pre-existence of the larger *tumah* could yield a true *"p'tur"*—and thus a *heter limud*—on the *baal keri*. But by *keri she'ra'ah zivah*, where the *keri* was classic *keri* when it hit first, no *heter* could be granted after the person became a *zav*, and Rabbi Yehudah would have to say *"chayav v'eino yachol,"* not *"patur."*

So in order to find out what Rabbi Yehudah means by *"patur,"* the Gemara seeks to know what he says by *keri she'ra'ah zivah*. If he says "*patur*" there too, it is clear that Rabbi Yehudah means "*patur*" from the requirement of immersion and allowed to learn without *tevilah*, not like *Rashi*. But if by *keri she'ra'ah zivah*, Rabbi Yehudah does not say "*patur*," it is arguable that where the *keri* hits first, the *baal keri* will not be allowed to learn (even if he goes ahead and immerses anyway!), because "*patur*" means exempt from the *tumas keri*, but completely liable to its *tevilah* requirement once it hits, a *tevilah* requirement that can only be satisfied if it yields *taharah* upon immersion.

This also explains why we need Tani Rabbi Chiya. Without it, it could still be that Rabbi Yehudah is lenient by a woman because she has no mitzvah of *Talmud Torah*, for which the need for *eimah*, *yirah*, *reses*, and *zei'ah* is what prompted *takanas Ezra* in the first place; but maybe he would still say "*chayav v'eino yachol*" by a *baal keri she'ra'ah zivah*! Rabbi Chiya leaves no doubt.

Endnotes

1. *Rambam, Mishneh Torah, Hilchos K'rias Shema* 4:4.
2. *Tur, Orach Chaim* 78.
3. *Rambam, Mishneh Torah, Hilchos Tefillah* 4:13.
4. *Shulchan Aruch* 78:1.
5. *Rambam, Mishneh Torah, Hilchos K'rias Shema* 3:10.

Chapter Four
Tefillas Ha'shachar

Berachos 26a

דף כו. (3)

מתני׳ תפלת השחר עד חצות רבי יהודה אומר עד ד׳ שעות וגו׳.

The morning [Shemoneh Esreh] prayer [can be said] until noon. Rabbi Yehudah says until four hours [into the day].

1. *Chachamim* and Rabbi Yehudah argue in the Mishnah over whether *Shacharis* can be said until *chatzos* (for illustrative purposes, let's call it 12:00 PM) or the [end of the] fourth hour (10:00 AM). Ordinarily, we would *pasken* like *Chachamim* in such a *machlokes*, but here we *pasken* like Rabbi Yehudah. Rav Kahana on 27b says this is because Rabbi Yehudah's opinion is cited in a Mishnah in the authoritative *Mesechta Eduyos*. But a look at that Mishnah reveals that all the Mishnah did was tell a story about the one time the lamb for the *korban Tamid* was found late and had to be processed at 10:00 AM. How does this incident prove the halachah is like Rabbi Yehudah? Even if the halachah were like *Chachamim*, the lamb would have been processed when it was found at 10:00 AM!

2. The Gemara, according to our *girsa*, after establishing that the *vasikin* standard for *z'man tefillah* is not a contradiction to our Mishnah, challenges *Chachamim*'s end time of *chatzos* from a teaching of Rabbi Yochanan that one can do a make-up *tefillah* for *Shacharis* after *chatzos*. The Gemara answers this by saying that on-time *tefillah* (*tefillah b'zmanah*) is only until *chatzos*. After *chatzos* (until the end of the day), you can still get *tefillah* credit, just not *tefillah b'zmanah* credit. This poses the following four difficulties:

דף כו.

a. If *tefillah* is a request for our needs, why are we talking about credit? One who failed to daven in the morning can no longer get his morning needs met in the afternoon!

b. Why was this even a challenge? For all we know at this point, *tashlumin* might be a special *chiddush* unrelated to the primary obligation of *tefillah*. The fact that one can do a *tashlumin* after *chatzos* should not have to mean that the *z'man tefillah* is not over at *chatzos*!

c. Those who *pasken* like Rabbi Yehudah bring *l'halachah* that you get *z'man tefillah* credit until 10:00 AM, and after-*z'man tefillah* credit **until chatzos**. Why is it that with the *Chachamim*'s *z'man* you get after-*z'man tefillah* credit all the rest of the day and with Rabbi Yehudah's *z'man* you get after-*z'man* credit only until noon, and how did the *poskim* even know this? Even according to Rabbi Yehudah, there is no reason the after-*z'man* time shouldn't continue to extend until the end of the day like it does for *Chachamim*!

d. According to the *girsa* of the *Rif* and *Rosh*, the teaching of Rabbi Yochanan is not a challenge at all, because in their version the phrase "*v'kulei alma ad chatzos v'su lo?*" does not exist as a preface to Rabbi Yochanan's statement. Instead, "*v'kulei alma ad chatzos*" is the end of the resolution of the question from *vasikin*. Rabbi Yochanan's statement stands alone as an independent teaching about *tashlumin* for missed *tefillos* (*Rosh* even brings this halachah in its own separate *siman*). How does *Rosh* understand this? What is an independent *sugya* of *tashlumin* for missed *tefillos* doing in the middle of our discussion of *z'man tefillah*?

3. After accepting a question about whether Rabbi Yochanan's *din* of *tashlumin* extends past the end of the day (enabling the making up of a missed *Minchah* at *Maariv*), the Gemara concludes that it does, suggesting that *tefillos* are not connected to the daily *Tamidim* (in which case we would say *avar yomo batel korbano*). How does this square with the statement on *amud*

215

beis in the name of Rabbi Yehoshua ben Levi—*paskened* by all *poskim*—that *tefillos k'neged tamidim niskenu*?

4. If the *Rosh paskens* like Rabbi Yehudah that *z'man Shacharis* is until 10:00 AM, how can he *pasken* that *z'man Musaf* is all day, when Rabbi Yehudah's opinion on *Musaf* is that it is only valid until 1:00 PM? [Apparently, some versions are so concerned about this discrepancy that they remove Rabbi Yehudah's *Musaf* position from the Mishnah entirely!]

5. The Gemara on *amud beis* quotes Rabbi Yose bar Chanina as saying the *tefillos* were established by the *Avos*, beginning with Avraham Avinu establishing *Shacharis*. The source for this is given as the *pasuk* in *Parashas Vayera* that Avraham rose early the next morning (after the destruction of Sodom and Amorah) and returned to the place where he had stood [in prayer] the previous day. At least according to the *Rambam*, the Biblical obligation to pray once a day already existed, so all Avraham could have established is that it be done in the morning. But the *pasuk* does not say he woke up early and prayed. It says he returned to the spot where he prayed the previous day. But if the previous day's prayer was his dialogue with G-d on behalf of the Sodomites, that took place in the afternoon, not the morning. We know this because the *malachim* arrived at noon (*k'chom ha'yom*) and left after a meal was served. They reached S'dom that evening. Avraham went out to escort them, and at the spot where he bid them depart, Hashem came to Avraham and the dialogue ensued. That would have been an afternoon prayer, not a morning one. What does it mean that Avraham established *Shacharis*?

6. *Pirkei Avos* tells us the world stands on Torah, *avodah*, and *gemilus chassadim*. Life in Gan Eden (pre-sin) included *avodah* (*l'avdah u'l'shamrah*) and *chessed* (*olam chessed yibaneh*), but there was no Torah in Gan Eden. How would life in Gan Eden have been sustainable, had there been no sin, without the pillar of Torah?

Yesod

All relationships require two fundamental types of interaction—giving and receiving.

In our world, Torah is the way we receive from God, and *avodah* is the way we give to God.

But what is it that we receive from God through our study of Torah? It is our sense of self. Torah, by connecting us to the Divine thinking process, connects us to the Source of Life, which gives us a confirmed sense of our own existence.

But in Gan Eden, it was different. Being in the unconcealed presence of God, as we were, we did not need to study Torah in order to have a sense of our existence. Our existence was inherently sensed through our acute awareness of God's permeating all of existence. Not needing to receive a sense of ourselves, then, what we received instead as part of our relationship equation was material bounty—all the abundance of Gan Eden! And how did we access the receiving of that material bounty? Through *tefillah*, using the mechanism explicitly referred to in *Bereishis* 2:5 as *avodah* (see *Rashi*, s.v. *ki lo himtir*)!

Evidently, pre-sin *avodah* performed the exact opposite function of post-sin *avodah*. In our world, *avodah* is the way we give to God. But in Gan Eden, *avodah* was the way we received from God!

Incidentally, how did we **give** to God in Gan Eden? We gave to God by guarding the Garden—doing *shemirah*! And that is the meaning of *l'avdah u'l'shamrah*. That was the original version of *Torah v'avodah*, with *avodah* first serving as our means for receiving, with *shemirah* as our means for giving. Only later did *avodah* flip its role to our means for giving, after Man's expulsion and disconnection from God's presence required a displacing of the receiving function of *avodah* (which was only effective for receiving bounty) in favor of a new kind of receiving made accessible just over two thousand years later with *Matan Torah* (effective for receiving a sense of existence).

This should not be such a surprise. This original function of *tefillah* was the very thing Moshe had been asked to reinstate when God asked him to speak to the rock. Communicating our needs and desires to nature and having nature respond with provisions is precisely what *Rashi* describes in Gan Eden when Adam would pray for rain and bounty would ensue! Of course, Moshe did not succeed, as his act of hitting the rock was more like the demanding, begging, and imploring styles of prayer with which we are more familiar.

This brings us back to the question of *tefillos Avos tiknum* versus *tefillos k'neged Tamidim niskenu*.

With Torah set to take over as the new catalyst for receiving, what was to be the new conduit for the function of our giving to G-d?

The answer is—*korbanos*, the *avodah* known as the sacrificial service. Prayer—formerly used to communicate and thereby receive—had no expected role in the new *avodah*-as-giving scenario. We would learn Torah to receive from God, and we would bring *korbanos*—primarily the daily *Tamidim*—to give to God. Prayer we would continue to engage in—once a day per Torah law—simply because we were commanded to do so, but it would have no role in the relationship matrix of God and the Jewish People.

THE AVOS WISHED to amend this plan. Aware that Torah was still several generations off in the future, they established the *d'Rabbanan* institution of *tefillah* as an interim way of receiving from God, or at the very least, *asking* to receive from God. The concept first came to Avraham as he was using *tefillah* to petition on behalf of the Sodomites. *Tefillah* can have a role in our Heavenly relationship, Avraham realized, even if it is not the one originally intended by the Creator and practiced in Eden. Although for it to be successful, it should not be left for the afternoon—after the trouble is already upon us—but it henceforth should be done in the morning as a prophylactic against troubles coming upon us during the day. Had I only davened for S'dom before God approached me with his plans to destroy the city, thought Avraham, I might have succeeded in averting that decree.

Shacharis was thus established. Yitzchak added *Minchah* and Yaakov added *Maariv*, with similar calculations in mind. Until Torah becomes the force that it will, we can use *tefillah* to receive—not bounty, but favors from Hashem that we still need *erev va'voker v'tzaharayim*.

According to Rabbi Yose bar Chanina, this set of enactments put in play by our Avos is the origin of our *seder tefillos d'Rabbanan* to this day.

Rabbi Yehoshua ben Levi says—no, that's not it at all.

Our *tefillos* are not from the Avos' use of *tefillah*. Our *tefillos* are from the *Anshei Knesses Hagedolah*'s alarm that the loss of the sacrificial service would leave us with no format for giving to God. Through Torah we will receive from God, but how will we give to God without *korbanos*?

The answer—*u'n'shalmah parim s'faseinu*. Our prayers will have to replace the *korbanos* in the role of *avodah*-as-giving.

What difference is there between the two approaches? The difference is massive. If our *tefillos* are from the Avos, they are a vestige of the original function prayer once had of **receiving from** God. If our *tefillos* are from the *korbanos*, they are serving in their newly acquired role as vehicles for **giving to** God.

I wish to suggest that the *machlokes* between the *Chachamim* and Rabbi Yehudah is that the *Chachamim* hold like Rabbi Yose bar Chanina that our *tefillos* today originate with the original-function *tefillos* established by the Avos, and Rabbi Yehudah holds like Rabbi Yehoshua ben Levi that our *tefillos* originate with the new-function *tefillos* put into place in lieu of *korbanos* by the *Anshei Knesses Hagedolah*.

More simply, the *Chachamim* hold our *tefillos* are for **receiving** from God; Rabbi Yehudah holds our *tefillos* are for **giving** to God.

To be sure, there is crossover. Rabbi Yehudah does not deny that in the process of performing our daily *tefillah* regimen, we are simultaneously fulfilling our *d'Oraisa* obligation of *l'avdo*—which we have already established to be an obligation of receiving, even if our primary mode of receiving is through learning Torah. And the *Chachamim* do not deny that without *korbanos*, we definitely do need a format for giving, and the *tefillos* might even serve *both* functions as a result.

But with this approach, we can begin to answer the questions that troubled us when we first encountered the *sugya*.

For one thing, we can understand Rav Kahana's proof from the source in *Eduyos*. The proof is not from the fact that they brought the *korban* at 10:00 AM. The proof is from the very fact that they linked the *machlokes Chachamim* and Rabbi Yehudah to the bringing of the

Berachos 26a

Tamid at all! That is evidence that the Mishnah held the *tefillah* issue over which the *Chachamim* and Rabbi Yehudah tussle is connected to the *korban* issue, which is a clear act of siding with Rabbi Yehudah over the *Chachamim*, for whom the dispute with Rabbi Yehudah over *z'man tefillah* would have been at most tangential, not central, to the incident of the delayed *korban Tamid*.

Next, we can understand how the *poskim* knew to limit after-*z'man tefillah* credit in Rabbi Yehudah to *chatzos* only. Like the *Chachamim*, *tefillah* is a Rabbinic extension of the *d'Oraisa* of *tefillah*—a once-a-day obligation that would have been perfectly acceptable done anytime during the day. Fixing a *tefillah* at *Shacharis* was no more than Avraham Avinu's gambit to make the prayer more successful. It would make no sense to cut off the afternoon from *tefillah*-credit when *m'd'Oraisa* such a thing remains a fully accredited behavior and the *d'Rabbanan* is anyway linked to that *d'Oraisa*.

But according to Rabbi Yehudah, our *tefillos* have little to do with the original *d'Oraisa* of *l'avdo*. That was about **receiving**. Our *tefillos* are now about **giving**. *Shacharis* was invented to parallel the *Tamid shel Shachar*. If we have a gift to give God, we should be giving it first thing in the morning—like the *Tamid* (and the way it is in fact done by the *vasikin*). At the very least, make sure to bring it *b'zmano*—by 10:00 AM. But by the afternoon, after *chatzos ha'yom*, it no longer has any ability to parallel the *Tamid shel Shachar*. That train has left the station! It is now time for the *Tamid shel Bein Ha'arbayim*. Maybe there is a new *chiddush* called a *din tashlumin* (that does not even exist by the *Tamidim*!), but the *tefillah* that was *niskan* after the morning *Tamid* is gone and can not be credited even as after-*z'man tefillah*. To the *poskim*, this was self-evident!

And we can now understand why the Gemara was not at all certain you could make up a missed *Minchah* at *Maariv*. If we could be *paskening* like Rabbi Yehudah, how could there be a *din* of *tashlumin*? Rabbi Yehudah links our *tefillos* to the *Tamidim*, and the *Tamidim* have no possibility of *tashlumin*! And even if you decide to look at all the day's *korbanos* as merged, certainly Rabbi Yehudah would say *avar z'mano batel korbano* by the end of the day!

דף כו.

When the Gemara quotes Rabbi Yochanan as permitting a *tashlumin* of *Minchah* at *Maariv*, the Gemara realizes that while the *tefillos* themselves might be linked to the *Tamidim*, the *din* of *tashlumin* is a completely separate concept, and might even be a nod to the original *d'Oraisa* desire to have prayer be a vehicle for *bakoshos rachamim*, welcome any time and subject to the expression *"u'l'vai she'yispallel adam kol ha'yom."* In other words, according to Rabbi Yehudah, I should fulfill my *tefillah*-as-giving obligation first thing in the morning. If not, I should certainly complete it within the time period mandated for the gift. If it is still technically within the gift's framework (a morning gift can only be called that as long as it is still morning), I can still get credit for bringing an untimely gift. After that, it will no longer be a valid gift, but I can still revert to the Torah level, at which *tefillah* is not a gift but a *bakashas rachamim* request to receive, and that is what we call *din tashlumin*.

And so there is no contradiction between denying *avar yomo batel korbano* and *paskening* that *tefillos k'neged tamidim nis'kenu*. The latter is addressing our primary halachic view that *tefillos* today perform the function of giving. The former addresses the back-up plan, known as *din tashlumin*, whereby our *tefillos* revert to their original function of asking for and receiving kindnesses and favors from Hashem.

Musaf is different, because it contains no aspect of receiving. Thus, it can have no *tashlumin*, it was not recited before *churban haBayis*, and it does not fall back onto the *d'Oraisa* level. That fact that the *Chachamim* hold of it at all shows that even the *Chachamim* agree to the level of giving now attached to *tefillos*, if not at a primary level like Rabbi Yehudah holds. But then why don't the *Chachamim* require that it be done by seven hours in the day like Rabbi Yehudah does? This exposes a new split between the *Chachamim* and Rabbi Yehudah. To Rabbi Yehudah, reciting the *tefillos* is like bringing the *korbanos*. The *korban Musaf* had to be brought by seven hours in the day, so *tefillas Musaf* must be done by seven hours in the day. But like the *Chachamim*, even at best, davening is not like bringing the *korbanos* themselves; *tefillos* only get their **time of day** parameters from *korbanos*. *Musaf* is *b'dieved* brought all day, so its time parameter is all day.

Berachos 26a

It turns out we may actually *pasken* like the *Chachamim*, not like Rabbi Yehudah. This may be dependent on the *machlokes Taz/Magen Avraham* versus *Darkei Moshe (Rama)* that we find in the issue of what ensues when a person reverses the order of his *Maariv tefillah* and his *tashlumin tefillah* on a Motza'ei Shabbos. See the next *shiur* for further discussion of this subject.

דף כו:

ת״ר טעה ולא התפלל מנחה בערב שבת מתפלל בליל שבת שתים טעה ולא התפלל מנחה בשבת מתפלל במוצאי שבת שתים של חול וגו׳.

The Rabbis taught: If one forgot Friday afternoon Minchah, he davens two Shabbos evening Maariv tefillos on Friday night. If he forgot Shabbos afternoon Minchah, he davens two weekday Maariv tefillos on Motza'ei Shabbos. [During those tefillos,] he adds the Havdalah in the first of the two Maarivs but not in the second. (Rashi—The first time around he davens for the immediate obligation and thus includes Havdalah in Chonen Ha'daas; the second is for making up the missed Shabbos tefillah; he does not include Havdalah.¹) And if he adds the Havdalah in the second but not in the first, his second [tefillah] counts [for his Motza'ei Shabbos prayer] but his first [tefillah] does not count [for anything, as he is not allowed to proceed with his make-up tefillah before having discharged his immediate obligation.² The second tefillah also does not count for his Shabbos make-up because, having included Havdalah, he reveals that it is not intended as a Shabbos tefillah; that it should be considered as Maariv.]

Gemara: Does this mean to say that leaving out Havdalah is like you didn't daven at all and we would make you go back? But don't we have a Tosefta that says that if you omit Mashiv Ha'ruach or V'sein Berachah/Tal U'matar we make you go back, but if you omit Havdalah we don't make you go back because you will anyway be making Havdalah over a cup of wine? It is a question.³

Berachos 26b

1. The *Beraisa* of *Ta'ah v'lo hispallel Minchah b'Shabbos mispallel b'Motza'ei Shabbos sh'nayim* begins with the *din* of *Ta'ah Erev Shabbos mispallel b'Shabbos sh'tayim*. It does not need to begin there, as proven from the fact that it does not begin with the other *dinim* of *tashlumin*. So why does it begin with *Ta'ah Erev Shabbos*?

2. The bigger question is: Why should it matter that he left Havdalah out of the first *Maariv*? That omission has no invalidating effect on the *Maariv*, so his first *Maariv* should have counted for his immediate obligation, at which point his second *Maariv* should be a completely legitimate *tashlumin*, and so what if it contains Havdalah? As simply understood (but see *Tosafos*, s.v. *Ta'ah* for an alternative view), the point of a *tashlumin* is not to capture the features of the missed *Shemoneh Esreh*—it is to make up for a missed *tefillah* with the *tefillah* of the next segment, whatever that happens to be (which is probably why this *sugya* begins by advising us that a second *Maariv* on Shabbos can make up for a missed Friday afternoon *Minchah* despite the fact that Shabbos *tefillos* are made up of completely different content than weekday *tefillos*)!

Yesod

The *lashon* of the Gemara is very telling. The *lashon* is: "*Mavdil ba'rishonah v'eino mavdil b'sh'niyah.*" Then it says "*V'im hivdil b'sh'niyah v'lo hivdil ba'rishonah, sh'niyah alsa lo rishonah lo alsa lo.*"

Why is the second statement presented backward? The order of the events as they transpired should have the Gemara saying: "*V'im lo hivdil ba'rishonah v'hivdil b'sh'niyah, sh'niyah alsa lo rishonah lo alsa lo.*"

I believe the Gemara is setting up a very specific set of circumstances. The reason the Gemara doesn't say, "*V'im lo hivdil ba'rishonah v'hivdil b'sh'niyah...lo alsa lo,*" is because if that were exactly what happened, his actions **would** be *alsa lo*. The problem scenario is where he davened *Maariv* and immediately realized he had left out Havdalah. Now he has two choices. If he says to himself, "No problem—I will make Havdalah on a *kos*," he is *yotzei Maariv* and he may now proceed to his *tashlumin*. If during that *tashlumin* he inadvertently included Havdalah, it would still be valid.

But if he says to himself, "Oy, I left out Havdalah! I'd better daven again!" he is mentally disqualifying his first *Maariv* from fulfilling his current obligation. Then, because his second *Maariv* will count as his regular *Maariv*, his first *Maariv* cannot and will not count as his *tashlumin*.

That is the *lashon*: "If he says Havdalah in the second *because* he had not said Havdalah in the first, the second counts [as his *Maariv* and therefore] the first doesn't count [as his *tashlumin*]."

דף כט:

אמר רבי תנחום אמר רב אסי אמר רבי יהושע בן לוי טעה ולא הזכיר של ראש חדש בעבודה חוזר לעבודה וגו'.

Rabbi Tanchum said in the name of Rav Assi, who said in the name of Rabbi Yehoshua ben Levi: If one erred and did not mention Rosh Chodesh in R'tzei [i.e., he omitted Yaaleh V'Yavo in Shemoneh Esreh], he returns to R'tzei. If he remembered in Modim, he returns to R'tzei. If he remembered in Sim Shalom, he returns to R'tzei. But if he concluded [Shemoneh Esreh], he returns to the beginning.

Said Rav Papa son of Rav Acha bar Adda: That which we say, "he returns to the beginning," we only say if he moved his feet. But if he did not yet move his feet, he returns to R'tzei.

[(He) (They) said to him: How do you know this? He answered, "From Abba Mari I heard this, and Abba Mari heard it from Rav."]

Said Rav Nachman bar Yitzchak: That which we said, "If he moved his feet he returns to the beginning," we only said when he is not accustomed to add supplications after his Shemoneh Esreh. But if he is accustomed to add supplications after his Shemoneh Esreh, he returns to R'tzei.

Another version—Said Rav Nachman bar Yitzchak: That which we said, "If he did not yet move his feet he returns to R'tzei," we only said when he is accustomed to add supplications after his Shemoneh Esreh. But if he is not accustomed to add supplications after his Shemoneh Esreh, he returns to the beginning.

דף כט:

1. Rav Papa seems to be arguing on Rabbi Tanchum, with Rabbi Tanchum setting the last point of returning to *R'tzei* at the end of the *tefillah* text, and Rav Papa setting it later at *akiras raglayim*. If so, why does Rav Papa use the phrase "that which we say (*ha d'amran*)," which implies he is merely commenting on Rabbi Tanchum, not arguing?

2. Rav Nachman bar Yitzchak requires that a person be accustomed to adding supplications after *Shemoneh Esreh* before allowing his *siyum ha'tefillah* to be extended until *akiras raglayim*. Why must the person be "accustomed" to adding the supplications? Why is it not enough that today he is adding supplications, thus making his *tefillah* not end at *Ha'mevarech es amo Yisrael ba'shalom* but rather after his supplications are complete, at a time that will be indicated by his *akiras raglayim*?

3. The *Tur* and the *Rosh* appear to *pasken* like Rav Nachman bar Yitzchak (second version), saying that one must return all the way to the beginning, unless one both has not yet moved his feet and is accustomed to adding supplications.[4] The implication of this is that if one has both factors, he gets to return only to *R'tzei*. This clearly disagrees with Rabbi Tanchum, who would say even if one had both of those factors, if he had already finished the *tefillah* text he could no longer return to *R'tzei*. But Rav Amram, cited in the *Tur*, *paskens* that the only factor is *akiras raglayim*. That seems to be the position of Rav Papa, but what is the logic that compels Rav Amram to accept Rav Papa's qualification of Rabbi Tanchum but reject Rav Nachman bar Yitzchak's qualification of Rav Papa?

4. The way the *Tur* rules, it comes out that, theoretically, if one had moved his feet before the end of *Sim Shalom*, he would have to go back to the beginning, because he is missing one of the factors enabling one to go back only to *R'tzei*. But why should

that be if his *akiras raglayim* in this scenario was clearly not the end of his *Shemoneh Esreh*? Furthermore, doesn't the Gemara explicitly state that if he remembered in *Sim Shalom*, he goes back to *R'tzei*—without any attention paid to the position of his feet?

5. The *Rambam* in *Hilchos Tefillah* (5:1) identifies a variety of *tefillah* preparations he calls *tikkun ha'guf*. Listed in 5:4, these preparations include placing one's feet together side by side. He tells us these preparations are ideal to be performed, but they are not *m'akev b'dieved*. Presumably, the *akiras raglayim* specified in this *sugya* is the undoing of this *tikkun ha'guf* step of placing one's feet together side by side. How can the official end of *tefillah*—which is *akiras raglayim* according to everyone but Rabbi Tanchum—be linked to an action that is not absolutely required as part of one's *Shemoneh Esreh* activities?

Yesod

In *Berachos* 6b, Rav Chelbo said in the name of Rav Huna, "Whoever is *kove'a makom* for his *tefillah*, the God of Avraham will come to his aid."

The *Rambam* surprises us by *paskening* that one should be *"kove'a makom l'tefillaso* **tamid**—to **consistently** establish a spot for his *tefillah*." This is surprising because the way *kove'a makom* is commonly understood, it means one should set a fixed spot in shul (or at home) from which one always davens. If this is the definition of *kove'a makom*, it would not be something that one would do "consistently." One would establish the fixed spot once, and then continue *using* the spot on an ongoing basis. But what could the *Rambam* mean by telling us to "be *kove'a*" the fixed spot consistently?

In Chapter One above, in the chapter on the Gemara on *daf* 6b, I suggested that the *Rambam* has a different understanding of *k'vias makom*. It means that one should make a determination that he is going to say his entire *Shemoneh Esreh* standing in one spot, not moving from that spot until his *tefillah* session is over. He lists this requirement in 5:6 as part of what he calls *tikkun ha'makom*, and, like *tikkun ha'guf*, it is an ideal practice but not *m'akev b'dieved*.

But wait, you might ask—Isn't standing fixed in place with one's feet together an absolute requirement of *Shemoneh Esreh*?

No, it actually isn't, at least not according to the *Rambam*. *Shemoneh Esreh* is known as *Amidah*, which means that it is a standing prayer. But standing does not have to mean rooted in one place with feet together. Standing can mean just not sitting. In theory, one could walk around during *Shemoneh Esreh* as long as he remains standing. And even if he is standing still, he could walk around between *Avos* and *Gevuros*, or between any other two paragraphs as long as he stands still when he is actually reciting the words. To actually agree to stand still, rooted in one place, and for the entire duration of the *tefillah* session—that is what *Rambam* calls being *kove'a makom l'tefillaso*.

As such, it becomes very difficult to link *siyum ha'tefillah* with *akiras raglayim*, as *kivun raglayim* is part of *tikkun ha'makom* and not an absolute requirement of *Shemoneh Esreh*. The only way *akiras raglayim* could be elevated to the level at which it could be seriously considered as a signal of *siyum ha'tefillah*, is if one has demonstrated consistency in being *kove'a makom l'tefillaso*. If, in the *Rambam's* words, one is *kove'a makom l'tefillaso* **tamid**, then we know his *akiras raglayim* is not a mere pause in his *Shemoneh Esreh*; it is a conclusion, and we can wait for it before declaring him ineligible to return merely to *R'tzei*. And only if his consistency extends to any extra supplications he adds to *Shemoneh Esreh* can we grant the extension of *siyum ha'tefillah* to the *akiras raglayim* that he does at the end of his regular supplications.

That is Rav Nachman bar Yitzchak's view, and that applies when the person has demonstrated consistency both in regularly adding supplications and in always maintaining his position through his entire davening session.

With a person who has not established regularity, *akiras raglayim* is an ineligible factor. He may be dislodging his feet simply to take a break! We revert back to the view of Rabbi Tanchum—he can return to *R'tzei* up until he reaches the end of the standard text of *Shemoneh Esreh*.

This is the *shitah* of the *Rambam*, as is clearly laid out in *Hilchos Tefillah* 10:10.

So what about Rav Amram?

Berachos 29b

Rav Amram disagrees with the *Rambam* that *kivun raglayim* is just a *l'chatchila*. Rav Amram holds like the *Bach*, who rules that *kivun raglayim* is *m'akev* according to the *Bavli* (and strictly *l'chatchila* only according to the *Yerushalmi*). If so, says Rav Amram, we cannot rule like Rav Nachman bar Yitzchak, whose qualification makes sense only if *akiras raglayim* is linked to some kind of personal commitment. We have to go with Rav Papa, who, in saying *"ha d'amran"* is saying as follows: That which Rabbi Tanchum says, [if one concluded *Shemoneh Esreh*] he returns to the beginning, that is said according to the view of the *Yerushalmi*, which does not consider *akiras raglayim*, because *akiras raglayim* is not an absolute requirement. But when **we** say it, following the view of the *Bavli*, we establish *siyum ha'tefillah* as *akiras raglayim*, because we consider *akiras raglayim* to be *m'akev*.

Indeed, it makes sense that **Rabbi Tanchum**'s approach would be that of the *Yerushalmi*, as the *Rosh* himself on *daf 6b paskens* the halachah of establishing a fixed *makom* for *tefillah* not from Rav Chelbo *amar* Rav Huna, but from **Rabbi Tanchum** b'Rabbi Chiya in *Perek Tefillas Ha'shachar* in *Yerushalmi*:

> צריך אדם ליחד לו מקום בבית הכנסת שנאמר
> ויהי דוד בא עד הראש אשר ישתחוה שם
> לאלהים—השתחוה לא נאמר אלא ישתחוה.

> *A person needs to designate a place for himself in the shul, as it says, "And David came unto the spot where he would bow there to God." "Bowed there" it does not say, rather "would bow there."*[5]

This fits with the *Rambam*'s understanding that no *chiyuv* of conventional *k'vias makom* can be learned from Rav Chelbo *amar* Rav Huna.

Rav Amram, who, of necessity, sees Rav Papa and Rabbi Tanchum as arguing, rejects the Rabbi Tanchum approach built on *Yerushalmi* in favor of the Rav Papa approach taken from the *Bavli*.

The *Rambam*, on the other hand, sees in the fact that the Gemara brings Rav Nachman bar Yitzchak—a position tenable only in light of the approach of Rabbi Tanchum—that the Gemara in fact prefers the approach of Rabbi Tanchum, and that is how he *paskens*. Indeed, according to the *Rambam*, Rav Papa and Rabbi Tanchum are not arguing. Rabbi Tanchum is simply addressing a case where the person has not established enough of a personal commitment to make *akiras raglayim* a factor; Rav Papa—as explained so clearly by Rav Nachman bar Yitzchak—is addressing a case where the person has.

Endnotes

1. *Rashi* is interesting. He does not say *l'fikach* (thus) on the second *tefillah*. In other words, the fact that it is a Shabbos make-up is not the reason not to include Havdalah. *Rashi* simply says, "He does not include Havdalah," as if to say, "He already said it." This is quite significant. I might have thought Motza'ei Shabbos is the time for Havdalah, so every *tefillah* said on Motza'ei Shabbos is incomplete without Havdalah. *Rashi* is saying no—Motza'ei Shabbos *tefillah* is not **incomplete** without Havdalah; you just need to say Havdalah at some point. Once you said it in the first *tefillah*, there is no need to say it in the second. But that produces a problem. How will *Rashi* learn the answer to "*kashya*" in the Gemara? As long as you have a plan for Havdalah, why can't the first *tefillah* be valid? And as long as being a Shabbos *tashlumin* is not enough reason on its own to omit Havdalah, why can't the second *tefillah* be valid as *tashlumin*?

2. The *Bach* writes, to explain *Rashi*, that the *mispallel* certainly did not advance his *tashlumin* prayer to the forefront, so his intention must have been to fulfill his immediate obligation. But for that it does not count, because he omitted Havdalah. *Rashi* then continues: If so, then, that his intention in the first prayer was on his immediate obligation, just that it did not work because he failed to include Havdalah, if indeed that is so, let his second *tefillah* count as his Shabbos make-up *tefillah*. After all, he never attempted to advance his *tashlumin* ahead of the immediate obligation—he just failed in fulfilling his immediate obligation! On that, *Rashi* avers that his inclusion of Havdalah in the second *tefillah* reveals that he had no intention to use the second prayer as his Shabbos make-up prayer.

3. Although there are answers. For example, Havdalah over wine will help you with Havdalah but it won't help your *tefillah* be a proper *tefillah*. So maybe where our objective is to say a *tashlumin*, we will make you go back despite your having a plan for the missed Havdalah. Or, maybe Havdalah over wine only helps when you will not be saying another *tefillah*, but here you did say a second *tefillah* with Havdalah, so the first *tefillah* does not have any way to avoid the stigma of having been an invalid *tefillah*.

4. Tur, Orach Chaim 422.

5. Rosh, Berachos 4:7.

Chapter Five
Ein Omdin

דף לב:

ת״ר מעשה בחסיד אחד שהיה מתפלל בדרך וגו׳.

The Rabbis taught: There was an incident where a certain chassid was davening along the road. A nobleman passed by and offered the chassid a greeting, to which the chassid did not respond. The nobleman waited until the chassid completed his Shemoneh Esreh and accosted him, "Fool! Doesn't your Torah require you to take measures to protect your life? When I greeted you, why did you not respond? Don't you know that for that impetuosity, I could have taken your life without a single consequence!" Said the chassid, "Wait a moment, and I will appease you with words."

The chassid went on. "If you had been standing before a flesh-and-blood king, and a friend of yours passed by and offered you a greeting, would you have responded to him?"

"Certainly not," declared the nobleman.

"And if you had, what would they have done to you?"

"They would have had me beheaded!"

"So the matter is only logical. If that were you, standing before a king of mere flesh and blood, who is here today but in the grave tomorrow, then all the more so I, who was standing in the presence of the King of all kings, the Holy One who lives forever and ever!"

Immediately, the nobleman was appeased and left the chassid to depart in peace.

דף לב:

1. It is difficult to understand what it was that was so novel and effective about the *chassid*'s explanation of his behavior to the nobleman. Surely, the nobleman could have already understood that the *chassid* was praying, and that was the reason for his failure to respond. What was it about the *chassid*'s illustrative parable that gave the nobleman reason to be appeased?

2. When the *chassid* spoke of the mortal king, he referred to him as one who is "here today and in the grave tomorrow." But that seems irrelevant. What difference does it make that someone who can cause me harm today will be dead tomorrow? In the meantime, it is now today, and he can cause me great harm! Why is his death after a time a reason for me to have less fear of him right now than I would have now of a king who will happen to continue living on forever afterward?

Yesod

The *chassid* realized that the nobleman had actually made a strong argument—but only because the nobleman was operating under a misconception about the *chassid*'s motivations.

The nobleman was assuming the *chassid* would be afraid to interrupt his *Shemoneh Esreh* out of fear of what his God might do to him as punishment for his insubordination. To that, the nobleman challenged the *chassid* by pointing out that whatever his God might do to him, a) it remained uncertain that there would be retribution, b) it would not necessarily be immediate, and c) with time and mercy, the *chassid* might even be spared entirely. In contrast, the nobleman standing there represented a definite and impending threat. Doesn't the Torah's own moral code demand that one react to save oneself first and foremost from a clear and present danger? "How dare he be ignoring me like that!" fumed the nobleman.

The *chassid* moved to deflect and undermine this misperception. "You assume I am motivated by fear for my life and my safety. But that is not it. My actions while in the presence of my God are actually motivated by the great respect I have for Him. Listen to my logic, and you will understand."

And so it was. As soon as the *chassid* presented a scenario in which the nobleman himself would refrain from interrupting **and then contrasted the lesser king to the greater one by invoking a factor—mortality—that has no bearing on the havoc a powerful figure can wreak in the moment**, it became instantly clear to the nobleman that the *chassid* was focused not on any fear for his own personal safety but rather on the tremendous respect he bore for **any** kind of greatness, allowing only that the figure in whose presence he had been standing was simply entitled to *more* respect, because the awesome nature a powerful **and eternal** being unarguably outranks the awesome nature of one who is powerful but not eternal. Notably, the *chassid*, in his description of kings, makes no reference to the punishment an offender would receive. That was cited only by the nobleman. Rapidly, the nobleman began to understand that the *chassid* was relating only to the sense of awe due to one with absolute power.

It is now easy to see why this presentation appeased the nobleman so well. Before, the nobleman was facing what he had perceived to be the degrading insolence of one with so seemingly little regard for his nobility that its presence did not even generate terror to the degree the fellow's own wisdom would impose. Instead, suddenly, he found himself exposed to a man so filled with respect for greatness—including the nobleman's own greatness, he understood—that if not for the simple matter of his being outranked by a superior greatness, the *chassid* would certainly have been stirred to attention by the greeting of the great nobleman.

How important it is to disarm our would-be adversaries by giving them a healthy feeling of their own value and importance in our eyes!

Chapter Six
Keitzad Mevarchin

Berachos 35a

דף לה.

מתני׳ כיצד מברכין על הפירות וגו׳.

Mishnah: How do we bless over fruits? On tree fruits, one says Borei Pri Ha'eitz, except for wine, on which one makes Ha'gafen. On ground fruits, one says Borei Pri Ha'adamah, except for bread, on which one makes Ha'motzi...

Gemara: How do we know this? For the Rabbis taught "Kodesh hilulim l'Hashem..."

1. The Mishnah asks: How do we bless over fruits? It answers by supplying various *berachah* texts for various types of produce. *Tosafos* points out that the Tanna clearly began with a presumption that we do make *berachos*. He only asks: What is the nature of those *berachos*? But then how could the Gemara begin, "*Mina hani mili?*" If the question is, "How do we know we say *berachos*?" there was no such message stated in the Mishnah! What are the words in the Mishnah that could prompt "*Mina hani mili*"?

2. Why is Rabbi Akiva's statement of, "It is forbidden for a person to taste a thing before he makes a *berachah*" inserted where it is? The Gemara is just about to develop its challenge against the *pasuk* of, "*Kodesh hilulim l'Hashem*" being the source for *berachos*. Isn't Rabbi Akiva's statement at this point premature? And what does it even mean? How can he derive such a restrictive halachah from the simple requirement that eating be surrounded by *berachos*?

3. Why does Rabbi Akiva say "to taste" and not "to eat"? Later, when the Gemara rejects the *pasuk* and learns *berachos* from a *sevara*, the language is: "It is forbidden for a person to 'benefit'

from this world without a *berachah*." Why does it not repeat Rabbi Akiva's formulation?

Yesod

The Gemara is not asking how the Mishnah knows we have to say *berachos*. *Berachos* we know from *v'achalta v'savata u'verachta*. What the Gemara is asking is, "How does the Mishnah know we must say *berachos* **before** eating?"

Saying a *berachah* after eating makes sense. We have enjoyed a benefit; we must say thank you. And the *pasuk* of *v'achalta v'savata u'verachta* confirms that it is an obligation. But what logic is there to saying thank you before eating? The Mishnah is telling us about *berachos* that the Torah requires us to say even before we have eaten anything. That is the "*mili*" about which the Gemara asks, "How does the Mishnah know this? This is a brand-new concept. Why should I have any prior restriction on eating food that has been given to me for my survival and that I have in my possession? Do I have to say a *berachah* before I drive the car I own that I bought with my own money? What is this new halachah?"

To that, the Gemara answers—It is a *pasuk*: "*Kodesh hilulim l'Hashem*." Two *hilulim*—Not only afterward, but also before.

Says Rabbi Akiva, if so, we now have a new *issur d'Oraisa*; it is thus forbidden to even taste any food before reciting a *berachah*.

The reason the Gemara mentions his opinion where it does is because it is about to discard the *pasuk* of *kodesh hilulim* as a source. The Gemara wants us to know, however, that it is not discarding Rabbi Akiva's opinion, just the source. Thus, when the Gemara ultimately concludes that *berachah rishonah* is a *sevara*, it is a *sevara d'Oraisa*, not a *sevara d'Rabbanan*. (In the end, Rabbi Akiva can still hold *berachah rishonah* is learned out from *kodesh hilulim*, since he could learn *kerem revai* from the *gezerah shavah* and *achlei v'hadar achlei* [אחליה והדר אכלי] from *maaser sheni* [see *Tosafos*].)

We thought food was just a tool of survival. We now learn that it is a lever by which we can connect with Hashem. Wherever Hashem is involved, there is some kind of *issur* that reflects its sanctity (like Shabbos

Berachos 35a

and Yom Tov). But now we know why Rabbi Akiva says "to taste." If there is going to be a connection to Hashem, there has to be some kind of *taam* involved. Water, which has no *taam*, cannot be part of a Godly relationship experience. That is, truly, just for survival, and thus any *berachah* on water is only *m'd'Rabbanan*.

And now we can explain why the Gemara at the end doesn't say "to taste." From *sevara*, you could never say that there is an *issur* to do something that gives you no real *hana'ah*. That you could only say if you have a *pasuk*. All you can say *m'sevara* is that one can be restricted from *hana'ah* until a *berachah* gives one the recognition that this *hana'ah* is coming to him as a gift from Hashem.

דף לה:

רבי חנינא בר פפא רמי וגו׳.

Rabbi Chanina bar Papa noted a contradiction. It says, "I will take away My grain in its time" (Hoshea 2:11), and yet it says, "You shall collect your grain" (Devarim 11:14). But this is really no contradiction: One is talking about when Jews are doing God's will, and the other is talking about when Jews are not doing God's will.

A Beraisa taught: Why does it say, "You shall collect your grain"? Because elsewhere it says, "Words of Torah shall not depart from your mouth" (Yehoshua 1:8). I might have presumed that this is to be taken literally [and allow for no activity other than Torah study], therefore the Torah says, "You shall collect your grain," i.e., engage in worldly endeavors. These are the words of Rabbi Yishmael. Rabbi Shimon Bar Yochai said: Is it possible that a man could plow at plowing time, sow at sowing time, reap at reaping time, thresh at threshing time, and winnow when the wind blows—What will become of Torah?! Rather, when Jews are doing God's will, their work will be done for them by others, as it says, "Strangers will arise and shepherd your flock." (Yeshayahu 61:5). But when Jews are not doing God's will, not only will they have to do their own work, as it says, "You shall collect your grain," but they will be forced to do the work of others, as it says, "You will serve your enemies" (Devarim 28:48).

Said Abaye: Many conducted themselves according Rabbi Yishmael and succeeded. Many conducted themselves according to Rabbi Shimon Bar Yochai and did not succeed.

Berachos 35b

> Rava said to the Rabbis: I implore you, do not appear before me during the months of Nissan [planting month] and Tishrei [harvest month], in order that you not be worried about your livelihood all the rest of the year.

The contradiction is between the verse in *Hoshea* and the verse in *Devarim*. But what exactly is the contradiction? And what is the purpose of the Gemara citing the *Beraisa*?

One possibility is that in *Hoshea*, God refers to grain as "My grain," whereas is *Devarim* He calls it "your grain." It is resolved by saying that God calls it "My grain" when we disregard His will; it is "your grain" when we obey Him. The *Beraisa*, then, is a challenge to this resolution. Rabbi Shimon Bar Yochai in the *Beraisa* says that "your grain" is used when we *disobey* God's will. So how can Rabbi Chanina bar Papa differ with Rabbi Shimon and read "your grain" as being positive?

This cannot be how the *Tosafos* understand the Gemara, because they ask this question on their own. If it is the Gemara's question, we don't need *Tosafos* to restate it.

But it does seem that it could be how *Rashi* understands the Gemara, as seen in his comment on the line, "*b'zman she'osin retzono*."

According to this reading of the Gemara, how does the challenge from the *Beraisa* get answered? Furthermore, Rabbi Chanina's statement is reversed. The first verse cited is *Hoshea*; the second is *Devarim*. He should have said, "One [i.e., the first verse] is talking about when Jews are *not* doing God's will; the other [i.e., the second verse] is talking about when they *are*." Why are these two phrases reversed? And what is being added by the statements of Abaye and of Rava?

Indeed, the *Beraisa* itself is very difficult. Rabbi Shimon is making a legitimate point.

How does Rabbi Yishmael answer him? Also, the context of the *pasuk* "*v'asafta daganecha*" clearly states that you will collect your grain as a reward for listening to God's commandments. How could Rabbi Shimon suggest that it is a negative?

Yesod

The *Beraisa* is indeed a *kashya* on the resolution of Rabbi Chanina bar Papa's contradiction. In Rabbi Chanina's resolution, "collect your grain" was positive and was the result of Jews doing God's will. In the *Beraisa*, Rabbi Shimon Bar Yochai declares "collect your grain" to be negative and the result of Jews *not* doing God's will, so Rabbi Chanina bar Papa's resolution is negated.

That brings us back to square one. How do we resolve the contradiction between *Hoshea* and *Devarim*?

Abaye supplies the answer.

Really, Rabbi Shimon Bar Yochai is right. God's will is that we study His Torah and our work will be done by others. But if we find that "many conducted themselves according to Rabbi Yishmael and succeeded," we have a right to say that this alternative approach *has become* God's will. Stunningly, we have the power to redirect God's will simply by feeling unable to adhere to His initial *ratzon* and by initiating an alternative on our own. The only requirements are that they be within the broader framework of Torah—that they be an organic development, i.e., "*many conducted themselves...*" and that they prove themselves a spiritual success.

We may find a similar parallel in the acceptance of *minhag* (custom). Known as "*Toras imecha*"—the Torah of your mother (i.e., Jewish instinct as opposed to Divine dictate), *minhag*, in certain cases, can trump halachah (Jewish law), but only if it has developed organically.

Rabbi Chanina bar Papa is thus justified in learning that "collect your grain" is the result of Jews doing God's will—it is simply referring to God's *revised* will, according to which worldly endeavors are laudable, as per Rabbi Yishmael.

SO WHAT HAPPENS to God's original will—the one maintained by Rabbi Shimon Bar Yochai?

Berachos 35b

It does not disappear, but it has a new limitation. It can still be followed successfully, but only by a select few. When "*many* conducted themselves according to Rabbi Shimon Bar Yochai," they did not succeed.

Rava adds one final point. To whom is Rava speaking? His rabbinical students. These are the ones who, faced with the personal dilemma over whether they should join the many and live like Rabbi Yishmael or strive to be the select few that follow Rabbi Shimon, might feel obliged to undertake the latter. His message to them is: Once you hear your Rebbe asking you to abandon the highest road of spiritual achievement and accept a lesser mandate, you can do so *l'chatchila*.

WITH THIS APPROACH, we can appreciate why Rabbi Chanina reversed his resolution statements. One verse—the second *pasuk*—is talking about when Jews are doing God's will. But by lining it up corresponding to the line about Jews not doing God's will, he means to hint that the very same *pasuk*—at least in the eyes of the great Rabbi Shimon Bar Yochai—is actually referring to when Jews *abandoned* God's initial will before redirecting it to one that more closely matched their own.

In today's world, we often find masses of Torah students following paths that may actually seem to conflict with fundamental and time-honored principles of general Torah conduct (for example, sitting and learning Torah for many years after marriage and being supported by the generosity of others). Beyond an emergency period of *eis la'asos l'Hashem* justified by the upheavals of twentieth-century Jewry, a case can be made that perhaps this was not God's initial will. But if many are conducting themselves this way and succeeding, that is *prima facie* evidence that the approach is now consistent with God's will—particularly if these disciples are following their *rebbeim* in adhering to it—yet we continue to leave open the path of God's initial will to those bold individuals who seek nothing less.

דף לו. (1)

קמחא דחיטי רב יהודה אמר בורא פרי האדמה ורב
נחמן אמר שהכל נהיה בדברו וגו'.

Wheat flour—Rav Yehudah says [the berachah is] Borei Pri Ha'adamah and Rav Nachman says [the berachah is] Shehakol Nihyeh Bid'varo…

1. Rav Yehudah and Rav Nachman differ over what the proper *berachah rishonah* should be for eating wheat flour. Rav Yehudah says *Borei Pri Ha'adamah*; Rav Nachman says *Shehakol*. Rava tells Rav Nachman he should not argue with Rav Yehudah, since both Shmuel and Rav Yochanan agree with Rav Yehudah. One can understand Rava *paskening* like Rav Yehudah because of the support for his position lent by Shmuel and Rav Yochanan, but what business does Rava have telling **Rav Nachman** what **he** should hold?

2. The support from Shmuel (and Rav Yochanan) is based on a position Shmuel takes regarding olive oil. Olive oil is *Borei Pri Ha'eitz*, the same as the olive. Says Rava: Just as Shmuel holds the *berachah* did not change when the olive was processed into oil, so too he would hold here that the *berachah* (in this case, *Ha'adamah*) does not change when the wheat kernel is processed into flour. But aren't there many distinctions one can make between oil and flour? How is Rava so sure that Shmuel would agree with the automatic application of his law on oil to the case of flour? On the other hand, in the Gemara's challenge to Rava where we do draw a distinction between oil and flour (*iluya acharina*), why should that distinction make a difference—why

Berachos 36a

should the fact that flour has an additional improvement ahead be a reason to affect what *berachah* it should get right now?

3. When Rava makes his point to Rav Nachman, the Gemara uses the phrase, "Rava said to Rav Nachman…" Later, when the Gemara presents the responding challenge to Rava, it begins directly with *Mi dami*, not preceding it with "Rav Nachman said back to him…" Why not?

4. When Rava brings his support from Shmuel, he seems to be establishing a principle based on Shmuel's position on olive oil. The principle is, "Even though [a food item] has undergone a change, it retains its original *berachah*." But then he continues and says, "Here too [by wheat], even though it has changed [to flour] it retains its original *berachah*." If Rava is reading Shmuel's position as being a principle, why does he have to repeat "*ha-cha nami*—here too"? Shouldn't it be enough just to state the principle that foods retain their *berachos* even after undergoing a change, and we will automatically understand that it should likewise apply to wheat processed into flour?

We have the principle:

וכי אית ליה עלויא אחרינא לא מברכינן עליה בורא פרי האדמה אלא שהכל.

When there is another improvement we don't bless on it Borei Pri Ha'adamah but rather Shehakol.

5. This phrase can be read either as a conclusion or as a challenge. If it is a conclusion, why is it so specific? Shouldn't the counterpoint here state simply that just because a food has undergone a change, it does not necessarily retain its *berachah*? Why limit its application to cases of *Ha'adamah*? This would seem to indicate that the phrase is, rather, the beginning of a challenge intended specifically for our case of flour. The challenge would be, "Is the *berachah* for wheat flour really *Shehakol*? But didn't Rav Zeira say the *berachah* for barley flour is *Shehakol*, implying that wheat flour is *Ha'adamah*?" But if that is the proper way to read the

phrase, why does it bother to begin with a repeated mention of *iluya acharina* when the only point of the challenge is to say that we have a source that contradicts Rav Nachman's halachah?

6. Rava seems to be saying that Rav Nachman is arguing with Shmuel. So how can he ask him a question from Rav Zeira—Rav Zeira was only quoting Shmuel! Obviously Rav Nachman will disagree with a source like that; he disagrees with Shmuel!

7. In Rava's understanding of Rav Zeira, how did Shmuel ever explain that barley flour should get *Shehakol* (in the *hava amina*—before we learned it causes worms)? Doesn't that sound more like the view of Rav Nachman, that when a food item has an additional improvement ahead it drops to *Shehakol* and does not retain its original *berachah*?*

Yesod

"*Af al gav d'ishtani b'milsei kai*" and "*Iss lei iluya acharina*" are code words, each describing a different approach to understanding what a *berachah* is all about. This *sugya* is actually a *machlokes* between Rava and the Gemara over which of the two approaches is the one adopted by Shmuel.

"*Af al gav d'ishtani b'milsei kai*" means, "Even though it has been processed, it retains its *berachah*." Why would something retain its *berachah* after it has been processed? Because from the standpoint of the *Borei*, it is still the same item He created, and He deserves the same recognition. "*Iss lei iluya acharina*" means, "It is not currently in its optimal edible state." Why should this matter? Because from the standpoint of the eater, processed food is a different eating experience than raw food. Just as the *berachah* for raw food is optimal because it is being eaten in the state that is optimal for raw food, the *berachah* for processed food will be optimal when it is eaten in the state that is optimal for processed food. When a processed food has a further improvement ahead, it is not currently in its optimal processed food state. Thus it gets only *Shehakol*. The first approach understands that a *berachah*, being praise of the Creator, must denote the action of the *Borei*. The second approach,

Berachos 36a

understanding that praise is a reaction to one's personal experiences, posits that a *berachah* must reflect the experiences of the eater.

Rava looks at Shmuel's position on olive oil and reads that Shmuel is holding like the first approach. This is why, opines Rava, the *berachah* is retained even after processing. Thus, without a question in Rava's mind, Shmuel would hold that the *berachah* on flour, also following the first approach, would be the same as for a wheat kernel, since it is still the same item as created by the *Borei*.

Rav Nachman does not answer Rava back. Rav Nachman has to accept Rava's contention, because he is not willing to argue with Shmuel, and he has no way other than through Rava to ascertain Shmuel's intent.

But the Gemara can and does challenge Rava: "How can you, Rava, be so sure that Shmuel's law would carry over to flour? Maybe he holds like the second approach, and the reason the *berachah* on oil is retained is not because it is still the same item as created by the *Borei*, but because oil is at the optimal state for processed olives. Flour, on the other hand, which is not at the optimal state for processed grain, would be *Shehakol*!"

To this, Rava fires off his response: "You are trying to tell me that *Iss lei iluya acharina* is Shmuel's operative position, and therefore the *berachah* [over grains] should be not *Ha'adamah* but *Shehakol*? I have proof that cannot be, as Shmuel himself is quoted by Rav Zeira in the name of Rav Masna as implying that the *berachah* for wheat flour is *Ha'adamah*! Only because barley flour causes worms is its *berachah Shehakol*, but evidently wheat flour [which does not cause worms] is *Ha'adamah*! This proves that Shmuel adopts the first approach."

The Gemara disagrees: "Shmuel could hold like the second approach, and he can hold that wheat flour is also *Shehakol*."

Rava: "Then why did Shmuel not state that wheat flour is *Shehakol*, as that would have been a bigger *chiddush* than to say barley flour gets *Shehakol*?"

Gemara: "Because Shmuel needed to teach that barley flour gets **at least** a *Shehakol* as opposed to no *berachah*."

Rava: "But why would anyone think barley flour gets no *berachah*—doesn't it have at least as much food value as salt and brine?"

דף לו.

Gemara: "It does, but there are those who would try to contend [as do many Rishonim, you will note, in the *sugya* of drinking olive oil] that when something is *mazik*, it gets no *berachah*, even if it has food value. To counter their thinking, Shmuel had to teach that barley flour does get a *berachah*—because the eater inevitably does get pleasure—but the *berachah* is only *Shehakol*, as it is for wheat flour, because flour is not the optimal state for an eater of processed grain.

(Rava is unable to consider the possibility that anybody might be thinking that something with food value gets no *berachah*. Why? Because in an earlier *sugya*, Rava accepted the view that whoever takes pleasure from this world without a *berachah* is guilty of *me'ilah*.[1] We noted at the time that none of the other opinions there are this definitive. The others preface their condemnations with the word *k'ilu* [as if]. According to Rava there simply is no legitimate *hava amina* that one could take pleasure without a *berachah* when at stake is the *issur* of *me'ilah*. Thus the only possible purpose behind Shmuel's exclusive mention of barley flour and its *berachah* of *Shehakol* is to teach by inference that wheat flour gets *Ha'adamah*. Rava cannot deny, however, that Shmuel in that same earlier *sugya* accepts a view of *k'ilu*, saying, "Whoever takes pleasure from this world without a *berachah*, it is **as if** he has taken [unauthorized] pleasure from the Sacred Reserve.")

While Rava does not capitulate, he is unable to defeat the Gemara's argument, thus the Gemara has shown that Shmuel could be understood either way, as taking the first approach or as taking the second approach. Without a clear mandate in Shmuel's *derech*, Rav Nachman is once again free to take the view with which he began—that the *berachah* on wheat flour is *Shehakol* because we look at a *berachah* as reflecting the standpoint of the eater, and that Shmuel says the *berachah* by oil is *Ha'eitz* only because olive oil is at the optimal state for the eater of that processed food. Rav Yehudah will say the *berachah* is *Ha'adamah* because we look at a *berachah* with an eye toward the standpoint of the *Borei*, and raw or processed it is the same food the *Borei* created. In Rav Yehudah's view, this will be Shmuel's rationale for olive oil retaining its *berachah*, and he would hold the same principle by wheat flour.

Berachos 36a

It comes out that according to the position of the Gemara, Rav Nachman and Rav Yehudah are not arguing simply over what the proper *berachah* is for wheat flour. They are arguing over what is Shmuel's philosophy of *berachos*. According to the position of Rava, Shmuel, based on what we can deduce from his *piskei halachah*, has only one possible philosophy of *berachos*, thus Rav Nachman and Rav Yehudah are compelled to be in agreement over what Shmuel would hold—and therefore what the halachah will be—by wheat flour.

The *Rambam paskens* like the Gemara over Rava, and like Rav Nachman over Rav Yehudah.

דף לו. (2)

קורא רב יהודה אמר בורא פרי האדמה ושמואל אמר שהכל נהיה בדברו רב יהודה אמר בורא פרי האדמה פירא הוא ושמואל אמר שהכל נהיה בדברו הואיל וסופו להקשות אמר ליה שמואל לרב יהודה שיננא כוותך מסתברא וגו׳.

Hearts of palm—Rav Yehudah says [the berachah is] Borei Pri Ha'adamah, and Shmuel says [it is] Shehakol Nihyeh Bid'varo. [Why does] Rav Yehudah say Borei Pri Ha'adamah? [Because] it is a pri [fruit]! [And why does] Shmuel say Shehakol Nihyeh Bid'varo? Since it will end up hard [as wood]. Said Shmuel to Rav Yehudah, "Clever one, your position makes sense, as the radish ends up hard and its berachah is Borei Pri Ha'adamah, but it is not correct…

1. How can Rav Yehudah disagree with his *rebbe*, Shmuel?
2. Why does Shmuel praise Rav Yehudah's position if he does not hold like him?
3. If Shmuel is saying *v'lo hi*, he is apparently not praising Rav Yehudah, so why does the Gemara end off with, "And even though Shmuel praised Rav Yehudah…"?
4. If the entire issue is about whether people plant the item with the intention of eating it or not, why bother with the issue of *sofo l'hakshos*?
5. Why does Shmuel not respond to Rav Yehudah's claim of *pira hu* by simply saying, "Yes, but people do not plant it for its fruitness"?

Yesod

Rav Yehudah and Shmuel are having an argument, but it is not an argument in halachah. They both agree that if there is a part of a tree or plant that is edible yet is not its fruit, the proper *berachah* is *Borei Pri Ha'adamah*. So on this issue, Rav Yehudah is not disagreeing with his *rebbe*, and he even earns Shmuel's praise. *Kura* (heart of palm, according to most Rishonim) is an edible part of the woody portion of the palm tree when still soft, thus to Rav Yehudah's way of thinking, it is from the ground, it is edible, and it is not the fruit, so the *berachah* should be *Ha'adamah*.

However, Shmuel sees *kura* as belonging to a different dimension of produce. Yes, there exists something called "fruit of the ground." But there is something else, one step below "fruit of the ground," something we might call "edible nature." *Kura* is edible nature, holds Shmuel, and thus its *berachah* is *Shehakol*.

The code phrase for edible nature is *"Sofo l'hakshos."*

Shmuel continues: You might have continued declaring the *berachah* to be *Ha'adamah* even had you accepted my distinction between ground fruit and edible nature, and your thinking would have been right, since the radish—also edible nature—is *Ha'adamah*.

But just as you were not aware of my distinction between ground fruit and edible nature, so too you are not aware of a distinction I make *within* edible nature. Edible nature that we eat, but did not plant for that purpose (because the eating is injurious to the tree's future growth), to that we give the *berachah Shehakol*. However, if there is a variety of edible nature that we plant with intention to eat, its *berachah* is *Ha'adamah*. The radish is an example, and the *berachah* on the radish is indeed *Ha'adamah*, as you would wish to say. But because the radish's *berachah* is not because it is edible ground produce but rather because it is edible nature that gets planted for an eating purpose, its *Ha'adamah* remains no proof that all edible things that grow from the ground and are not tree fruit receive *Ha'adamah*. The *berachah* for edible nature is *Shehakol*.

Shmuel's praise of Rav Yehudah was for his **logic**—which was sound—but not for his halachic conclusion, which was made without awareness of Shmuel's halachic categories.

To clarify Shmuel's view, the **product** of a tree that is not its primary fruit (*ikar pri*) receives a *berachah* of *Ha'adamah*. Understood is that if planters had in mind to make that product primary, it rises one *berachah* level to *Ha'eitz*. But the **tree itself**, or other woody parts of nature that happen to be edible, are called "edible nature" and receive a *berachah* of *Shehakol*. If planters had in mind to harvest these parts deliberately, they rise one *berachah* level to *Ha'adamah*.

There is contemporary halachic significance to this understanding. We eat hearts of palm all the time. Should their *berachah* be *Shehakol* or *Ha'adamah*? The way we are learning—that they are classified as edible nature—it will depend on the intention behind the planting of the palm trees. If they are planted to be date or coconut palms, and the premature harvesting of the hearts enables us to eat the hearts but sacrifices their potential to produce actual fruits, they would receive the standard *berachah* for edible nature—*Shehakol*. But if they are planted by the growers for the purpose of harvesting the hearts, their correct *berachah* is *Borei Pri Ha'adamah*.[2]

Berachos 36a

דף לו. (3)

Fruit by Choice—Shitas Rambam on Kafrisin shel Tz'laf

אמר רב יהודה אמר רב צלף של ערלה בחוצה לארץ זורק את האביונות ואוכל את הקפריסין וגו'.

Said Rav Yehudah in the name of Rav: A caper-bush that is orlah—outside of Eretz Yisrael one should discard the berries but may eat the shells. Is this meant to imply that the berries are considered fruit, but the shells are not considered fruit? But don't we find a contradiction...

In the previous Gemara, Shmuel held that *kura* (palm heart) is *Shehakol* because it was *sofo l'hakshos* (going to end up as wood), and as such it could not be called *pira* (fruit). Rav Yehudah disagreed and held *kura* is a fruit (of the ground, and its *berachah* is *Ha'adamah*). But all understood that if something were to be classified as a non-fruit, its proper *berachah* would be *Shehakol*. Even Rav Yehudah accepts this.

THIS BRINGS US to the *sugya* of *kafrisin shel tz'laf*. Rav Yehudah is quoted as saying that regarding their *din orlah* outside of Eretz Yisrael, we must toss the caper-berries but may eat the shells.

The Mishnah in *Orlah* (3:9) tells us the uniqueness of *orlah* of *chutz la'aretz*: It is learned not from a *pasuk*. What is the significance of this? Where *orlah* is learned from a *pasuk*, we are able to include in the *chiyuvei orlah* all items learned from *diyukim* in the *pasuk* (for example: "וערלתם ערלתו את פריו," where the extra word *es* comes to teach us to include that which is secondary to the fruit, e.g., a fruit peel, as being obligated in *orlah*). While these items may not be fruit, they are, thanks to the *diyukim* from the *pasuk*, still *chayav* in *orlah*. Thus, in Eretz Yisrael, there exists no one-to-one correlation between fruit and *chiyuv orlah*, since non-fruits can also be *chayav* in *orlah*.

But in *chutz la'aretz*, as we've said, the *chiyuv orlah* does not come from a *pasuk*; thus all that can be deemed *orlah* outside of Eretz Yisrael is that which is most logical to be *orlah*—the fruit! So back to Rav Yehudah. He says that in *chutz la'aretz* you are to throw away berries of *orlah* but you can eat the shells. Now, why should this be? If you want to tell me that both the berries and their shells are considered fruit, but in the laws of *orlah* there remains some kind of distinction between the two (like, maybe one is considered the primary fruit of the tree and the other is just a secondary fruit product), then why limit that distinction to *chutz la'aretz*? Why not use whatever distinction there is to permit the eating of caper-berry shells even in Eretz Yisrael? It can only be that Rav Yehudah holds *kafrisin* are not fruit and are thus not subject to *orlah* outside of Eretz Yisrael, and are only forbidden as *orlah* in Eretz Yisrael because non-fruits can be included in *chiyuvei orlah* in Eretz Yisrael where *orlah* is learned from a *pasuk*.

BUT IF RAV Yehudah holds *kafrisin* are not fruit, based on the previous *sugya* the *berachah* ought to be *Shehakol*! Rav Yehudah himself would have agreed to that. So how will he explain a *Beraisa* that teaches that on *kafrisin* the *berachah* is *Borei Pri Ha'eitz*?

The *Beraisa* says:

> על מיני נצפה על העלים ועל התמרות אומר בורא פרי האדמה ועל האביונות ועל הקפריסין אומר בורא פרי העץ.

> *Regarding types of caper-bush edibles: On the leaves and shoots, one says Borei Pri Ha'adamah; on the berries and the shells, one says Borei Pri Ha'eitz.*

(Somewhat parenthetically, keep in mind that even though both Shmuel **and** Rav Yehudah are in agreement that if an item is not a fruit, its *berachah* should be *Shehakol*, the *Beraisa* of *al minei nitzpah* is not a *kashya* on Shmuel. Shmuel can simply say that while *kura* may be a non-fruit and get *Shehakol*, *kafrsisin* are fruit and get *Ha'eitz*. The only consequence of this position is that he will have to hold they cannot be eaten when they are *orlah*—neither in Eretz Yisrael nor in *chutz la'aretz*. But Rav Yehudah, who says *kafrisin shel orlah* **can** be eaten in *chutz la'aretz*, is by definition saying that *kafrisin* are not fruit. If so, how could the *berachah* be anything other than *Shehakol*?

But why isn't the *reisha* [first part] of the *Beraisa*—which says, "On the leaves and edible green shoots say *Borei Pri Ha'adamah*"—a *kashya* on Shmuel? Shmuel holds non-fruits get *Shehakol* while the *Beraisa* gives their *berachah* as *borei pri Ha'adamah*. How will Shmuel explain this?

Shmuel will say what he has already said: "*Tz'laf nat'i inshi a'da'ata d'shusa.*" According to *Rashi*, this means people plant caper trees intending to eat the leaves and shoots, as, unlike with *kura*, consuming these items does not harm the tree. Thus, they are "fruit"—thanks to people's intentions—and their *berachah* of "*Borei Pri...*," according to Shmuel, is legitimate. It is only for Rav Yehudah that our *Beraisa* poses a problem.)

The Gemara offers to resolve the problem for Rav Yehudah. The *Beraisa*, says the Gemara, is the view of Rabbi Eliezer in the Mishnah in *Maasros* (4:6), who holds that *temaros*, *evyonos*, and *kafrisin* (caper tree shoots, berries, and shells, respectively) are all fruit (and will therefore get a *berachah* of "*Borei Pri...*"—either *Ha'eitz* or *Ha'adamah* depending on additional factors; see below). As fruit, none of these items could be eaten when they are *orlah*; not in Eretz Yisrael, nor in *chutz la'aretz*. Rav Yehudah, on the other hand, follows the view of Rabbi Akiva that only *evyonos* are fruit. *Evyonos* get *Borei Pri Ha'eitz* and cannot be eaten as *orlah* (anywhere). The other parts of the caper tree are not fruit, can be eaten as *orlah*, and get *Shehakol*. But he doesn't go with Rabbi Akiva completely, for if he did, he would eat *kafrisin* of *orlah* even in Eretz Yisrael. Rather, he embraces the principle that when it comes to agricultural halachos, "where there is a dispute about which way to hold in Eretz Yisrael, the halachah follows the lenient view for *chutz la'aretz*," not only for something like *maaser* on vegetables, which is *d'Rabbanan*, but even for *orlah*, which is *d'Oraisa*.

דף לו.

AT THIS POINT, it would seem that Rav Yehudah actually holds like Rabbi Eliezer (albeit like Rabbi Akiva in *chutz la'aretz*, because of the above principle), that *kafrisin* are fruit, that they are subject to *maaser* (like any other fruit), that its *orlah* is forbidden in Eretz Yisrael, and that its *berachah* is *Borei Pri Ha'eitz*. And it would seem that the halachah follows him from the fact that the later Amora, Mar bar Rav Ashi, did this same practice of eating *kafrisin shel orlah* in *chutz la'aretz*.

BUT OUR PROBLEM is that the *Rambam* does not support this conclusion. According to the *Rambam* (*Hilchos Berachos* 8:6), the *berachah* on *kafrisin* is *Ha'adamah*, not *Ha'eitz*. So to understand the *Rambam*, we have to ask how the *Rambam* believes Rav Yehudah learns; or, alternatively, like whom is the *Rambam paskening* if not Rav Yehudah?

Let us stop briefly and ask ourselves what Shmuel's position might be at this moment.

In regard to *kura*, we know that Shmuel holds that this is not a fruit. So according to Shmuel, *kura's berachah* is *Shehakol* and it is obligated neither in *maaser* nor *orlah*.

With *temaros* and *alin*, we also know what Shmuel holds. When the Gemara tells us, "*tz'laf nat'i inshi a'da'ata d'shusa*," *Rashi* says that people plan to eat the caper's shoots and leaves, since the tree's growth is not impeded by this.

Shmuel thus considers the shoots and leaves of the caper tree to be "fruit," but not because they are a natural botanical fruit. **They are considered fruit because people elevate them to that status by planting the caper tree with the intention of eating the shoots and the leaves**. If the planters did not intend to eat the shoots and leaves, these items would be called non-fruit and the *berachah* for anyone who did eat them would be *Shehakol*, like by *kura*. As it is, they are "fruit" on account of the planters' intentions, or what I call "Fruit by Choice." As fruit, they are entitled to a *berachah* higher than the general *Shehakol*. But because their status as fruit was acquired not because God made them to be fruit but because people elected to plant them and treat them as fruit, they are not entitled to the highest *berachah* of *Borei Pri Ha'eitz*. They get only *Borei Pri Ha'adamah*. They are fruit but not primary fruit, and

Berachos 36a

for the same reason they are not subject to *orlah*. With regard to *maaser*, shoots are "fruit" enough to be subject to *maaser* while leaves are not, as per Rabbi Eliezer in *Mesechta Maasros*.

WE MIGHT DEDUCE that regarding *evyonos* and *kafrisin*, Shmuel holds like the *Beraisa* and like Rabbi Eliezer. As primary fruits, they will get *Ha'eitz* and be subject to *maaser* and *orlah*.

But thanks to the above-cited *Rashi*, it is possible that Shmuel differs with Rabbi Eliezer and the *Beraisa* on one key matter. The *Beraisa* definitely holds *kafrisin* are considered primary fruit ("*ikar pri*"). But from *Rashi*, who only mentions how people plant the caper tree to eat the shoots and the leaves, it seems that Shmuel holds that people no longer plant caper trees intending to eat the *kafrisin*. As such, there is no way *kafrisin* can continue to be called *ikar pri*, even when someone does plant the caper tree for its *kafrisin*.

So according to Shmuel, *kafrisin* could be at most *Borei Pri Ha'adamah*, not like the *Beraisa* that declares them to be *Borei Pri Ha'eitz*. Basically, according to Shmuel, *kafrisin* are non-fruit (based on the above *Rashi* that besides for the berries, people plant caper trees only for the shoots and the leaves, but not for the *kafrisin* shells). Their *berachah* remains *Borei Pri Ha'adamah*, however, because they have a strong enough connection to "fruit" status through the minority of people who do plant it for *kafrisin*. They have no *din maaser* unless and until someone actually plants it for the *kafrisin*, and they have no *din orlah* even if someone did plant it for the *kafrisin*, because *orlah* (like the *berachah* of *Ha'eitz*) is only for *ikar pri*. This is *shitas* Shmuel.

(BOTH SHMUEL **AND** the *Beraisa* could be right if we allow that at one point in time people did eat the shells right along with the berries and at a later time in history not only did they stop eating the shells along with the berries but they generally stopped eating the shells at all.)

WELL, NOW THAT we are aware of *shitas* Shmuel, maybe *shitas* Shmuel is all we need. The previous Gemara told us that despite the accolades heaped upon Rav Yehudah by Shmuel, the halachah still follows Shmuel. That was said relative to the *din* of *kura*, but since the whole point of our *sugya* is to pose a contradiction against what Rav Yehudah learned from Shmuel in the *sugya* of *kura* (namely, that on non-fruit the *berachah* is *Shehakol*), our *sugya*, it would seem, would still be covered by the blanket pronouncement of the halachah going like Shmuel.

THIS WOULD FIT in beautifully with the *Rambam*. In studying his rulings, it becomes clear that he *paskens* precisely like Shmuel:

1. ***Berachah***—*Kafrisin* are no longer recognized as a *pri* the way Rabbi Eliezer and the *Beraisa* once considered them to be, so they are no longer *Borei Pri Ha'eitz*. They are now "non-fruit" unless the tree was planted specifically for the purpose of eating the *kafrisin*. The only *berachah* they can get now is *Borei Pri Ha'adamah*. This is *shitas* Shmuel, as we have just shown. And this is indeed how the *Rambam* rules in *Hilchos Berachos* 8:6: "The caper-berry shell receives the *berachah Borei Pri Ha'adamah*, because it is not a fruit."

2. ***Maaser***—With regard to *maaser*, *kafrisin* are not considered a *pri* unless and until they are planted with a specific intent for the *kafrisin* to be eaten. When they **are** planted with such intent, they become *chayav* in *maaser* and are considered to be a *pri*, which is enough reason to upgrade their *berachah* even without the elevating intent, and thus they get the *berachah* of *Borei Pri Ha'adamah*. This is the *Rambam* in *Hilchos Terumos* 2:4, where he says:

> תמרות של צלף וקפריסין של צלף פטורים מפני שאינן פרי בד"א כשזרען לזרע אבל זרען לירק הרי אלו חייבים וכן אביונות של צלף חייבים מפני שהן פרי.
>
> *Caper shoots and caper-berry shells are exempt [from maaser] because they are not classified as fruit. When is this so? When they are planted for seed. But when they are planted as food, they are obligated, and also caper berries are obligated, because they are classified as fruit.*

Berachos 36a

Do not be misled into reading the closing phrase of this *Rambam* (*"mipnei she'hein pri"*) as referring to just the berries. For if this were the correct way to read the *Rambam*, the phrase *"v'chein evyonos shel tz'laf chayavim"* would make no sense. *Evyonos* would be the only part of the caper tree *chayav* in *maaser* under all conditions. The proper word would not be ***v'chein*** (**and also**). The phrase would be ***aval*** (**however**). What the *Rambam* is actually saying is that *kafrisin*, when they are grown to be eaten, as well as *evyonos* under all conditions, are *chayav* in *maaser* because they are both "fruit."

3. **Orlah**—*Kafrisin* are *patur* from *orlah* in both Eretz Yisrael and *chutz la'aretz* according to Shmuel because they are not fruit, and the fact that they could become fruit by having someone plant the tree specifically to eat the *kafrisin* can only bring it to the *Borei Pri Ha'adamah* level—not the *ikar pri* level you would need in order to make it *chayav* in *orlah*. The *Rambam paskens* like Shmuel. This explains why in *Hilchos Maaser Sheini* 10:3, the *Rambam* includes the law of *tz'laf* in with the law of *s'yag* (planting fruit trees as a fence) to which the laws of *orlah* do not apply, due to lack of intent for the fruit.

> זה שחשב עליו למאכל חייב בערלה וזה שחשב עליו
> לסייג, או לעצים פטור שהדבר תלוי בדעתו של נוטע
> והצלף חייב בערלה האביונות בלבד אבל הקפריסין
> מותרות.

> ...*The [tree] that was intended for its fruit is liable for orlah, while the one that was intended as a fence or for its wood is exempt, for the matter depends on the intent of the planter; and as for the caper bush—the berries alone are liable for orlah, but the shells are exempt.*

The point of his closing phrase is that *kafrisin shel tz'laf* is to be understood in contrast to the law of *s'yag*. *"Aval ha'kafrisin mutaros*—But *kafrisin* are exempt (from *orlah*)," **even if you planted the tree specifically to eat the *kafrisin*** (unlike the law of *s'yag l'inyan orlah* and unlike the law of *maaser* where specific intent can incur a *chiyuv*, as we just saw at the beginning of this halachah and in *Hilchos Terumos* above).

Only one problem remains: Rav Yehudah and Shmuel are committed to the *berachah* of *Borei Pri Ha'adamah* for *kafrisin* because *kafrisin* can be elevated to fruit status via *machshavah*. This we derived from the fact that Rav Yehudah ate *kafrisin* in *chutz la'aretz* but did not say "halachah k'Rabbi Akiva," which would have indicated he held *kafrisin* are non-fruits, period, and the *berachah* would have been *Shehakol*. By saying to throw away the *evyonos* and to eat the *kafrisin* in *chutz la'aretz* and concluding that whatever (opinion) is lenient in Eretz Yisrael, the halachah is like him in *chutz la'aretz*, he is indicating that he holds like Rabbi Eliezer that *kafrisin* belong in the world of fruit.

But just because Rav Yehudah does not align himself with Rabbi Akiva, how do we know he holds *kafrisin* are a fruit? Maybe he holds they are a "fruit-protector"? That would make them non-fruits but still *orlah* in Eretz Yisrael (because of the *pasuk* that includes some non-fruits in the *din* of *orlah* in Eretz Yisrael). If he held this way, there would be no lenient opinion to rely on for *chutz la'aretz*, leaving the only rationale for his eating *kafrisin shel orlah* in *chutz la'aretz* the fact that a *shomer l'pri* is simply not a *pri*, and, where no *pasuk* exists to include it (i.e., in *chutz la'aretz*), it is *mutar* regarding *orlah*. Its *berachah* should thus be *Shehakol*, not *Borei Pri Ha'adamah*!

To answer this problem, the Gemara gives us the story of Mar bar Rav Ashi. Ravina found Mar bar Rav Ashi eating *kafrisin* of *orlah* in *chutz la'aretz*. Ravina presumed he was following Rabbi Eliezer fundamentally, while relying on Rabbi Akiva as the lenient opinion, enabling him to eat *kafrisin* in *chutz la'aretz*, and proceeded to ask a follow-up question based on that presumption. The Gemara asks: How did Ravina know Mar bar Rav Ashi was not relying on a different principle—that *kafrisin* are a *shomer l'pri* and not a fruit?

That would make them subject to *orlah* in Eretz Yisrael, but permissible to eat in *chutz la'aretz*, and then the *berachah* on *kafrisin* should be *Shehakol*! The Gemara concludes that *kafrisin* do not qualify as *shomer l'pri*. Thus, Mar bar Rav Ashi—and, by implication, Rav Yehudah and

Berachos 36a

Shmuel—**must** be in essential agreement with the *Beraisa* and Rabbi Eliezer. Thanks only to modified usage of the caper-berry shells, *kafrisin* came to be seen as non-fruits capable of becoming "Fruit by Choice"—elevated to *pri* status by way of *machshavah*, a condition that renders its *berachah* "*Borei Pri...*," but only *Borei Pri Ha'adamah* and not *Borei Pri Ha'eitz*.

With this, we can begin to explain how the *Rambam* must understand the ensuing *sugya* of *pilpilei* (pepper).

פלפלי רב ששת אמר שהכל רבא אמר לא כלום וגו׳.

Pepper [i.e., the spice]—Rav Sheishes says [the berachah is] Shehakol; Rava says it gets no berachah...

For pepper, all the *poskim* rule like Rava that it receives no *berachah*. The Gemara asks on Rava: Then what do we do with Rabbi Meir, who says we learn to include pepper trees as having a *din orlah* from the extra word "*ma'achal*" in the *pasuk*? From this word, we learn to include a tree that is called an *eitz ma'achal*—a phrase in the Torah that refers to a tree whose wood and bark has the same taste as its fruit, the embodiment of which is the pepper tree. That hardly sounds, asks the Gemara, like a tree whose product should receive no *berachah*!

The Gemara answers, *ha b'r'tivta ha b'yabeshta*. When fresh, pepper is a berry and it is *chayav* in *orlah*; dried, it receives no *berachah*. According to the *Tur*, the berry's *berachah* is *Borei Pri Ha'eitz*, while the dried peppercorn has no *berachah* ("*lo klum*") because it is inedible.

Now, what happens if you take a dried peppercorn (or some ground dry pepper) and make it edible by adding sugar? According to the *Tur* and other *poskim*, it could no longer be *lo klum*, as it is no longer inedible. So what would the *berachah* be? Well, the *Tur* (*Orach Chaim* 202) says that candying dried ginger brings it back to being *Borei Pri Ha'adamah*, but no higher, as even fresh ginger was never more than *Borei Pri Ha'adamah*. But fresh peppercorns, according to the *Tur*, were originally *Borei Pri Ha'eitz*. Yet, we don't say sweetened dried pepper is now *Ha'eitz*. Evidently, drying pepper has not only cost it its *berachah*, it has even cost it its original status as a fruit! Why should this be?

דף לו.

The *Rambam* here fits in much more easily, because he never declared peppercorns to be *Ha'eitz*, even when fresh. But our questions are on him as well:

1. Why does he **not** *pasken* that fresh peppercorns are *Ha'eitz*?
2. Why does he not bring *l'halachah* that sweetened pepper reverts at least to *Borei Pri Ha'adamah*?

But with what we've just said about *kafrisin*, we can explain. Let us propose that the *Rambam* differs from everyone else in two fundamental ways.

Rabbi Meir's *derashah* about *pilpilin* and *orlah* tells the *Rambam* that *pilpilin* is like *kafrisin*, a non-fruit elevated to fruit status by decision only—a "Fruit by Choice." It has *din orlah* only because of a *derashah* (similar to a *shomer l'pri*), but not because it is a primary fruit (*ikar pri*). The most such an item can get as a *berachah* is *Borei Pri Ha'adamah*. And what makes it a non-fruit other than when it is planted with the intention of being eaten as moist peppercorns? The fact that it is a spice. **A spice (*tavlin*) is not a food—it is an enhancer of food**. And anything that is not a food does not get a real *berachah*. Yes, the Sages can assign it a *berachah*—like they do for water, which is also not a food, but here Rava, echoed by the *poskim*, rejects Rav Sheishes' position that the Sages assigned *tavlin* a *berachah* of *Shehakol* like they did for water. So, even mixed with sugar, says the *Rambam*, pepper will remain a spice and have no *berachah*. Fresh peppercorns will be *chayav* in *orlah* but will have only a *berachah* of *Ha'adamah*, as they are only "Fruit by Choice."

(PARENTHETICALLY, WHY DOES the Torah even want the pepper tree to have a *din orlah*? Because of its symbolism. Its character of *taam eitzo v'ta'am piryo shavin*, as discussed in *Sukkah* 35a, makes it *chashuv*—it is the only tree that still reminds us of Hashem's original plan for Gan Eden. [The esrog also has this quality, but it is a *yerek*, not an *ilan*; see *Tosafos*, *Kiddushin* 2b, s.v. *shaveh l'ilan*.] The Torah is letting us know that Eretz Yisrael is not lacking anything—not even trees with strictly symbolic value. But pepper trees' *din orlah* is not because of the peppercorns' status as fruit.)

Berachos 36a

THE *SUGYA* OF *pilpilin*, then, according to the *Rambam*, becomes the final step in a three-part Talmudic discussion of the appropriate *berachah* for edible parts of trees that are other than their classic fruits. The *sugya* of *kura* teaches us that non-fruits get a *Shehakol*. The *sugya* of *kafrisin* teaches us that non-fruits can become "Fruits by Choice" and can earn a *"Borei Pri"* berachah but not a *Borei Pri Ha'eitz*. And the *sugya* of *pilpilin* teaches us that when the reason for something being a non-fruit is because it is not even a food, then it receives no *berachah* at all, but nevertheless it can still be elevated to a *berachah* of *Borei Pri Ha'adamah* if designated a "Fruit by Choice."

דף לז:

אמר רב יוסף האי חביצא דאית ביה פרורין כזית וגו׳.

Rav Yosef said: Chavitza, when its pieces are a k'zayis in size, receives the berachah of Hamotzi...

1. The Gemara wants to know what the *berachah* is for *chavitza*. *Rashi* explains *chavitza* as bread that has been subsequently broken down and cooked. *Tosafos* differs and says it means bread that has been kneaded together with soup or honey or some other foreign substance. While Rav Yosef wanted to argue that if it had gotten broken down into pieces smaller than a *k'zayis*, it loses its *Hamotzi* and becomes *Mezonos*, the conclusion in the halachah is that whether or not it got broken down into pieces of smaller than a *k'zayis*, it still retains its *berachah* of *Hamotzi*, provided that it still retains the look of bread. It is difficult to understand the *hava amina* of Rav Yosef. A peanut butter sandwich cut into quarters would seem to fit the requirements of being smaller than a *k'zayis* and having the bread mixed with a foreign substance. Does anyone believe he would have us making a *Mezonos* on such a thing?

2. The *Rambam* (*Hilchos Berachos* 3:8) seems to contradict himself. He says that bread broken down into pieces, and either cooked or kneaded with soup, retains its *berachah* if either the pieces are *k'zayis*, or they are less than *k'zayis* but the look of bread remains. That would imply that to lose *Hamotzi*, the bread would have to undergo two changes—lose its *k'zayis* size and lose its look of bread. But then he says: If the bread pieces are smaller than *k'zayis* **or** they have lost their appearance of bread, the *berachah* is *Mezonos*. How could that be? What if the bread pieces

Berachos 37b

are smaller than *k'zayis* but still have the look of bread? Are they *Hamotzi*, like the first half implies, because they look like bread, or are they *Mezonos*, like the second half implies, because they are smaller than *k'zayis*?

Yesod

There are two basic ways that bread can lose its *berachah* of *Hamotzi*. Bread is cohesive—it comes in a loaf and it sticks together. If it loses that cohesion by being broken down into little pieces, it loses its *berachah*. Now, it is not sufficient here to simply have the bread broken down—broken-down matzah can still be used for the mitzvah of matzah, so it is obviously still bread. Rather, it must be broken down and cooked, and then it will lose its *Hamotzi* by virtue of having lost its cohesion.

Another thing that bread has is its appearance. The way bread loses its appearance is not by being broken down. It is by having foreign substances added to it such that its look changes. If it gets mixed with a foreign substance like soup enough that its look changes, it loses its *berachah* of *Hamotzi*. That is the second way bread can lose its *berachah*.

But there is also a third way. Bread could be physically intact and have no added elements and no change of appearance. But if it has been cooked so long that it has undergone an internal change such that in its essence it is no longer bread, it has lost its bread-essence and loses its *berachah* of *Hamotzi*.

This is all in the precision-tuned language of the *Rambam*. All the commentators seem to have read the *Rambam* as we presented it above. But with the shift of one comma, the *Rambam* can be read differently. Instead of being phrased like this:

הפת שפתת אותה פתים ובשלה בקדרה או לשה במרק אם יש בפתיתין כזית או שניכר שהן פת ולא נשתנה צורתה מברך עליה בתחלה המוציא.

it could be phrased like this:

> הפת שפתת אותה פתים ובשלה בקדרה או לשה
> במרק אם יש בפתיתין כזית או שניכר שהן פת ולא
> נשתנה צורתה מברך עליה בתחלה המוציא.

Bread [either] broken down into pieces and cooked, or kneaded with soup retains its berachah if either the pieces are k'zayis [in the case of its being broken down and cooked] or if its appearance has not changed [in the case of its being kneaded with soup].

This reading reflects the first two ways to downgrade the *berachah* of bread—destroying its cohesiveness (by breaking it down into small cooked pieces) and destroying its appearance (by adulterating it with a foreign substance). The *Rambam* then continues (because he has not yet told us what *berachah* a downgraded bread form will receive):

> ואם אין בהן כזית או שעברה צורת הפת בבישול
> מברך עליה בתחלה בורא מיני מזונות.

If the bread pieces are smaller than k'zayis [in the case of breaking down and cooking], or if the bread [is intact and retains its appearance but] has totally forfeited its bread-essence via overcooking [the third way to downgrade bread], its berachah is Mezonos.

Included in that last line is the obvious understanding that if the bread had lost its appearance through adulteration, the *berachah* would be *Mezonos*. That is simple logic—if the total loss of its essence still leaves it at *Mezonos*, the simple loss of its appearance would certainly bring it no lower than *Mezonos*. Thus we have the entire concept nesting precisely in the *Rambam*'s language.

The Jewish People merited leaving Egypt because, according to the midrash, they did not change their language, their clothing, or their names. According to our understanding, this would be in perfect consonance with the *Rambam*. Changing language breaks down the cohesiveness of a group; changing dress destroys its appearance; changing

Berachos 37b

names undermines its essence. The three things that allow bread to keep its *berachah* of *Hamotzi* are those same three things that enabled the Jewish People to be redeemed from Egypt.

And this is perfect, because the language of the *berachah*—*Hamotzi lechem min ha'aretz*—is parallel to the Torah's description of Hashem's efforts for the Jewish People—*Hamotzi eschem me'eretz Mitzrayim*. Just as the *Hamotzi* on bread can only happen when there has been no change in the cohesion, appearance, and essence of the bread, so too *Hamotzi* of the Jewish People from Egypt can only have happened because there had been no change in their cohesion, appearance, or essence.

Endnotes

1. *Berachos* 35a.
2. Rav Moshe Heinemann of the Star-K argues that the *berachah* for hearts of palm is *Ha'eitz*, because today's growers of commercial palm hearts grow the palms for the purpose of harvesting the hearts, thereby making them the *ikar pri*. If not for our analysis of the Gemara, I might have agreed; but with our identification of "edible nature," which as postulated above can never reach a level of *Ha'eitz*, because they start at *Shehakol* and go up only one level when planted purposefully, I stand by my conclusion. See also the chapter below on *Kafrisin Shel Tzlaf* (36a). *L'halachah*, consult your own Rav.

Chapter Seven

Sheloshah She'achlu

דף מה.

על ברכת הזימון ועל ברכת המזון

כתב הרמב"ם פ"א הלכות ברכות ה"א מצות עשה מן התורה לברך אחר אכילת מזון שנאמר ואכלת ושבעת וברכת את ה' אלקיך. (פ"ב הלכה א') וסדר ברכת המזון כך היא ראשונה ברכת הזן שנייה ברכת הארץ שלישית בונה ירושלים רביעית הטוב והמטיב. ובפ"ה הלכה ב' שלשה שאכלו פת כאחד חייבין לברך ברכת הזימון קודם ברכת המזון ואיזו היא ברכת הזימון אם היו האוכלין מג' עד עשרה מברך אחד מהם ואומר נברך שאכלנו משלו והכל עונין ברוך שאכלנו משלו ובטובו חיינו והוא חוזר ומברך ברוך שאכלנו משלו ובטובו חיינו, עכ"ל. (הלכה ג') ואחר כך אומר ברוך אתה ה' אלקינו מלך העולם הזן את העולם עד שגומר ד' ברכות והן עונין אמן אחר כל ברכה וברכה עכ"ל.

והנה בטור או"ח סי' קצ"ג כתב ז"ל אם היתה חבורה גדולה מסובין יחד ואינן יכולין כולם לשמוע הברכה מפי המברך ואינן רשאין ליחלק לחבורות של י' י' מפני שנצטרכו לברך בקול רם וישמע בעל הבית ויקפיד עליהם יכולים ליחלק לחבורות של ג' ג' ולברך בנחת שלא ישמע בעל הבית ויקפיד—זה טוב להם ממה שלא יצאו ידי חובת ברכת המזון שהרי אינן יכולין לשמוע מפי המברך.

והקשה הבית יוסף מהו פירושו של לא יצאו ידי חובת ברכת המזון? בשלמא ידי חובת ברכת הזימון בשם לא יצאו אם לא ישמיעו למברך, אבל ברכת המזון יכולים כל אחד ואחד לברך בפני עצמו, ולמה לא יצאו אם לא ישמעו מפי המברך? ולכן החליף הגירסא בטור וכתב דצ"ל ממה שלא יצאו ידי חובת ברכת הזימון, עי' לשונו.

אבל הב"ח כתב דאינו כן אלא גירסתו נכון הוא דכך הוא העיקר דבג' צריך שיצטרפו ביחד לכתחלה בכל הברכות ואינם יכולים לברך לעצמם, ואף בלחש, ולכן אם לא ישמיעו להמברך לא יצאו ידי חובת ברכת המזון, וכמש"כ בטור.

נראה דהרמב"ם ס"ל כשיטת הב"ח ממה שכתב והוא חוזר ומברך ברוך שאכלנו משלו ובטובו חיינו ואחר כך אומר ברוך אתה ה' אלקינו מלך העולם הזן את העולם כולו בטובו עד שגומר ארבע ברכות והן עונין אמן אחר כל ברכה וברכה, ע"כ, הרי אף לשיטת הרמב"ם המסובין צריכין לשמוע ברכת המזון מפי המברך.

והראה לי אחד מחברי דרבינו תם לכאורה ג"כ סבירא לי' הכי ממה שכתב בתוספות ב"ב דף פ"א ע"ב ד"ה למעוטי אדמת עכו"ם, מהא דלא הי' מניח רבינו תם לגרים לברך ברכת הזימון לפי שאינו יכול לומר שהנחלת לאבותינו ארץ טובה. ואם אין המברך מוציא את הרבים אלא בברכת זימון בלבד, מה בכך אם

דף מה.

אינו יכול לומר שהנחלת, שהוא בברכת המזון, והלא ברכת המזון כל א' וא' מברך לעצמו, ומאי נפקא מינה אם הגר יברך ברכת הזימון.

אלא נראה בשיטת הני ראשונים—ר"ת והרמב"ם והב"ח—דכשג' אוכלים כאחד המברך אומר ברכת הזימון וכל ברכת המזון בקול, והמסובין עונים הזימון ועונין אמן ויוצאין ידי חובתם ככה בזימון ובבה"מ.

וצריך לדעת מהו מקורו של הדין הזה? ידועה, ומובא בש"ס וברמב"ם, דמקור ברכת המזון הוא הפסוק בפרשת עקב ואכלת ושבעת וברכת את ה' אלקיך. מקור דין זימון מובא בש"ס מן הפסוק כי שם ה' אקרא הבו גודל לאלקינו. האחרונים חולקים אם דרשה גמורה היא זו או רק אסמכתא בעלמא, ובראשונים עצמם הדבר סתום, אבל הפרי מגדים כתב שרוב הפוסקים סוברים דברכת הזימון דרבנן היא וקרא אסמכתא בעלמא. ונראה דזו היא שיטת הרמב"ם מהא דלא כתב מצוות עשה מן התורה לברך ברכת הזימון שנאמר כי שם ה' אקרא הבו גודל לאלקינו, כמו שכתב גבי ברכת המזון. אבל מ"מ ברור דשני דברים נפרדים הם—ברכת המזון וברכת הזימון. והנה בדיני ברכת המזון, בידוע שכל מי שירצה יכול לצאת ידי חובתו בשמיעת ברכת חבירו מדין שומע כעונה, וכדהזכיר הרמב"ם עצמו בפ"א הל' י"א, אבל לעולם לא מצינו שחייבין לצאת ככה, ומאי שנא הכא דחייבין? ועוד, בדיני שומע כעונה יכולים לצאת אף בלא ענית אמן, וכמש"כ הרמב"ם שם, וא"כ למה כתב כאן דצריכין המסובין לענות אמן?

והרי יש מן הראשונים שרצו לבאר דזימון כמו שתקנוה חכמים אינו רק ברכה נוספת אלא שינוי בעצם ברכת המזון.

ומייסדים את הפירוש הזה על מחלוקת ר' נחמן ור' ששת בברכות דף מ"ו ע"א בענין עד היכן ברכת הזימון ר' נחמן אמר עד נברך ור' ששת אמר עד הזן. רש"י מפרש ר' ששת כפשוטו, דברכת הזימון באמת עד הזן ומשמע דברכת המזון לעולם אינו מתחיל אלא מנודה לך, ואפילו ליחיד. אבל שאר ראשונים, שלא נחית להם האי פירושא, מפרשים באחד משני אופנים. האחד—לפסוק כר' נחמן כנגד ר' ששת, ודלא כדקיימא לן ר' נחמן ור' ששת הלכה כר' ששת, וכאופן זה פסק הרי"ף. השני—כמש"כ, והיינו דאע"פ דברכת הזימון עצמה פסקה בברוך שאכלנו משלו ובטובו חיינו, אבל תורת זימון פועלת לעשות שינוי בעצם ברכת המזון ג"כ והיינו לחייב המסובין לשמוע למברך עד שהוא גומר ברכת הזן, ועי' בהתוס' והרא"ש.

אבל לעולם אין כל זה מועיל כלל לקושייתינו, דהלא אף אם תמצא לומר דהרמב"ם ס"ל כשיטת התוס' והרא"ש, אמאי בעינן כל ד' ברכות לשמוע להמברך, והלא לא איירי ר' ששת אלא עד הזן, וכאן בעינן המסובין לשמוע ולענות אמן אחר כל ד' ברכות. ולכן עדיין קושייתינו עומדת—מהו מקורו של הדין הזה.

יש שרוצים לתרץ שמקורו הוא ברוב עם הדרת מלך, היינו דכשיש כמה אנשים חייבים במצוה אחת בשעה אחת, ראוי להם להצטרף מפני כבוד המלך, ולכן ראוי שאחד יוציא את הרבים ידי חובתם.

האי ענין דברוב עם הדרת מלך באמת מצינו בהלכה. כתב הטור בסי׳ קצ״ג ששה שאכלו כאחד נחלקים כיון שישאר זימון לכל חבורה, וכן עשרים כיון שישאר זימון בשם לכל חבורה. והב״ח הביא על זה דברי הרב בהגהות ש״ע דפי׳ דכשהם עשרים יכולים ליחלק אם ירצו אבל טפי עדיף שלא יהיו נחלקים דברוב עם הדרת מלך וכן ששה נחלקים אם ירצו אבל טפי עדיף שלא יהיו נחלקים, עכ״ל. וכתב הדרכי משה דמשמע כן מפירוש רש״י ג״כ וכתב דכן הוא המנהג משום דברוב עם הדרת מלך.

ובענין אחר כתב הרא״ש, הובא בבית יוסף שם, ז״ל, מצוה לחזר אחר ג׳ כל מה שיכולים משום ברכת זימון דברוב עם הדרת מלך, עכ״ל.

והרמ״א בסי׳ קצ״ג סעי׳ ב׳ הזכירו לענין שלשה שאכלו אבל לא קבעו את עצמם מתחלה, דבזה רשאין ליחלק ולא לזמן, אפילו הכי עדיף טפי לזמן משום ברוב עם הדרת מלך.

אבל גם זה אינו נוגע לעניינינו, דכל הני הלכות אינן מדברות אלא לענין זימון—דלזמן עדיף טפי משלא לזמן משום ברוב עם הדרת מלך, והמרבה בזימון הרי זה משובח. אבל לענין ברכת המזון לא מצינו דלהוציא אחרים ידי חובתם עדיף טפי משכל אחד יברך לעצמו, ובפרט אחר שכבר הצטרפו לזימון וכבר יש בכח זו ענין הצטרפות אף אם יברכו לעצמם.

ואדרבה, משמע מסוגיא דיהודה בר מרימר בדף מ״ה ע״ב דאין כאן ענין להצטרף לברכת המזון. איתא בגמרא יהודה בר מרימר ומר בר רב אשי ורב אחא מדפתי כרכי ריפתא בהדי הדדי לא הוה בהו חד דהוה מופלג מחבריה לברוכי להו בריך איניש לנפשיה אתו לקמיה דמרימר אמר להו ידי ברכה יצאתם ידי זימון לא יצאתם, ע״כ. וא״כ דבעינן להצטרף משום ברוב עם הדרת מלך, למה היו אומרים לברך כל אחד בפני עצמו, נהי דזימון לא היה להם, אבל ברוב עם בוודאי היה להם, ולמה לא חשו לדין זה?

ועוד, דאי סבירא ליה להב״ח דטעמא דדין זה הוא משום ברוב עם הדרת מלך, יהא קשה גם עליו לשון הטור. הטור שהבאנו לעיל כתב ז״ל זה טוב להם ממה שלא יצאו ידי חובת ברכת המזון. וא״כ דחיוב הצטרפות שלהם משום ברוב עם הדרת מלך הוא, היה צריך לומר ממה שלא יצאו ענין ברוב עם הדרת מלך, דהא חובת ברכת המזון וודאי יצאו אף אם יאמרוה כל אחד בפני עצמו. ולא יהא עדיף ממה שהקשה הב״ח גופא על הבית יוסף כשהחליף הוא את הגירסא בטור.

ואם אין מקורו של דין הצטרפות בברכת המזון מחמת ברוב עם הדרת מלך, אמאי חייב המזמן להוציא את הרבים ידי חובתם בברכת המזון. ועוד, הראה לי

274

דף מה.

הרב חיים כהן, שליט״א, שיש להחזיק את הקושיא מסוגיא בפרק מי שמתו. איתא בפרק מי שמתו, ברכות דף כ׳ ע״ב, אמר [הקב״ה] וכי לא אשא פנים לישראל שכתבתי להם בתורה ואכלת ושבעת וברכת את ה׳ אלקיך והם מדקדקים על עצמם עד כזית ועד כביצה, ע״כ. ומבואר ברש״י לר׳ מאיר וכביצה לר׳ יהודה הוו שיעורי דרבנן דהא מדאורייתא ואכלת ושבעת וברכת כתיב דבעינן שביעה גמורה. ועוד איתא שם א״ל רבינא לרבא נשים בברכת המזון דאורייתא או דרבנן למאי נפקא מינה לאפוקי רבים ידי חובתם אא״ב דאורייתא אתי דאורייתא ומפיק דאורייתא אלא אי אמרת דרבנן הוי שאינו מחוייב בדבר וכל שאינו מחוייב בדבר אינו מוציא את הרבים ידי חובתם, ע״כ. ופשיטא דאין לחלק בין דרבנן זה לדרבנן אחרינא, אלא ודאי דבכל מקום לא אתי בר חיוב מדרבנן ומפיק חיוביה דבר חיוב מדאורייתא. וממאי דאוקים תלמודא האי דבן מברך לאביו בכגון דאכל האב שיעורא דרבנן, נראה ברור דכל מי שחיובו מדרבנן או מטעם קטנות או מטעם אישיות או מטעם שיעור אכילתו אינו מוציא בברכת המזון את מי שחיובו מדאורייתא.

וא״כ בדוכתא דידן כשנותנים לאחד לברך והוא בעי להוציא את האחרים ידי חובתן, אמאי לא בעינן לשאול אותו אם שבע הוא אם לאו, דהא אם לא שבע רק שאכילתו היה יותר מכזית, הרי אינו מחוייב אלא מדרבנן והאיך מוציא אותם שאכלו כדי שביעה ידי חובתן בברכת המזון שלהם.

ויש לעיין טובא בסוגיא דינאי מלכא ושמעון בן שטח בדף מ״ח ע״א דקיהבו ליה לשמעון בן שטח כסא לברוכי אף דלא אכל אמר היכי אבריך ברוך שאכל ינאי וחביריו משלו שתייה לההוא כסא יהבו ליה כסא אחרינא ובריך. ולא הודו לו חכמים אלא הצריכו שיאכל המברך כזית דגן כדי להוציא את הרבים אבל בכזית מיהו סגי. והלא יש להקשות, בכזית אינו חייב אלא מדרבנן והאיך יכול להוציא אחרים דשבעו, דחיובם מדאורייתא הוא. [ובאמת אפילו כדי שביעה בדגן אינו חייב בברכת המזון מדאורייתא אלא בפת, אבל יש לומר דחייב מ״מ במעין מ״מ שלש דהוא בגדר דאורייתא, וצ״ע.] וכן הקשו כמה ראשונים והעלו תירוצים שונים:

רש״י תירץ דיכול להוציא אף דלא אכל אלא כזית משום דכיון דמיחייב מיהו מדרבנן מחוייב בדבר קרינן ביה.

תוס׳ תירץ בעניין אחר דמעיקר הדין היה יכול להוציא אף דלא אכל כלל מטעם כל ישראל ערבים זה לזה, וכזית דגן אינו צריך אלא כדי שיוכל לומר שאכלנו משלו.

הבעל הלכות גדולות (בה״ג) חולק וכתב שבאמת אי אפשר להוציא אחרים ששבעו עד שיאכל עמהם כדי שביעה.

הראב״ד תירץ בע״א לגמרי דבאמת מה שעשה שמעון בן שטח מעיקר הדין היה—דקיי״ל כזית וכביצה דאורייתא נינהו, ודלא כסוגיא דפרק מי שמתו.

275

הרמב"ם ודאי לא סבירא ליה הכי דהא כתב בריש הלכות ברכות ז"ל ואינו חייב (בברכת המזון) מן התורה אא"כ שבע שנאמר ואכלת ושבעת וברכת ומדברי סופרים אכל אפילו כזית מברך אחריו, עכ"ל.

נראה דשיטת הרמב"ם כשיטת הבה"ג מהא דכתב בפרק ה' הלכה ט"ו בן מברך לאביו ואשה מברכת לבעלה בזמן שאכל ולא שבע אבל אם אכל ושבע שהוא חייב בברכת המזון מן התורה בין אשה בין קטן אין מוציאין אותן שכל החייב בדבר מן התורה אין מוציאין אותן מידי חובתן אלא החייב באותו דבר מן התורה כמותו עכ"ל. הרי דלשיטתו אי אפשר להוציא אחרים ששבעו עד שיתחייב כוותייהו, וכמש"כ הבה"ג. ועל הא דאיתא אצל האי מעשה דשמעון בן שטח אין מוציאין את הרבים עד שיאכל כזית דגן. דמשמע דבכזית סגי, כך השיב לחכמי לוניל דלא בא לחדש אלא דבעינן דגן ולאפוקי יין או שאר ז' מינים, אבל לעולם שיעור כזית מהני להוציא את מי שחייב מדרבנן דוקא, ושיעור כדי שביעה בעינן להוציא את מי שחייב מדאורייתא, כדקיי"ל בפרק מי שמתו.

וא"א יותר תקיף קושייתנו, דלשיטת הבה"ג והרמב"ם אינו יכול להוציא אחרים אא"כ חייב עמהם באותו חיוב אכילה שלהם, א"כ בכל פעם שאחד בא להוציא אחרים ששבעו צריכים לבדקו אם שבע הוא אם לאו, ולענין זה כתב הרמב"ם בהלכה ט"ז במה דברים אמורים (שבן יכול להוציא את אביו, וכו') בזמן שאכל ולא שבע, אבל אם אכל ושבע אין מוציאין אותו עכ"ל. אבל לפי מה שפירשנו לעיל לשיטת הרמב"ם כשיטת הב"ח, דבכל מקום שאחד מברך ברכת הזימון חייב הוא להוציא האחרים ידי חובתן בברכת המזון ג"כ, א"כ כל מזמן צריך להיות שבע, דהא מן הסתם צריך להוציא אף שבעים, ולמה השמיט הרמב"ם דין זה אצל הלכות זימון ולא כתבו אלא לאחריו אצל הלכות בן מברך לאביו, והלא בכל זימון וזימון שייך הלכה זו.

ואולי אפשר לתרץ הכי. עמדנו עד כאן בהנחה קדומה דמצות עשה דואכלת ושבעת וברכת חל על כל אחד ואחד מישראל שאכל כדי שביעה. ואחר שעיינתי בפרשת עקב נראה לי דאולי אינו נכון. בכל פעם בקרא שמדבר משה רבינו עם כלל ישראל מדבר באחד משני אופנים, או בלשון יחיד או בלשון רבים. מן הסתם הוי אומר דכשמדבר לכלל ישראל מדבר בלשון רבים וכשמדבר לכל יחיד ויחיד מדבר בלשון יחיד, והרי ואכלת ושבעת וברכת בלשון יחיד כתיב, יהיה נראה לומר דמצוה היא על כל יחיד ויחיד.

אבל נראה דאינו כן, ואדרבה כשמדבר קרא בלשון רבים, כגון והיה עקב תשמעון, אכל יחיד ויחיד קאי, כלומר אתם תשמעון. וכשמדבר בלשון יחיד, כגון ברוך תהיה (ולא תהיון) מכל העמים וכגון ואכלת את כל העמים, אכלל ישראל כחבורה אחת קאי. וכזה ראיתי בפירוש בספר תוספת ברכה להרב ברוך הלוי עפשטיין, מחבר ספר תורה תמימה.

דף מה.

ואם כן, אפשר דהנחתינו אינו נכון, אלא נוכל לומר דכשאכלו שלשה כאחד—שעשו את עצמם כחבורה אחת—אינו חל עליהם אלא מצות עשה אחת, דפסוק ואכלת ושבעת וברכת בלשון יחיד נאמר, לשון המדברת אל הכלל ולא אל היחיד.

וא"כ חיוב ברכת המזון על חבורה שאכלה אינו חיוב פרטי על כל אחד מן המסובין, אלא חיוב אחת על כולם כאחד, שאנשי החבורה חייבים למנות אחד מהם שליח לברך בשביל החבורה, ולהצטרף עם ברכתו על ידי עניית אמן.

וממילא פשוט הוא דבמקום זימון, כשלשה אכלו כאחד, פשיטא דבעי המזמן לברך ד' ברכות בשביל כולם, דהא זו עיקר ברכת המזון שלהם מאחר דהצטרפו לאכול כאחד ועכשיו חל עליהם רק מצות עשה אחת.

ונראה לי דזו היא שיטת הרמב"ם במה דהצריך דהאוכלים ישמעו ברכת המזון של המזמן כדי שיצאו חיובם מפני שחיובם אינו של כל אחד ואחד בפרט אלא של החבורה בכלל, ואם לא ישמעו לא יצאו.

וממילא פשיטא דלא הביא הרמב"ם האי דין שהוא חייב מדרבנן אינו יכול להוציא את מי שהוא חייב מדאורייתא, דדין זה לא שייך אלא היכא דאחד באמת מוציא את חבירו בחיוב פרטי שלו. אבל הכא, אין ברכת המזמן פועל בתורת מוציא את חבירו אלא בתורת ברכת החבורה, וא"כ אף אם הוא בפרט אינו שבע, כל זמן שהחבורה שבע יכול כל אחד שירצה להמנות שליח, כי חיוב ואכלת ושבעת וברכת אינו חל עליו בפרט אלא על החבורה. וא"כ לא בעי הרמב"ם להעתיק האי דינא דהמחוייב מדרבנן אינו מוציא את מי שחייב מדאורייתא אלא התם אצל בן מברך לאביו וכיוצא בו שרק התם מדבר בתורת א' מוציא את חבירו.

ובזה מיושב בקל דין דהביא הטור לפי גירסת הב"ח דטוב להם ליחלק לחבורות של ג' ג' ממה שלא יצאו ידי חובת ברכת המזון, דזה פשוט דמאחר שחל עליהם חובת ברכת המזון בחבורה אינם יכולים להוציא את עצמם אלא בחבורה.

ולענין הלכה, קיימא לן כשאר ראשונים ולא כהרמב"ם, וכמש"כ בבית יוסף הנ"ל, והיינו שכל אחד ואחד מהמסובין יברך ברכת המזון בפני עצמו. וזהו לשון השו"ע או"ח סי' קפ"ג ס"ז נכון הדבר שכל אחד מהמסובין יאמר בלחש עם המברך כל ברכה וברכה ואפילו החתימות, ע"כ. אבל מן הט"ז והמשנה ברורה שם נראה דאפילו הכי שורש הדין כמו שכתבנו. וזהו לשון המשנה ברורה שם סקכ"ז נכון הדבר היינו אף דמדינא היה יותר נכון שישמעו המסובין כל ברכת המזון מפי המזמן והוא יוציאם בברכתו ובעצמן לא יברכו כלל מ"מ בעבור שמצוי בעוונותינו הרבים שהמסובין מסיחין דעתם ואינם מכוונים לדברי המברך כלל ונמצא שחסר להם ברכת המזון לגמרי ומבטלין עשה דאורייתא בידים לכך נכון כהיום יותר שהמסובין יאמרו בעצמן בלחש כל מלה ומלה עם המברך, עכ"ל.

וא"ת דמזה אינו ראיה, דזה אינו משמע אלא דמעיקר הדין צריך לנהוג כשיטת הרמב"ם אבל לאו דוקא מטעמא שאמרנו.

וראוי לעיין בסי' קפ"ב ס"א בדין כוס של ברכה בברכת המזון, דהדין הוא דברכת המזון טעונה כוס יין, והמנהג שלנו שלא לברך על הכוס אלא בשלשה. והנה, אין לומר דדין כוס אינו אלא חלק מהלכות זימון, דהא הביא המחבר שיטות דבעינן כוס אפילו ביחיד. וא"כ מן ההכרח דדין כוס הוי חלק מהלכות ברכת המזון. וא"כ מן הראוי שכל אחד ואחד שחייב בברכת המזון טעונה כוס בפני עצמו. והכי הוא הדין לדעה זו, כמו שממשיך הש"ע ואומר ז"ל ולפי זה אם שנים אוכלים יחד צריך לקחת כל אחד כוס לברכת המזון, עכ"ל.

וא"כ כששלשה אכלו כאחד, אם כן דחל חיוב ברכת המזון על כל אחד ואחד מהמסובין, היה מן הראוי שכל אחד ואחד יקח כוס לעצמו. אבל הדין אינו כן, דאפילו לדעה זו, בשלשה ויותר לא בעינן אלא כוס אחד, וכמש"כ במשנה ברורה שם סק"ג, ונראה דהוא מטעמא דביארנו.

Chapter Eight
Eilu Devarim

דף נא:

מתני׳ אלו דברים שבין בית שמאי ובין בית הלל בסעודה וגו׳.

Mishnah—These are the issues of difference between Beis Hillel and Beis Shammai in matters relating to meals: Beis Shammai say one makes the blessing over the day [Mekadeish Ha'Shabbos] first, and then the blessing over the wine, while Beis Hillel say one makes the blessing first over the wine and then over the day.

Gemara: Beraisa—Issues [of difference] between Beis Shammai and Beis Hillel regarding meals: Beis Shammai say bless the [Shabbos] day first and then bless the wine because the day is what causes the wine to be brought out. Also, the day was sanctified first and the wine only second. Beis Hillel say bless the wine first and then bless the day because the wine is what causes kiddush ha'yom to be said. Another reason is that a blessing over wine is a more common occurrence than a blessing over the Shabbos day, and the rule is that the more common takes precedence over the less common [Tadir v'she'eino tadir, tadir kodem]. And the halachah is established in accordance with Beis Hillel.

Why do Beis Hillel have the need to tack on "another reason…"? Is it because Beis Shammai had two reasons and Beis Hillel only one? That cannot be, as Beis Hillel also had two reasons, that 1) Wine causes the kiddush, and 2) Tadir!

"And the halachah is established in accordance with Beis Hillel." This is obvious [p'shita], for we already know that a bas kol has emerged and declared the halachah to be like Beis Hillel in all matters!

[There are two answers:]

If you prefer [iba'is eima], I can answer that this halachic ruling was taught prior to the emergence of the bas kol.

Or if you prefer [iba'is eima], I can answer that the ruling was taught even subsequent to the bas kol, but the Beraisa's ruling is in line with Rabbi Yehoshua, who—in the famous case of Tanur shel Achnai—denied the bas kol any authority in our rulings.

1. Beis Shammai gives two reasons for his position that *Birkas Ha'yom* comes before *Birkas Ha'yayin*. Why does he need two reasons, and what is the difference between them?
2. Why are Beis Hillel's two reasons treated differently than Beis Shammai's two reasons, with Beis Hillel's second reason being doubted as a second reason up until the Gemara's *maskanah*? Indeed, what changed? Why did the Gemara at first question Beis Hillel having a second reason before deciding they do have one? And why is it introduced as a *"davar acher"* when Beis Shammai's second reason was not introduced with that phrase?
3. *Tosafos* worries that we have a contradiction in halachah *paskening* both like the *bas kol* (that declared *halachah k'Beis Hillel*) and like Rabbi Yehoshua who rejects the *bas kol*. *Tosafos* answers that we embrace the *bas kol* when it is supported by a majority (*rov*); we reject the *bas kol* when it goes against the *rov*. If the *bas kol* is only embraced when it is supported by a *rov*, who needs a *bas kol* at all—we have a *rov*, and the *pasuk* tells us *"acharei rabim l'hatos"*!
4. *Tosafos* says Rabbi Yehoshua's *bas-kol*-rejectionist position is incorporated here even though our *bas kol* has a majority in its support, because Beis Shammai—despite being in the minority—is known to be intellectually superior (*mechadedi t'fei*).

Berachos 51b

> If a *bas kol* only works when supported by a majority, and even then can be overturned by the minority being superior, what good is a *bas kol*?
> 5. Why does Beis Shammai ignore the halachah of *tadir v'she'eino tadir, tadir kodem*?
> 6. If Beis Shammai is so intellectually superior, why in fact is the halachah in our case like Beis Hillel (even according to Rabbi Yehoshua)?
> 7. Why does the Gemara ask a question ("Why do Beis Hillel have the need to tack on "Another reason…?") and then never answer it?[1]

Yesod

The Gemara **is** answering its question. The existence of two "*iba'is eima*"s to the question of *p'shita* is the answer to its question of why Beis Hillel needed to tack on a *davar acher*. Let me explain.

According to the first *iba'is eima*, *bas kol* requires a supportive majority, but when it has that, it is strong enough to overcome even a superior intellect in the minority.

According to the second *iba'is eima*, *bas kol* is valuable only when both sides are equivalent—in number and wisdom. Otherwise, it is unnecessary when backed by a majority and powerless when opposed by an intellectually superior minority.

Like the first *iba'is eima*, no *bas kol* has yet emerged, and we have no prejudice as to which side is intellectually superior. Halachah by halachah, whichever side provides a stronger logic will have the halachic ruling be like them. In our case, Beis Shammai opens with a strong point that since there would be no wine without the *yom*, the *yom* is primary and therefore it must be recited first. Beis Hillel matches that logic and surpasses it—*yom* may indeed be the prime cause, but in our living world we relate to immediate causes, and the immediate cause of making *kiddush* is having wine over which *kiddush* can be made. Wine is therefore primary and should be blessed first. Touché! But Beis Shammai has a second reason—Shabbos was here before the wine came. For that, Beis Hillel has a rejoinder—wine is more common, so its *berachah* goes first even if it arrived second.

But like the second *iba'is eima*, the die has already been cast. Beis Shammai has been declared intellectually superior to Beis Hillel. If you accept the *bas kol*, you can rule like Beis Hillel. But if, like Rabbi Yehoshua according to *Tosafos*, you are required to reject the *bas kol* if faced with an intellectually superior minority, we must *pasken* like Beis Shammai! And where do we see in our *sugya* that Beis Shammai is intellectually superior? Clearly, it must be from the fact that they provided two reasons for *yom* to precede *yayin* while Beis Hillel provided only one! *Tadir v'she'eino tadir* is not a viable argument here. If it were, intellectually superior Beis Shammai would have acknowledged it. The halachah should be like Beis Shammai!

So why isn't it?

That's the *davar acher*. True, Beis Hillel does not have a superior argument. But they have a trump card. It's called *tadir v'she'eino tadir, tadir kodem*. But it is not being brought as a *sevara* about wine and the day of Shabbos. According to the second *iba'is eima*, this principle is not being brought by Beis Hillel as a rejoinder to a Beis Shammai argument. That was only in the first half of the sentence ("*birkas ha'yayin tadirah u'birkas ha'yom eina tadirah*"). The rest of Beis Hillel's comment (*tadir v'she'eino tadir, tadir kodem*) is a statement that **superiority does not always win**. There is a concept in Torah that consistency and other similar good *middos* can count more than greatness. So if two people are in line for an honor, and one is greater than the other, but the other is more consistent, we give *kadimah* to the one who is lesser but more consistent. This concept is known as *tadir v'she'eino tadir, tadir kodem*.

Says Beis Hillel: Yes, you have two arguments while we only have one. But the reason we were selected by the *bas kol* was not because of our intellectual greatness. It was because we consistently presented your views first before we presented our own. And so, we may have lost to you on the intellectual battlefield, but we win because our consistency earned us the imprimatur of the *bas kol*. And this *maaleh* we have even if you are *mechadedi t'fei*.

Berachos 51b

This is the *davar acher*, and it is needed precisely as a *davar acher* because of the unique way it has to address the second *iba'is eima*. Yes, *halachah k'Beis Hillel* because *tadir v'she'eino tadir, tadir kodem*, but in this setting it refers to the *tadirus* of Beis Hillel, not the *tadirus* of *Birkas Ha'yayin*.

Endnotes

1. There is another way to read the Gemara that **does** have the Gemara answering its question: "Why do Beis Hillel have the need to tack on 'Another reason...'?" It is so that if the objection is raised that Beis Shammai has two reasons while Beis Hillel has only one, it can be answered that Beis Hillel also has two reasons: 1) Wine causes the *kiddush*, and 2) *tadir v'she'eino tadir, tadir kodem.*

   My difficulty with this approach is that in order for this to be the reading, the correct phrase would have been "*d'ki teima,*" not "*v'ki teima.*" Indeed, the *Tzlach*, who uses this alternative approach, brings the phrase as "*d'ki teima.*" Our *girsa*, however, is "*v'ki teima,*" and so I choose to stay with my reading of and approach to the Gemara.

Chapter Nine
Ha'roeh

Berachos 57a

דף נז.

הבא על אמו בחלום יצפה לבינה וגו'.

One who cohabits with his mother in a dream should anticipate [becoming imbued with] understanding [binah], as it says, "Binah is called 'Mother'" (Mishlei 7:4).

One who cohabits with a betrothed maiden [in a dream] should anticipate Torah, as it says, "Moshe commanded us in the Torah, an inheritance of the community of Yaakov" (Devarim 33:4)—do not read "inheritance" [morasha], rather read "betrothed" [m'orasa].

One who cohabits with his sister in a dream should anticipate wisdom, as it says, "Say to wisdom—You are my sister" (Mishlei 7:4).

1. What is the significance of dreams that they should play such a large role in our waking world, and why do they take up such a major portion of a chapter in *Mesechta Berachos*?
2. How can it be explained that the arrival into a person's life of such holy and pure concepts as understanding, wisdom, and Torah should be heralded by such unseemly images as cohabiting with a mother, a sister, and a betrothed maiden?
3. "Say to wisdom—You are my sister" sounds very similar to Avraham's request of Sarah when they were about to enter Egypt: "Please say you are my sister." What is the connection between Sarah Imeinu and this *pasuk* in *Mishlei*?

Yesod

Yosef HaTzaddik almost succumbed to the temptation of *eishes Potiphar*. And he had every reason to. He was young and vigorous, inflamed with passion, and powerfully desired. What made him resist?

His dreams.

Aware that he had seen dreams of spiritual greatness for his future, he flashed on those dreams as well as on a vision he suddenly had of his father's face. In this new vision, his father warned him that he stood to lose all the greatness his dreams portended for him should he give in to his passions. From those dreams and visions, he gathered the strength to say no to the sinful liaison.

Dreams changed the nefarious plans of non-Jews as well. Avimelech was terrified by a nocturnal appearance of God, warning him in a dream against bringing harm to the prophet Avraham. Lavan reversed his plans to harm Yaakov Avinu after God came to him in a dream. Alexander the Great spared the Jews of Jerusalem upon meeting and discovering that it was the face of Shimon HaTzaddik that dominated his dreams the night before every victorious battle.

Dreams have altered the world of modern figures as well. The mass gatherings of the followers of Reverend Martin Luther King, Jr., could easily have given way to violent demonstrations but for their leader's message: "I have a dream." Somehow, the presence of a dream gives such security about an inevitable future that agitation over that future can be calmed.

What is a dream?

It has been suggested that a dream is a fantasy image that enables one to hope despite reality. I believe it is just the opposite.

That which we call reality is actually the fantasy. A dream is a snippet of reality superimposed upon our fantasy world.

We know our world is fantasy because Chazal refer to this world as *Olam Ha'sheker*. Dreams are the means by which Hashem insinuates a whiff of the world of truth into our *Olam Ha'sheker*. This is the source of the power dreams have to shake us up, restrain us, and redirect us.

Berachos 57a

So first of all, this is why dreams come when we are sleeping. Sleep loosens the bonds we have to our world. With less to bind us to the falsity of our existence, we are more open to the truth that comes with dreams.

But now we can also explain our question about the unholy images. In the real world that exists beyond ours, things have value not as articles for practical use, but as symbols for deeper meanings. The clearest place to see this is in the *Mishkan*, where a Menorah symbolizes wisdom, a Table symbolizes abundance, and an Incense Altar symbolizes harmony. The *Mishkan*, much like a dream, serves as an inlet for the higher world into our lower world, and thus its implements serve as symbols more than as functional articles. Another such inlet is the holiday of Rosh Hashanah, which propels us out of our world into a world in which we see *malchus Shamayim* on display and vivid books of destiny lying open before us. There too, we see how food items serve as symbols, as we use the *simanim* foods to nudge our lives into the success column, based solely on what the names of those foods symbolize.

It is the same with the images in our dreams.

Intimacy plays a powerful role here in this world, so powerful that it needs to be strongly regulated in order to prevent its descent into cesspools of fantasy. This is what gives us the *issurei arayos*. But in the world of truth, all our relationships, all our emotions, and all our physical activities are merely symbols for deeper and transcendent meanings. So in the world of dreams, which takes its language from the *Olam Ha'emes*, "mother"—who has a natural perception of her child's wants and needs—symbolizes understanding; "betrothed maiden"—who even in this world suggests excitement, preciousness, and potential for growth—symbolizes Torah; "sister" symbolizes wisdom; and cohabitation symbolizes intense connection. It quickly becomes clear how in the world of our dreams, it is perfectly natural for an oncoming strong connection to Torah, for example, to be symbolized by cohabitation with a betrothed maiden. We need only choose to see it from the perspective of the World of Truth from which it came.

That brings us to the question of why the *pasuk* seems to want to link *chochmah* with Sarah Imeinu.

דף נז.

There is actually a choice every human being has to make anytime he is presented with a tantalizing treasure of this world. Does he look at it with wonder and admiration—hoping to learn about it, discover its essence, and connect with its Designer—or does he just grab it and indulge in whatever gratification it provides?

A sister is an example of a relationship that, because it includes no carnal component, cannot be tainted by the indulgence in gratification. Any love we have for a sister is love built on appreciating her qualities and character and the sharing of common bonds of origin. By saying, "*emor l'chochmah achosi at*," *Mishlei* is exhorting us to relate to wisdom for its inherent greatness and for the ability it has to reflect the brilliance of its Source, not for any selfish advantage it may be able to offer us.

Sarah Imeinu was entrenched in this same issue. Sarah possessed unparalleled beauty. Avraham Avinu, for his part, was so removed from self-indulgence that he was not even aware of the extent of his wife's attractiveness until he saw her reflection in the Egyptian river. But he knew all about the decadence of Egypt. On the simple level, Avraham had Sarah say she was his sister in order to save his life. But thanks to the link from *Mishlei*, we see there was another level as well. By telling her, "*Imri na achosi at*"—Please say that I can relate to you as a man relates to a beloved sister—Avraham was actually charging Sarah with the task of educating the cultural savages that it was possible for a person of beauty to be appreciated for her character, her bearing, and her inner grace—the way a brother appreciates a sister—all in spite of her overwhelming beauty and attractiveness. Understood like that, all of *yeridas Mitzrayim* can be seen as part of Hashem's grand plan to send us out to inspire the world to wean itself off its culture of gross self-gratification. Only once the world understands that great gifts are not to be exploited but are to be cherished will its population be able to absorb the radiance of the Torah's sublime beauty and wisdom as it will be revealed in all its glory at the End of Days, and not transform it into a tool for enhancing their selfish pleasures.

With this backdrop, we can now see how this chapter about dreams not only belongs in *Mesechta Berachos* but actually sums up the entire message of the *mesechta*. Food is one those things that gives us the basic

Berachos 57a

choice we identified above. One can relate to food with indulgence, gluttony, and crass gratification of the taste buds, or one can relate to food as evidence of God's immense kindness to us—as a source of wonder over the intricacies of food's design and its capacity to nourish and satisfy, and as a means to unite and bond with one another as we use mealtimes to encourage praise of Hashem and to share thoughts from the wisdom of His Torah.

The halachos found in *Mesechta Berachos* address precisely these loftier choices. After first laying out for us how *berachos* of *k'rias Shema* and of *tefillah* can be used to elevate our daily routine from the mundane to the meaningful, the *mesechta* shifts into the ability that *berachos* have to elevate our consumption of food to an activity infused with God-awareness. We learn how the simple recital of a *berachah* transforms our eating from an act we share in common with the animals to an act of manifest devotion to the Creator of food. We discover how breaking bread together is a bonding mechanism and leads to an ever-greater ability to shower praise upon our Benefactor. Finally, we learn how the choice we are bidden to make between indulgence and transcendence is parallel to the choice we are bidden to make between reality and fantasy, with dreams serving as the aroma of reality wafting through our loosened minds otherwise mired in the falsity of limited perception. *Mesechta Berachos* virtually walks us through the proper way of responding to God's great challenge found at the end of the Torah: "Behold I place before you life and good, and death and evil...*u'vacharta ba'chayim*—choose life."

Mesechta Berachos, by teaching us how to make meaningful choices in our everyday lives, teaches us how to choose life.

About the Author

Rabbi Chaim Goldberger, a disciple of HaRav Yaakov Weinberg, *zt"l*, and, *ybc"l*, HaRav Yochanan Zweig, *shlita*, has spent over twenty years in the rabbinate, serving congregations in Lowell, Massachusetts, and Minneapolis, Minnesota. His first *sefer*, *The Six Steps of Bitachon* (Mosaica Press, 2016), is a Jewish bestseller—and has already changed thousands of lives.

Comments and questions are welcome.
Please address them to the *mechaber*
at rabbi@kenessethisrael.org.

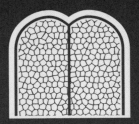

Elegant, Meaningful & Bold

info@MosaicaPress.com
www.MosaicaPress.com

The Mosaica Press team of acclaimed editors and designers is attracting some of the most compelling thinkers and teachers in the Jewish community today. Our books are available around the world.

HARAV YAACOV HABER
RABBI DORON KORNBLUTH